The Federal Government and Urban Housing

SUNY Series in Urban Public Policy

Mark Schneider and Richard C. Rich, Editors

The Federal Government and Urban Housing

Ideology and Change in Public Policy

R. ALLEN HAYS

State University of New York Press

Published by
State University of New York Press, Albany

© 1985 State University of New York

Printed in the United States of America

For information, address State University of New York
Press, State University Plaza, Albany, N.Y., 12246

Library of Congress Cataloging in Publication Data

Hays, R. Allen, 1945–
    The federal government and urban housing.

    (SUNY series in urban public policy)
    Bibliography: p. 267
    Includes index.
    1. Housing policy—United States—History.
2. Housing—United States—History. I. Title.
II. Series.
HD7293.H394 1985   363.5'8'0973   85-2732
ISBN 0-88706-105-2
ISBN 0-88706-106-0 (pbk.)

10 9 8 7 6 5 4 3 2

Contents

List of Figures

Tables

Acknowledgements

The roots of my current scholarly interest in housing policy lie in my five-year stint in the Community Development Department of the Richmond, Virginia Redevelopment and Housing Authority. Therefore, I would like to express my appreciation to John Baker, Bob Everton, Duane Finger, and the rest of the staff. They provided me with much valuable experience and insight in the field of housing. I would also like to thank Professors Robert Ross, Christopher Silver, and Robert O'Connor for their useful comments at various stages of the manuscript, and Sarah McCowan for her very useful advice. Finally, I would like to thank my wife, Pam, for helping me keep up my morale and for carrying more than her usual 50 percent share of domestic duties during the final stages of this work.

Introduction

This book is an attempt to describe and to understand recent changes in national urban housing policies. Its principal focus will be on the changes which occurred in the 1970s, a decade which, in many respects, was a pivotal one for housing policy. It began with large federal housing subsidy programs in full swing, producing more units than ever before. The federal government was also heavily involved in a variety of community development activities related to housing such as urban renewal and model cities. Some of these programs had existed for many years while others were spawned in the surge of federal legislative activities which occurred between 1964 and 1968 under the aegis of Lyndon Johnson's "Great Society." In either case, the early 1970s saw funding levels peak and benefits broaden to include a wider segment of the population.

Yet, the early 1970s also witnessed a growing chorus of criticism of these programs. Even as housing programs were booming they were being attacked for high costs, poor quality, and lack of equity. Meanwhile, federal categorical programs in general were being criticized as too complex, as mutually contradictory in purposes, and as too inflexible with regard to the differing needs and purposes of local communities.

The Nixon Administration did not oppose continuation of these programs at first; however, it gradually took the lead in criticizing them and in attempting to formulate alternative approaches. The criticism culminated in the declaration of a moratorium on the implementation of all such programs in early 1973. This action paved the way for congressional approval of the Housing and Community Development Act of 1974.

The new law represented a major change in the direction and design of federal housing and community development efforts. First, it incorporated a modified version of Nixon's special revenue sharing proposal by consolidating seven categorical programs into the Community Development Block Grant, under which local governments could allocate funds subject only to very broad federal guidelines. Second, funding was reduced in cities which had competed actively for categorical funds and was spread among a broader range of communities through a system of formula entitlements. Third, Section 8 of the act directed housing subsidies at consumers through direct rent subsidies rather than incorporating them as cost reductions to builders, and it encouraged the use of existing and rehabilitated units, as well as new units, for subsidized housing.

A gradually reduced federal administrative role in housing and community development signalled the beginning of a long term reduction in federal involvement in these problems. The Ford Administration continued Nixon's basic approach, and the Carter Administration, while professing a commitment to solving urban problems in order to please the Democrats' traditional urban constituencies, had higher priorities than urban housing. Funding levels for the new Section 8 programs moved higher, under pressure from the program's immediate constituency of builders and local officials, but federal attempts to solve urban housing problems had lost much of their momentum. Then, after Ronald Reagan took office in 1981, the movement toward retrenchment accelerated, and even the newer urban programs saw their funding cut drastically. Thus, a decade that began with an active and relatively well-funded federal role in urban areas also encompassed a slow, strategic withdrawal from that role, and ended with a precipitous federal retreat in the offing.

This drastic change was directly related to issues and problems which were unique to the areas of housing and community development. Various approaches to the provision of improved housing were tried, acquired an image (deserved or undeserved) of failure, and were replaced or supplanted by other approaches. However, this change was also related, I believe, to an underlying change in the values and perspectives of those public officials in key national decision-making roles. Changing economic conditions helped to produce a changing climate of opinion, particularly among political elites, and this new climate brought forth political leaders with different philosophies toward the role of government in urban areas.

The major task of this book will be to show the relationship between specific policy developments in the area of urban housing and these changes in climate and leadership. However, it will also be shown that recent changes reflect attitudes and values of much longer duration — in particular, the profound ambivalence with which American policymakers have always viewed government efforts to solve the problems of cities and their disadvantaged residents.

The focus of this book will be restricted to housing policies affecting urban areas. In making this limitation, I do not mean to denigrate the importance of housing in rural areas. These areas have their own uniuqe problems to deal with, including some of the most physically deteriorated housing in the nation. However, urban areas contain the largest and most visible concentrations of inadequate housing and neighborhood conditions, and these conditions exist in a complex inter-relationship with other facets of community life. Because of this, much of the energy and controversy in housing and community development policy has been centered in these areas. Thus, the scope of the undertak-ing is made more manageable by giving it an urban focus, while the underlying dynamics of the policy process are more clearly revealed.

Any such effort to understand the changes and continuities in values and perceptions of political elites and the impact of these changes on a specific policy area requires as its starting point a general conceptual framework outlining the nature of the policy-making process. The con-cepts and the proposals which shape policy in a given area do not emerge in a vacuum, and the policy debate cannot be treated simply as an in-tellectual exercise. Rather, policy decisions must be linked to the under-lying distribution of power which has shaped them. The phrase "values and perceptions of political elites" implies that a reasonably clear elite-mass distinction does exist; therefore, the underlying model must describe the nature of the elite groups under consideration. This phrase also implies that values and perceptions do have a significant impact on policy; therefore, some explicit propositions as to the role of these at-titudinal variables in shaping policy decisions are needed.

In a study of one policy area, the full range and complexity of these theoretical issues cannot be fully addressed. A complete discussion of these issues would quickly swallow the analysis of the issues at hand. However, if such a study is to contribute to a broader understanding of the policy-making process, the theoretical and empirical assumptions which guide the analysis must be made explicit. Therefore, in Chapter 1, some broad theoretical issues relevant to an understanding of the policy-making process will be discussed, with special emphasis on the role of ideology in shaping public policy.

In Chapter 2, the specific ideological frames of reference which have influenced housing policy will be discussed. In Chapter 3, the social and demographic changes which have shaped urban housing submarkets will be discussed, and overall trends in housing production and prices will be examined in terms of their impact on these submarkets. Finally, the chapter will touch on the complex question of determining the extent of housing needs.

Chapters 4, 5 and 6 will look at the development of the wide range of housing subsidy programs for the disadvantaged which were enacted before and during the 1970s. Chapter 4 will trace the major policy developments prior to the 1970s which set the stage for events during that decade. Chapter 5 will concentrate on the crucial events from 1969 to 1973 which led up to the Nixon moratorium. Chapter 6 will examine the period from the moratorium until 1980, with special emphasis on the new subsidy program, Section 8, which grew out of Nixon's initiatives.

Chapters 7 and 8, will examine the impact of community development policy on urban housing. In Chapter 7, the history of federal involvement in community development prior to the Nixon Moratorium will be traced. Chapter 8 will examine the subsequent history of the Community Development Block Grant program.

Chapter 9 will first provide a brief account of the housing and community development struggles which have occurred since Ronald Reagan took office in 1981. It will conclude with a discussion of the future of housing policy.

CHAPTER 1

Power, Ideology and Public Policy

Power And Ideology: Theoretical Considerations

The study of policy and the study of power are inextricably intertwined. Power is usually operationally defined in terms of policy outcomes — that is, as the ability of a political actor to influence the behavior of other actors in such a way as to gain a preferred outcome. Students of political power and of policy-making generally assume that power is not distributed temporarily or haphazardly among the population as a whole but rather, that any society develops stable influence patterns in and around governmental and nongovernmental institutions. In short, power is exercised within some kind of power structure, no matter how changeable and ambiguous that power structure may at times be.

For many years, the prevailing paradigm among political scientists was the pluralist model of the U.S. power structure. In this model, power in the United States is not controlled by a single ruling elite (as in the "minority" view expressed by Mills, Kolko, and others) but by fragmented elite groups which are divided both geographically and functionally. Though the ordinary citizen does not participate actively in this system, it is still seen as providing a reasonable approximation of democratic representation for at least three reasons. First, the leadership of organized interest groups represents the concerns of many citizens who are not directly involved in the political process. Second, the democratic rules of the game help insure the openness of the system to new groups of citizens who are activated by some compelling need for government action; and this openness is further encouraged by the fact that no single elite controls many or all areas of policy. Third, popularly elected officials act, in the pluralist view, as brokers who combine and balance competing interests into compromise and/or consensus on the direction of public policy.

This prevailing view was, however, challenged by writers such as Grant McConnell (1970) and Theodore Lowi (1979). Their critique was further reinforced by studies of "subgovernments" in the public administration and policy literature (Freeman, 1965). Finally, leading pluralists such as Robert Dahl and Charles Lindblom have modified their views considerably since the publication of their initial works. Though the views of these scholars are diverse, several common elements may be discerned in their critiques and revisions of pluralism.

These critics agree with the pluralist conclusion that power in American society is highly fragmented, with different collections of interests surrounding and controlling the decision-making process with regard to policies of immediate concern to them. Their conclusions as to the representativeness and openness of this system are, however, quite different from those of earlier pluralist writings. They stress that the operation of interest groups is not, in itself, a democratic process in which citizens freely combine to select representatives who express their views to public officials. Rather, most interest groups are internally controlled by a small elite which is mainly responsive to the larger economic units within the group. McConnell also stresses that these groups often exert control over key segments of the market economy, thus making compliance with group norms a precondition of economic activity in that area. Thus, his analysis fits with the notion of an 'administered' private sector, more fully developed by Michael Reagan, (1968) John Kenneth Galbraith, (1967) and others.

This model also questions the openness of the system to entry by new groups. In this view, existing groups more often than not succeed in excluding from the decision-making process new groups with differing views or interests. The principal strategy for such control is the development of close alliances with key members of Congress and with administrative agencies having a direct stake in existing policies. These "subgovernments," to use the well-known phrase coined by J. Leiper Freeman (1965), strongly resist intervention not only by competing groups but by top level political leaders representing broader constituencies, such as the president and congressional party leaders.

Lowi further argues that the operation of the U.S. power structure may vary according to the nature of the issues involved. He suggests that, with regard to issues raising fundamental questions about the existing distribution of wealth among large groups within the population, a much greater degree of top level control exists than in other policy areas. That is, policy change is highly dependent on initiatives made at the highest levels of the Executive Branch, and the formulation of these initiatives will be done by small groups of presidential advisors, assisted by specialists in the area. Thus, the power structure, though basically fragmented along policy lines, is capable of accomodating high level coordination when fundamental "redistributive" issues are at stake (Lowi, 1964; see also Ripley and Franklin, 1980, for an elaboration of Lowi's policy categories).

These revisions to the pluralist model clearly bring it much closer to the reality of U.S. politics. However, while those writing from this perspective suggest some widely shared U.S. political values which give legitimacy to the system of interest group power, they do not give full weight to the effects on the political process of fundamental similarities and differences in value perspectives among political actors which cut across fragmented power centers. Thus, an examination of another element of political reality — ideology — becomes critical to the development of a more complete understanding of the U.S. power structure than is provided by the revised pluralist model.

The relevance of ideology to the study of power was forcefully argued by Peter Bachrach and Morton Baratz in their classic article, "The Two Faces of Power" (Bachrach and Baratz, 1962). They pointed out that strong limits are placed on the total range of decisions possible in the system by the shared values and assumptions of its participants. They argued that certain societal problems, or certain alternative means of solving them, are simply never discussed or debated by decision-makers due to their shared assumption that these problems or solutions are not legitimate topics for political debate. They refer to these tacit acts of exclusion as "non-decisions."

While introducing the need to look at shared beliefs, or ideologies, as part of the study of power, Bachrach and Baratz's discussion of non-decisions does not take us very far in understanding *how* the beliefs held by participants really shape the decision-making process. They suggest that non-decisions operate to the advantage of established groups and to the disadvantage of "outsiders" such as the poor. However, ideologies clearly do more than provide criteria for those whose concerns are "in" and whose concerns are "out." To begin to understand the impact of ideology on political decision making, it is first necessary to explore the general structural features of ideologies.

Ideology

An ideology is a widely shared set of interrelated assertions about the world which guides the behavior of individuals and groups. To many, the term *ideology* conveys the notion of a complex, logically structured set of beliefs which has been refined to a fairly high level of intellectual sophistication. Certainly this is true for such ideologies as 'democracy' and 'capitalism'. Yet, other equally powerful and pervasive systems of beliefs exist which are much less sophisticated and come close, in the minds of most believers, to more primitive, emotional 'we-they' distinctions. Racism, sexism, and nationalism fall into this category, although each has its intellectual defenders. For present purposes, I will include such beliefs under the term *ideology*.

Most ideologies contain three types of statements. First, they contain assertions about reality—that is, statements which purport to be empirically valid generalizations about the nature of the world or of human beings. Second, they contain ethical prescriptions for human behavior derived from the assertions they make about reality. Third, they contain, as a special case of their ethical precepts, prescriptions for the arrangement of social institutions in ways consistent with their central values. No ideology is a totally consistent package which satisfactorily explains all aspects of reality. Most have major internal contradictions which emerge more clearly as they are applied and elaborated. Furthermore, the institutions these ideologies purport to justify do not exist in a vacuum. Complex societies contain several types of institutions—familial, economic, political, religious—each of which is legitimized by slightly different ideological principles. In any stable society, these institutions and ideologies reinforce one another to a significant degree, but there is also competition for influence between institutions. Major inconsistencies often exist between beliefs supporting different institutions of the same society; for example, the complex agreements and contradictions existing between democracy and capitalism.

As a result of these pressures, ideologies which enjoy wide acceptance in a society usually develop a set of 'operational' assumptions and values which may deviate significantly from the 'pure' ideals contained in formal statements of the ideology. The ideals set forth clearly and consistently what is to be valued most by believers. However, these moral absolutes rarely enter directly into the political process except as vague symbols, brought out on ceremonial occasions to legitimize the system as a whole. The operational form of the ideology, in contrast, stresses the concepts and behavior patterns most crucial to the long term survival of the institutions which the ideology justifies, and it incorporates the compromises those institutions have made to survive among other institutions.

As such, the operational ideology is much more likely to have a direct influence on political behavior, and it is only when we look for ideologies in their operational form that we can fully gauge their impact. It should also be emphasized that an operational ideology, as here defined, is more than a haphazard bundle of exceptions to the pure ideal. Rather, it is a transformation of the ideal into another, fairly consistent set of concepts which seem to correspond more closely to current 'reality.'

Because ideologies are so closely related to institutions and because individuals and organizations tend to interpret common ideologies in ways that match their unique situations, there has been a tendency among Western political analysts to see ideology as a dependent variable which is shaped by a much more potent source of human motivation—interests. An *interest* may be thought of as consisting of two elements; (1) an need experienced by an individual or a group; and, (2) an external object or state of affairs which is seen by the individual or group as fulfilling their need. As such, interests are immediate and concrete, and they are believed to be the main driving force behind political behavior. Material interests are usually seen as the most important type, but other needs such as power, security, prestige, or growth also serve to inspire political involvement. In this view, individuals and groups use ideology primarily to rationalize the pursuit of their interests to others and to convince themselves of the justice of their cause.

A more thorough examination of the relationship between ideologies and interests shows, however, that it is much more complex than this view suggests. At the heart of this complexity is the fact that interests, when examined more closely, do not turn out to be the concrete, self-evident motivators that interest-based notions of politics make them out to be. Of the two elements constituting an interest—a need plus an object or state of affairs which is seen as satisfying that need—the need element would appear to be the least ambiguous. Although there is wide disagreement among students of motivation as to what are the most basic human needs, one can generally identify some widely shared human need behind most political actions. The other element of an interest—the object which can satisfy that need—is much more variable and ambiguous. Any given human need can be satisfied in a large variety of ways, and, in most situations, it is far from clear in advance which of several alternative future states will best satisfy a need.

Thus, in order to pursue his or her interests, the individual must first identify which object or state of affairs will best satisfy his or her needs. Then means must be chosen to achieve the desired future state, and these means often involve intermediate goals and objects which also appear on the political scene as interests. Moreover, these choices must often be made on the basis of limited information as to the full costs and benefits of any alternative and in the face of unpredictable responses from others with a stake in the decision.

If interests are more accurately viewed as points in a complex decision-making process, rather than fixed, self-evident motivators, then one must ask what are the common methods by which actors determine their interests in a given situation. Many studies of the political decision-making process emphasize the large amounts of policy-relevant information from a variety of competing sources which the typical decisionmaker is asked to interpret (see, for example, Nakamura and Smallwood, 1980; Kingdon, 1984). He or she must also attempt to predict the actions and reactions of multiple sets of competing actors. The typical actor lacks the time, resources, and expertise to fully and rationally analyze the costs and benefits of each alternative. As a result, actors try to maintain established patterns of behavior which they regard as successful and tend to evaluate new data in terms of simple, preconceived decision rules which they feel have worked in the past. Aaron Wildavsky's analysis of the decision rules used by the House Appropriations Committee is a classic portrayal of these tendencies (Wildavsky, 1979).

It seems clear that widely shared ideologies can and do serve as potent and readily available sources of the expectations and of the preconceived decision rules brought into any situation by political actors. As noted above, ideologies contain both descriptive and prescriptive elements. Thus, they create expectations as to the behavior of others in concrete situations. To the extent that these expectations become operative as predictors of the future, ideology becomes deeply intertwined in the process of interest formulation. Actors use ideology not only to justify behavior but also to interpret data from their own experience and to predict the costs and benefits of future actions. To be sure, they may deliberately manipulate shared ideological precepts to cloak self-seeking behavior. But the world view upon which they draw for this "symbol manipulation" has also shaped their own perceptions of the situation and through these perceptions the very interests they pursue.

To suggest that ideological categories are used as a source of decision rules is not, however, to suggest that a uniform set of values guides the thinking of all or most political actors. Widely shared ideologies are broad enough in their structure to permit wide variations in interpretation. It is quite natural, of course, that there should be idiosyncratic variations between individual interpretations of shared values. However, an equally common pattern in contemporary societies is the development of two or more distinct sets of interpretive frameworks, each held by a certain subgroup within the society's active decisionmakers, which involve different notions of how common ideologies should be applied to concrete social problems. Each of these interpretive frameworks supplies a different set of decision rules to be used in specific situations, and the differences in these approaches generate much of the day to day political conflict over policy alternatives. The choice of one framework or another is usually influenced by the concrete interests of the actor; however, similar viewpoints are likely to be shared by a broad spectrum of actors from a variety of institutional roles. A succinct label for these competing interpretive frameworks is *coalition ideologies*, because they link together actors whose specific interests may vary.

The competing coalition ideologies which will be discussed in this work are subsumed under the terms *liberal* and *conservative*. While I will argue later that the principles widely attributed to these two viewpoints are not accurate reflections of their actual operational values, it is clear that these two terms symbolize distinct interpretations of a common ideology, democratic capitalism, which dictate different solutions to common problems. Both of these ideologies have been influenced by other belief systems besides capitalism. Liberals have incorporated socialist ideas to some degree while many conservatives adhere to notions of government enforcement of morality which predate and even contradict Adam Smith. Nevertheless, in their actual usage, these two outlooks are firmly rooted in a common capitalist world view. They both support the central economic institutional arrangements of capitalism, but they differ as to how these institutions, and the social order which supports them, can best be stabilized and perpetuated.

Shared ideologies may also be elaborated into more specific sets of preconceptions about particular areas of public policy. While widely shared ideologies encourage continuity in the way political decision-makers respond to a variety of problems, each substantive area of public policy has its own unique history, which tends to create shared assumptions among those involved about what can be and what should be done to solve problems in that area. Both Heclo (1978) and Kingdon (1984) suggest that policies are framed within distinct policy communities, composed of interest groups and governmental specialists concerned with a particular set of issues. Participation in these communities may, at times, be fluid, but common ideas and assumptions do develop. These assumptions are linked to the immediate interests of the actors involved, but their roots can also be traced to the ideological frameworks within which the policy developed. In part, they represent guidelines as to the application of general ideological principles to that policy area.

It should be stressed that the description of ideological preconceptions just presented applies primarily to political elites who are directly involved in the decision-making process. In addition to these activists, there often exists an attentive public, consisting of a small porportion of the total citizenry, who are concerned enough about an issue to develop an articulated set of beliefs about it. (Cobb and Elder, 1981) Beyond this, however, the great mass of citizens is generally poorly informed about specific issues and does not have a clear ideological framework within which policy preferences are organized. They may have absorbed some of the ideal statements about American society which are purveyed by the media and the educational system (such as the value of free enterprise), yet they have rarely worked out the application of this to specific, complex policy decisions. Therefore, they are vulnerable to symbol manipulation by elites wishing to justify their policies. (Edelman, 1964)

If, in fact, ideologies penetrate the decision-making process as pervasively as has just been suggested, then they may be expected to exert a profound influence on public policy outcomes. As suggested above, this influence will be in the direction of an underlying continuity in assumptions and approaches across a variety of policy areas, even when each area is dominated by different functional groups. There are at least two ways in which shared ideologies act to generate such continuities. The first and most obvious impact of shared ideological preconceptions is as intellectual and emotional filters through which policy initiatives must pass before they are considered acceptable and responsible proposals. Again, this "filtering" is often seen as a matter of interest protection—that is, proposals will not be considered which seriously threaten the power, wealth, or status of groups or individuals currently active. However, this is only part of the picture, for these preconceptions strongly influence judgements as to *whether* an alternative is threatening or not threatening to the interests of those who hold power. Thus, a proposed expansion of governmental activity will, in part, be evaluated by affected groups on the basis of its short-term concrete benefits, but they will also look at its long-term effects. If they have strong ideological biases against any government involvement in their affairs, this assumption will create the expectation of long-term harm which may override their desire for short-term gains.

Closely related to the ideological filtering of policy initiatives is the ideological filtering of participants in the political process. On the surface, it would appear that the U.S. system allows for the expression of a wide variety of concrete interests. Industry groups compete vigorously for government favors and protection, while labor unions, farmers, and groups of "public spirited" citizens also enter the fray, often with direct challenges to the pursuit of profit by particular firms. Yet, underlying this seeming plurality of interests are shared assumptions, often unstated, as to which groups and which types of individuals can be trusted to follow the rules of the game—i.e., to confine their pursuit of interests to methods which will not disrupt or threaten the system as a whole.

The most obvious set of criteria for the inclusion or exclusion of participants consists of the manifest beliefs of the individual or group in question. Those who espouse ideologies which are opposed to prevailing beliefs will find it difficult to move into positions of permanent stable influence, due to the profound distrust they engender in other participants. In addition, biases concerning social class and education act as selection criteria. Upper middle class and upper class businessmen and professionals find access to the political process much easier than the poor or working class, and where the working class or poor are represented it is by leaders who have been coopted into the prevailing value structure. Finally, institutional position itself is a criterion for inclusion in the larger decision-making arena. A person who has risen to a position of authority in a large public or private organization is not only recognized as a spokesperson for that organization, but is also presumed to have demonstrated the skill, reasonableness, and social conformity necessary to be a "responsible" participant in the larger political process.

This line of argument suggests that, while it may be too simplistic to talk, as Mills (1959), Dye (1983), and Kolko (1962) have, of a small, tightly knit "ruling elite," it makes much more sense to think of a "ruling stratum" of people of similar education, skills, and values who dominate most of the key economic and political institutions in American society. This ruling stratum is, of course, a very complex entity. Different institutional roles recruit persons of varying training and values, and individuals are idiosyncratic in their beliefs. Also, there are important inequalities within this stratum. A few members control larger institutions which set broad policy direcions while most direct policy only in their own specialized areas. Nevertheless, the recruitment process insures that their underlying similarities in background and values outweigh their differences and make them a reasonably distinct group within American society as a whole.

Having noted these very general types of filters which apply to virtually all aspects of U.S. political decision making, I will now look at some of the more specific institutional expressions of broad ideological perspectives in the political process. The revised pluralist model described earlier performs an important service by calling to our attention the narrowness of the concerns and interests which motivate many political actors. Yet, to view government as exclusively composed of a series of discrete, isolated decision-making arenas would be a distortion.

One must also take into account the institutions that permit and encourage the formation of broader ideological coalitions which have an important impact on the political process.

The most prominent of these institutions is the presidency. Writers on the presidency such as Neustadt (1980) have justifiably emphasized the limits on the power of the president — the need for him to bargain with and persuade not only Congress but segments of the bureaucracy which he nominally heads. Yet there is also tremendous power inherent in the administrative and the agenda-setting role of this office. Interest groups and agencies, entrenched in their "iron triangles", may be able to defeat the president on specific issues, and they may be able to rewrite the detailed language of legislation so as to maximize its benefits or minimize its costs to them, but the president has a powerful influence on the overall political atmosphere. He is the source of most major policy initiatives, and so interest groups often find themselves in a reactive position vis-à-vis issues he has forced them to address (Kingdon, 1984).

It is also clear that each administration has a distinct ideological flavor. Each president chooses a team of advisors and cabinet officers who reflect his own ideological perspective. Usually his views correspond with one of the broad liberal or conservative ideologies prevalent at that time. The voters who elect the president may not be clear on the values or issue positions of the candidate they choose, but party elites and other active, informed groups are, and they are ready to see their world view put into action when a sympathetic president is elected. More than any other single political leader, the president is expected to respond to issues with a coherent philosophy, rather than with adjustments to interest group pressures.

Ideological motivations are also prominent in Congress. It is certainly true that most members of Congress are policy specialists with strong commitments to interest groups and programs in their districts and in their specialized areas of expertise. Voting patterns on these issues of immediate concern may, therefore, follow subgovernment loyalties, which are not always ideologically consistent. Yet, on the vast majority of issues, each member has little intimate knowledge and no overwhelming commitments. On these issues, ideology becomes an important predictor of voting behavior (Savitch, 1979; Caraley, 1976). In addition, the election of an individual by a certain constituency will often reflect that constituency's ideological flavor, and the recruitment of a particular member to one or the other of the specialized policy subsystems may be strongly influenced by that individual's value preferences.

Ideology and Policy Change

One other important dimension of the influence of ideology on the policy-making process must be dealt with before these general comments can be applied to the creation of an analytical model appropriate to the examination of housing policies. This is the dimension of change in ideological perspectives. A common way to look at the process of change in beliefs is to think of them as shaped by events occurring in the external environment. In this view, the actor may, like Voltaire's Candide, start out with certain preconceptions about the world (i.e., Dr. Pangloss's optimistic dictum that "this is the best of all possible worlds"). These beliefs are then crushed or altered or expanded by the sheer impact of reality—by glaring inconsistencies between the actual behavior of others and the behavior predicted by one's initial beliefs.

However, as suggested in the above discussion, the separation between events and beliefs is a somewhat artificial one for several reasons. First, the expectations with which actors enter a situation strongly affect their behavior and, therefore, shape the reality of that situation. Second, unless the impact of a policy on an actor is direct and powerful, there is always room for interpretation as to whether the policy has actually failed or succeeded. Political leaders are bombarded with feedback about program outcomes from a variety of sources, and they can choose to listen to and believe those sources which confirm their predispositions. Finally, even when unanticipated and/or harmful consequences are too obvious to ignore, the actor will often try to account for the failure of initial plans through explanations which maintain the overall structure of his or her world view intact. There is no doubt that genuine changes in attitudes can and do occur, but they are likely to be incremental and actors will often deny that any real change has occurred. And, the resiliency of beliefs in the face of changed circumstances leaves open the possibility that the same mistakes or problems will occur repeatedly.

Looking at the larger political arena, another possible response to changing circumstances becomes apparent. Since shared ideologies are broad enough to be subject to conflicting interpretations which crystallize into coalition ideologies, it becomes likely that in the face of the failure of the environment to respond as predicted by the overall ideological system, political leadership will shift back and forth between differing ideological coalitions. Rather than question the relevance of their fundamental assumptions, political elites may simply struggle for the power necessary to try out their conflicting applications of these assumptions to the current situation. Out of this struggle, gradual change may emerge, as one coalition or the other incorporates new ideas. Yet, such a struggle may also produce drifting or incoherent policies, as none of the solutions which are acceptable in terms of current beliefs proves to be relevant or effective.

An awareness of the struggle between competing ideological perspectives also draws our attention to the centrality of compromise between those representing competing perspectives. Compromises occur on hundreds of technical and substantive points during the policy process; however, beyond these specific concessions, it appears that policies which have long term success exist in a kind of political equilibrium between opposing groups. Proponents of a particular program must usually push it through in the face of considerable opposition. In the process, they must make modifications which draw marginal supporters into the fold and satisfy key interest groups. The final product, if it is to survive over the long-term, must be acceptable not only to a short-term coalition of supporters but to a more stable majority, because opponents will make continuing efforts to weaken or eliminate it. If the program continues to gain support, these opponents will reduce their efforts at drastic change and concentrate on containment of its impact, often through the budgetary process. At this point, even if these opponents succeed in preventing the program from attaining the degree of impact desired by its most ardent supporters, the program will have obtained a secure niche in the system and will remain a stable part of policy until conditions generate broader support for new directions. Programs attaining this state of equilibrium usually contain provisions which make them palatable to a rather broad range of ideological perspectives.

This notion of policy as shaped by an equilibrium between opposing ideologies might, at first glance, appear incompatible with some recent research on public policy making. Kingdon (1984) and others stress the fluid, almost haphazard way in which problems and proposed solutions emerge, and they emphasize the changing cast of actors moving in and out of various policy arenas. However, this incompatibility is more apparent than real, since it is not being suggested here that ideological orientations rigidly dictate specific policy options. Within shared ideological perspectives, various options can be and are put forth by a wide variety of actors. Nevertheless, Kingdon stresses that the source of an idea is not as important to its adoption as the existence of an overall political climate in which that idea may be attended to and taken seriously. He also suggests that the ideological predisposition of decision-makers are an important part of that climate (Kingdon, 1984, pp. 75-82).

Summary and Conclusions

Perhaps the best way to summarize the argument made in the last few pages is to represent schematically the broad analytical framework suggested here. This is done in Figure 1.

As is readily apparent, the decision-making subsystems surrounding each distinct policy area form a central element in this schema. These subsystems will, in some policy areas, be organized along the lines of the subgovernment alliances suggested by Freeman (1965). In other policy areas, participation may be more fluid and open, as suggested by Heclo and Kingdon. In either case, these subsystems play a central role in shaping the problems which reach the public agenda and the alternatives which are considered. Moreover, each of these subsystems has its own

FIGURE 1
POLICY DECISIONS AND IDEOLOGY: A SCHEMATIC REPRESENTATION

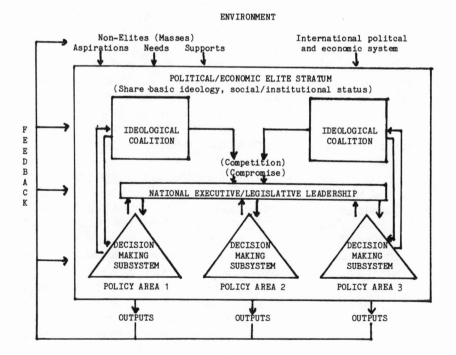

history, in which certain approaches have been accepted as technically or politically viable. This fact tends to create resistance to change within each area which, as the incrementalist model of decision making suggests, tends to make new proposals differ as little as possible from the status quo.

Because of the importance of these subsystems, the use of broad ideological orientations and coalitions as a major variable in explaining policy decisions should not be seen as an attempt to substitute some idealized, bipolar issue conflict for the complex and convoluted processes by which ideas and decisions emerge. Rather, ideological conflicts must be seen as a central element in the broader political environment within which more specialized policy subsystems operate.

The schema also outlines some of the processes by which ideological orientations influence policy subsystems. Broad ideological coalitions within the political/economic elite compete for control of legislative and executive institutions. One coalition or the other may be in a dominant position but rarely so commanding that compromise between competing coalitions is not also necessary. However, the coalition in the strongest position will, based on its ideological orientation, generate strong messages to policy subsystems concerning the kinds of general policy directions considered acceptable or unacceptable. These messages will then be interpreted by the participants in these subsystems and applied to the problems with which they are concerned. The nature of the national leadership will also affect the ideological makeup of participants in various subsystems, either directly through key appointments or indirectly through the types of ideas viewed as current or acceptable. Thus, in discussing housing policy under Nixon, it will be shown that Nixon's general preferences for cash (rather than in-kind) social welfare benefits and for block grants (rather than categorical programs) stimulated housing policy proposals along these lines.

Finally, the schema presented in Figure 1 also suggests that the outputs created by each policy subsystem generate feedback, which is utilized in the broader ideological debates over the direction of public policy. Conclusions about the positive or negative effects of various programs are publicized in the media, and programs are evaluated by various governmental and nongovernmental institutions. These conclusions are usually interpreted differently by those with different ideological perspectives and, thus, become 'ammunition' in the ideological struggle. Thus, it will be shown in Chapter 5 that Nixon used the well-publicized scandals associated with Section 235 and other housing programs to support his general assertion that federal bureaucracies do a poor job of providing housing for the disadvantaged.

Scholarly treatments of specific public policy areas generally tend to take one of two routes to an understanding of an area. One is to examine the broad historical sweep of policy change within the area and to account for change in terms of shifting conditions and attitudes. The other route is to narrow the focus to specific decisions and look in detail at participants and processes. The present study generally follows the first of these routes, and it is from this perspective that ideology emerges as such an important influence on the course of public policy. However, this study also attempts to give sufficient details about various crucial policy choices so that the impact of longer-term changes on specific policy outcomes may be illuminated. Therefore, on the theoretical level, I have tried to suggest patterns by which long-term changes in ideological climate and national leadership may influence more narrow decision-making processes. The schema presented here will implicitly and explicitly guide the treatment of housing policy decisions in subsequent chapters.

CHAPTER 2

The Ideological Context
Of Housing Policy

In this chapter, in order to develop a framework for an analysis of recent changes in housing policy, I will attempt to fill in the outline of ideological structures and impacts just presented with some specific content. In Part I, the broad coalition ideologies which have shaped this and other areas of public policy will be examined. In Part II, the attitude sets which are more directly linked to policy outcomes in the housing field will be described.

Coalition Ideologies in the Twentieth Century

Numerous attempts have been made to describe the broad ideological framework within which U.S. politics operates (Dolbeare, 1971, provides an extensive bibliography). Most have placed at the center of U.S. political ideology the set of beliefs which supports and legitimizes the capitalist economic system. Certainly, the fundamental issues concerning the role of government in the economy which are raised by housing policy suggest the particular relevance of these beliefs in this policy area. Kenneth Dolbeare suggests that, as capitalism emerged in the nineteenth century, the following three tenets became the most central to its justification:

1. The belief that the basic driving force behind human productive activity is the individual human being's desire to enhance his or her material well-being and to compete with others for recognition and advancement. The chief corollary is that society must encourage and reward acquisitiveness and competitiveness if it is to achieve the highest overall level of material well-being.

2. The belief that the free market is the most efficient and least coercive allocator of goods and services for the society as a whole, since its operation enables the desire of each invidual to maximize wealth and to consume what he/she likes to be automatically harmonized with the society's collective development.
3. The belief that government should play a secondary and supplementary role to the private market in regulating human interactions, leaving individuals to make their own consumption choices and private firms to produce whatever goods they wish (Dolbeare, 1971, pp. 22-32.

Taken together, these beliefs form an *ideal* image of the U.S. system which still functions as a potent symbol in political transactions. Public disagreement with these tenets can make a political actor vulnerable to criticism as untrustworthy or extremist. Yet, the profound changes which the U.S. economic and political system has undergone during the twentieth century have placed this belief system in tension with new realities and have also exposed some of its inherent internal contradictions. The main response has been to adopt modified perspectives on the system which retain the central validity of these beliefs while adapting them to changed conditions. These new views constitute the *operational* ideology of contemporary capitalism. Let us briefly explore them.

First, the model of the ideal economic actor as the acquisitive entrepreneur has been altered by the reality of modern organizational life. Certainly, materialism remains central to the U.S. value system. Nevertheless, the vast, complex, corporate entities which produce most essential goods and services require a different mind-set with regard to the actual process of getting and maintaining material status. The element of competition remains strong, but the individual must also be a cooperative team player in order to function effectively.

More importantly, a set of norms associated with the term *professionalism* has emerged. The complex skills and disciplines considered essential to modern production have produced a series of occupations which stress rational problem solving and task accomplishment as ends in themselves. In addition to material rewards, these professionals seek peer recognition based on those criteria of performance unique to their profession, and they seek enhancement of their collective status in the larger community. Engineers, doctors, accountants, professional managers, and many other groups have laid claim to unique problem-solving abilities which are of collective benefit.

The direction and scope of the development of various professions has always been strongly influenced by the holders of capital, but, at the same time, professionalism has had an important reciprocal impact on the development of capitalism. In addition to their impact within the corporate structure, the norms of professionals point beyond an economy in which entrepreneurial self-interest is controlled only by the workings of the "invisible hand." Instead, they suggest the deliberate choice of objectives and the pursuit of those objectives by scientific means. Such planning and coordination suggests, in turn, a more active role for government, which is traditionally the major vehicle for deliberate societal choices. It is no accident that growth in the use of government for problem-solving activities coincides historically with the growth of professionalism in all areas of social endeavor. Private sector professionals took the lead in demanding more professionalism in government, in the name of running government more like a business.

Ironically, the new groups of professional public managers and planners generated by these reforms soon developed a pride and expertise which put them in potential conflict with the claim of private sector professionals to be the most efficient economic and social decisionmakers. Moreover, new groups of professionals began to assert control in education, social work, and other human service occupations, areas not traditionally covered by the private sector except through charitable organizations. As a result, these new professions came to see the growth of government financing for such activities as an enhancement of their power and effectiveness and they became an effective new constituency for governmental social activism. This constituency has since come to be seen by many in the private sector as a major threat to their prerogatives.

The second major tenet of traditional capitalism, the belief in the free market as the principle allocator of goods and services, has also changed in the twentieth century. Though the economic model of "perfect competition" was never more than an approximation of reality, it is clear that the U.S. economy has moved farther and farther away from it, due to the growth of huge corporations and oligopolistic markets within most major industries. Large firms are able to influence both supply and demand, and they desire a predictable environment in which to do long-term planning. Therefore, they tacitly agree to restrict price competition, to focus on maintaining a steady rate of return, and to limit the competitive struggle to marginal changes in market share. Critics of this system view an increased economic role for the government as necessitated by the lack of traditional market controls over prices and efficiency (Galbraith, 1967; Best and Connolly, 1982).

In contrast, defenders of the continued validity of the free market ideology stress the continued dependence of corporate decisions on consumer preferences as evidence for the lack of excessive corporate power. They also stress the strong element of profit-motivated competition that continues to exist, even in oligopolistic markets, and they see this as a source of superior efficiency in the private sector. In addition, they argue that the dominant firms in an industry are in that position because of their superior technical abilities and business acumen; and, therefore, it is to society's benefit to preserve the power of these "market winners."

As can readily be seen, the differences in perspectives which have emerged in connection with the first two ideological premises outlined by Dolbeare rather quickly lead to debates about the third tenet, the belief in "limited government." In one sense, the notion of *laissez-faire* has always been partially a myth. Private enterprise has, throughout its history, turned to government for financial and legal support, and business interests have not hesitated to manipulate public power for private purposes. Nevertheless, the role of government has expanded greatly in the twentieth century, and the issue of the proper degree of government involvement in a wide range of activities has been joined more intensely and directly than in earlier periods.

The Progressive movement early in this century brought about a variety of new government interventions; and, subsequently, the Great Depression was an even greater catalyst for increased government activity. Efforts to relieve this crisis led to vastly increased public aid to those who had lost out in the economic struggle. Efforts to prevent similar crises in the future also led to government regulation of key market transactions, such as banking and securities. Though this phenomenon is well documented, analysts disagree as to its exact meaning and impact. As mentioned earlier, the traditional way to conceptualize the ideological divisions over the governmental role is the liberal/conservative dimension. In this view, liberals are those who favor an increased government role in all areas of social and economic life, while conservatives favor holding the line or decreasing governmental activity. But, a number of observers offer good reason to quesiton whether or not this conceptualization really captures the true lines of division in the dispute which has accompanied governmental growth.

Theodore Lowi takes us part way toward an understanding of the ideological issues involved with his notion of "interest group liberalism." In his view, the issue of whether or not the government should intervene in the workings of the private market has become moot. Numerous private industry groups demand government intervention to stabilize or enhance their economic position, and they form subgovernmental alliances with agencies and congressional specialists in order to maintain governmental protection. Such actions are legitimized, according to Lowi, by the shared ideology of interest group liberalism, in which government is viewed as an arbiter of conflict between economic interests and as an institution which necessarily plays an active role in meeting the demands of conflicting groups. The system is made fair and workable not by a competitive market detached from government intervention but by its openness to access by various groups and the freedom groups have to bargain and to mobilize support (Lowi, 1979).

However, Lowi's analysis fails to give sufficient weight to continuing ideological divisions over the direction of government growth. H. V. Savitch, in his recent treatment of public policy decisions affecting urban areas (1979), suggests a set of distinctions which takes more fully into account these pivotal ideological differences. Savitch emphasizes, as does Lowi, that the mainstream of U.S. politics does not seriously call into question the basic powers and prerogatives of the private market economy and of those corporate and financial entities which dominate it. He also suggests, as does Lowi, that there is an elite consensus supporting an active role for government in subsidizing and supporting many key market activities. In light of this basic consensus, the traditional designation of liberals as for big government overstates their challenge to the fundamental private economic structure, while the traditional view of conservatives as against big government understates the willingness of most conservatives to utilize government for a variety of purposes.

The true distinction between liberals and conservatives lies, Savitch asserts, in the purposes considered legitimate for governmental action. While a few conservatives continue to espouse a genuinely laissez-faire position, the majority of conservative political actors support government interventions which strengthen and encourage additional productive activity by those economic actors who are already winners in the private market struggle and interventions which reinforce the direction the market system is taking on its own. They tend to see the competitive, entrepreneurial thrust as very much alive in the private sector, and they see it as the main source of creativity and productivity in contemporary society. Government interventions which attempt to alter the distribution of wealth resulting from market transactions or which change the course of market decisions tend to reduce efficiency and productivity and thus to weaken the total system. In contrast, government actions such as infrastructure subsidies, selective tax breaks to encourage investment, or regulation of excessive competition—all interventions which stimulate and support ongoing market activities—have come to be seen as legitimate uses of government power. Savitch prefers to call this outlook the *reinforcing* rather than the conservative outlook, in order to avoid the antigovernment connotations of the more common term. However, this work will use the more familiar term, *conservative*, with the new meaning suggested here.

Liberals, on the other hand, believe in the more active use of government to restrain and channel the activities of the private market. They, too, believe in the basic strength and legitimacy of the private market system, and they frequently support the kind of interventions on behalf of market winners which conservatives also favor. However, they believe that in order to survive and to preserve its positive aspects, the system must make important adaptations to the demands of its environment. Programs are required in order to redistribute wealth in such a way as to ameliorate the conditions of life for those at the bottom of the economic scale, thus curbing their resentment and potential for rebellion. Survival also requires vigorous regulatory control of destruction of the natural environment; of occupational health and safety; and of the quality and safety of consumer goods, to prevent these perceived abuses from weakening the system as a whole. Although their long-term goal is still to preserve, rather than fundamentally alter, the existing order, liberals tend to view a government which more actively plans and orders social relationships as essential to that preservation. Savitch uses the term *meliorist* in place of liberal to avoid the connotation of any fundamental challenge to the power of the private sector. Again, I will retain the more familiar term.

Savitch's characterization fits many of the policy positions consistently taken by the competing elite coalitions which continue to play an important role in public policy making. The actions advocated by liberals, from the New Deal onward, have tended to be minor modifications of market outcomes which address those specific problems causing conflict in the system. The adjustments made often seem to lack intellectual consistency, and in most policy areas there have been frequent changes in the direction of liberal interventions (Aaron, 1978). Yet, over time, these seemingly inconsistent policies are tied together by the belief that private market outcomes must be constantly adjusted and modified by government action in order to maximize the public interest. Conservatives, in contrast, have found such constant "tinkering" to be abhorrent. In their view, the system has to be allowed to work on its own terms in order to survive. Government reallocations of wealth may solve short-term problems, but they create long-term inefficiency and divert resources from their most productive uses. The government may have to be used from time to time to correct glaring inequities, but these interventions must be kept at an absolute minimum.

Savitch's description of the major coalition ideologies also fits the trends in the capitalist world view discussed earlier. In the conservative view, the emergency of a wide range of professional skills is essential to modern technology and organization, but the professionals' penchant for planning must be kept in check so as not to squelch the entrepreneurial dynamism of the system. Planning and problem solving must be used in support, not in contravention, of "natural" market outcomes, which are ultimately in the best interest of society. In practical terms, this has meant criticism of growing intensity against those professional groups which have attached themselves to an enlargement of the government's role. In the last decade in particular, professional public administrators, teachers, social workers, and scholars have been accused, first by Nixon and later with more intensity by Reagan, of fattening themselves at the public trough while bogging down productivity with needless regulations. They are also characterized as lacking the competence and motivation to make intelligent decisions. Conversely, the private sector is defended as the true repository of socially useful expertise.

To define these general positions is not to suggest that they are totally controlling in national public policy decisions. Interest groups focused on immediate economic gains play a powerful role, particularly in shaping the detailed provisions of legislation directly affecting them, and their judgment as to the proper government action in matters directly affecting them may not correspond to the ideological distinctions just delineated. Nevertheless, these general ideological predispositions do play a critical role in a wide range of issues and must be taken into account in any comprehensive model of the political process. To see how they affect housing policy in particular, one must examine more closely how these general orientations have been applied and elaborated in connection with the specific concerns addressed by housing policy.

Housing Policy and Ideology: Multiple Frames of Reference

As was suggested in Chapter 1, the application of the broad liberal and conservative ideologies just described to decisions in a particular policy area is shaped by the unique traditions, values, and interests associated with that policy area. On the one hand, one can predict that the type of response liberals or conservatives will make to housing policy will be similar to responses made in other policy areas. On the other hand, housing policy has a history all its own which influences the decisions being made at any given time. In the ongoing policy process, alternative programs are proposed, debated, implemented, evaluated, and either maintained or rejected. Each stage of the process is influenced greatly by what has gone before — by the success or failure attributed by various actors to various programs.

Yet, delineating the particular values which influence a policy area is never a simple process. The notion of "policy areas" suggests that the various activities of government can be meaningfully divided according to the substantive problems at which these activities are directed; e.g., transportation, defense, health, housing, etc. However, the numerous problems faced by individuals and communities in contemporary societies exist in a complex web of interdependence, in which a program usually cannot define and address any particular problem without also having an impact on a number of related problems. Such multiple impacts are often the result of deliberate attempts by decisionmakers to please diverse groups with a single program, or they may be the unanticipated consequences of governmental action. In either case, both the way in which a policy subsystem evolves and the way in which national leadership of varying ideological persuasions may view specific programs are greatly influenced by the sets of problems or issues seen as forming the *context* of a particular program. If the primary goal of a program is seen as X, that program may be linked, in the eyes of decisionmakers, to a whole set of values and assumptions about programs of X-type. If a program is viewed as primarily directed at Y, another set of assumptions related to Y-type programs may influence their thinking. Policy subsystems often contain different sets of actors who view the same programs as X or Y programs, a fact which can either weaken or broaden program support, depending on the circumstances.

Therefore, if the impact of broader ideologies on policy outcomes is to be fully understood, one must look at the various contexts or frames of reference within which a given policy or program has been viewed. The intended and unintended consequences of programs often cause them to be linked with more than one set of problems simultaneously, and broadly shared ideological assumptions may be applied to programs in different ways, depending on the primary frame of reference in which the program is being viewed at any given time. In the case of housing policy, there are three frames of reference within which housing programs have been viewed. First, and perhaps most importantly, housing has been viewed as one of a set of programs subsumed under the label *social welfare policy*. Second, housing has also been viewed as a *community development policy*. Finally, housing policy has been viewed in the larger context of *macroeconomic policy* which has influenced a wide range of government programs. In the next few pages, these frames of reference will be described in general terms. These descriptions will serve as an introduction to the more detailed analysis presented in Chapters 5 through 8.

Housing as Social Welfare Policy

A social welfare program may be broadly defined as any program which utilizes public resources—in the form of direct financial aid, in-kind assistance, or publicly funded expertise—to alleviate problems confronted by individuals and families which are considered beyond their means or abilities to deal with on their own. Since housing has traditionally been viewed as part of the basic package of benefits necessary to a minimum standard of living (along with food, clothing, medical care, and education) decisions concerning housing programs have been heavily influenced by the overall history of social welfare efforts.

Though social welfare programs can, and do, serve other groups in the population, it is the poor who are their most frequent clients. Therefore, U.S. cultural and political orientations toward poverty play a major role in shaping the scope, design, and implementation of such programs. The central problem of poverty may be briefly stated in the following way. The "natural" working of the market system—that is, the way it allocates resources in the absence of intervention by government or other authoritative institutions—provides vastly unequal material rewards for various roles in the process of production and virtually no rewards for nonparticipation. People at the lower end of this reward structure often cannot afford the level of consumption of basic goods and services which our society defines as adequate or decent. Therefore, a group of people exists who, in their own eyes and the eyes of others, are impoverished. Material deprivation is often accompanied by social and psychological stress which contributes to above average incidences of psychological disorders and social conflict among this group.

The size and composition of the group labelled *the poor* has changed substantially over time. While the overall distribution of wealth in the United States has stayed relatively constant over the last 100 years, rapid increases in productivity have brought about a general increase in the nation's standard of living. Yet, it is a truism of modern social policy that a substantial group remains at a level of existence far below that of the majority—the "other America" which Michael Harrington brought so forcefully to the nation's attention over 20 years ago (Harrington, 1971). Housing which falls below widely accepted minimum standards of quality has been a significant and visible feature of the poverty of this group.

The three central beliefs of the capitalist ideology outlined in Chapter 1 have as one of their major corollaries a justification of the social inequality created by the market. Two arguments are central to this justification. One stresses the *necessity* of poverty as an element in the stable functioning of the economic system. In this view, the threat of poverty serves as an incentive for individuals to contribute their labor to the economic system and to advance within its hierarchies. Without such a threat, the overall productivity of the system would decline, resulting in a smaller 'pie' for the whole society to divide. Also, the price of labor (particularly unskilled labor) is kept low by the threat of even worse deprivation as a result of unemployment. This, in turn, reduces the cost of goods and services to the rest of society.

Another central argument relates to the justice of poverty as a fate which befalls individuals. This defense of poverty rests mainly on the premise that impoverishment is a result of the individual's lack of character and discipline—an unwillingness to make the effort and sacrifices necessary to advance or a cynical attempt to take a free ride at the expense of society. Such a justification of poverty is, of course, close- ly related to a more sweeping defense of the whole system of inequality. Not only do the poor deserve to be where they are, but those at various higher rungs of the economic ladder are there because they have ex- hibited hard work and strength of character. Therefore, they deserve to enjoy the fruits of their labors undisturbed by governmental redistributive efforts or by guilty consciences. In addition, those at the highest levels may justly exercise a disproportionate share of economic, political, or social power due to the wisdom and virtue which their posi- tion purportedly reflects.

For many Americans, hostility toward the poor extends beyond an intellectual defense of inequality to include a visceral dislike of the poor as a group. Many undesirable traits are attributed to them, including laziness, slovenliness, dishonesty, an inability to plan for the future, and a propensity to drug addiction and violence. These perceptions are used not only to justify resistance to social welfare efforts, but also to justify the geographic and social isolation of the poor. In addition, the process of defining one's own status in the U.S. system of stratification is often linked to the ability to enjoy a certain standard of living and to limit the social interactions of oneself and one's family to persons of equal or greater socioeconomic status. As a result, if social programs such as housing subsidies locate the poor in physical proximity to higher status groups or enable them to enjoy a comparable quality of life they are seen as a threat to the status of these groups.

Though there is no logically necessary association between hostility toward the poor and racism, the two are often closely associated in a cir- cular, self-reinforcing thought process. Discrimination in employment leads to disproportionate concentrations of blacks and Hispanics among the poor which leads, in turn, to an automatic association in the minds of many between the characteristic black or Hispanic and the negative characteristics attributed to the poor. This association leads to further discrimination since it reinforces the belief that such groups lack the character or intelligence for higher status occupations. It also intensifies demands for geographic and social isolation of poor persons who are members of racial or ethnic minorities, and the notion of providing services to the poor in general becomes associated with racial integration of those services.

The attitudes just described are widespread in American society and affect political actors at both ends of the political spectrum. However, clear differences have emerged between liberals and conservatives as to how these cultural values have been modified, interpreted, and applied. In particular, the issue of the proper *governmental* response to the problem of poverty divides, perhaps more clearly than any other single issue, the liberal and conservative ideologies described in Part I. Therefore, a brief examination of these two competing attitude sets is necessary in order to understand clearly their impact on housing policy.

THE CONSERVATIVE VIEW. Conservatives are generally characterized by a stricter adherence to the two central justifications for poverty just mentioned, in contrast to liberals who have qualified their support for market-generated inequalities in important ways. However, what most clearly distinguishes the conservative position is the linkage of these justifications of inequality to a rather complex set of attitudes toward the role of government in solving social problems. The strict laissez-faire position stresses the potential economic inefficiency of *any* government role in the allocation of goods and services. However, as previously noted, this outlook is not the operational ideology of most conservative political actors. Instead, they tend to support those forms of government intervention which protect or enhance the opportunities of market winners, while, in contrast, government interventions which force market participants to reallocate resources in uncongenial ways receive the full force of the laissez-faire critique. Clearly, programs directed at alleviating poverty fall into the latter category.

The type of social welfare program which most arouses conservative resistance is one in which the government takes over a segment of the productive apparatus and/or becomes a direct provider of goods and services, thereby placing itself in actual or potential competition with the private sector. Nationalization of key industries or transportation facilities, the direct employment of surplus labor by the government, and publicly owned housing or health facilities have all been bitterly opposed on the grounds that they confer too much power on the public sector and are inefficient uses of resources.

Somewhat more acceptable have been programs in which the government subsidizes private firms in order to make the provision of low cost goods and services profitable. As shall be discussed in Chapter 4, this form of housing subsidy program became very popular in the 1960s. Although arrangements vary from program to program, the basic design is as follows: the provider charges what is determined to be a fair market price for the item; the impoverished consumer pays whatever price governmental guidelines say he or she can afford; and the government pays the difference. Such programs are defended on the grounds that private entities can produce the desired goods with less overhead and less red tape than public sector agencies, a factor which is said to make up for the cost of subsidizing the private firm's profit margin. They are also defended on the grounds that they create less government bureaucracy, which is to say they confer less overall power on the public sector than would be the case under direct government control of production. Finally, such subsidies are said to provide additional economic benefits by stimulating production in key private industries. Subsidies to the poor become subsidies to market winners as well, thus bringing them closer to the type of governmental intervention acceptable to most conservatives.

Some conservatives have found even this type of government intervention to be too extensive, and they have advocated direct cash payments to the poor as an alternative. Milton Friedman has laid out the essential argument for such a system. The private market, he asserts, is ethically justified in large part by the fact that it allows individuals the freedom to choose what mixture of goods and services they wish to consume. One family may choose to consume a lower quality or quantity of food or clothing in order to purchase a better quantity or quality of housing, while another may make the opposite choice. By allowing such choices, the market not only enhances individual freedom, but it also guarantees that society's resources will be utilized in the most efficient way.

Friedman goes on to argue that an in-kind subsidy of housing or any other good by the government represents an intervention in the type and quantity of goods and services consumed which inevitably reduces efficiency. To be sure, individuals are constrained in their consumption choices by the value which the market places on their labor as a commodity, and if this value is too low, a degree of deprivation which is ethically unacceptable may result. However, the corrective to this, in

Freidman's view, should be a direct cash grant to the deprived person, so that the market system is disrupted as little as possible (Friedman, 1962). In Chapter 6, it will be shown that this debate over cash versus in-kind subsidies has been a central one in housing policy.

Another major strand in conservative opposition to social welfare programs relates to the total amount of resources devoted to such programs. Often the debate over programs to alleviate poverty has hinged on the total scale of such efforts rather than yes or no choices as to government involvement. If proposals appear too costly at the outset or are perceived as rising too rapidly in cost, they will be opposed vigorously. The criterion for what constitutes excessive costs is generally an incremental one; i.e., costs must not surpass those of previous levels of effort by too much, too quickly. If so, the program is denounced as a drain on the Treasury which the country cannot afford, often without regard for the relationship between the current level of expenditures and objective measures of the need for the program. Underlying such objections to rapid increases in the scale of such programs is, of course, a desire to contain the power of the public sector and to limit the amount of national resources which are being allocated by nonmarket mechanisms.

This emphasis on controlling the scale of government intervention introduces a paradox into the conservative stance on programs for the poor. Their basic belief that the individual's status is determined by hard work and self-discipline would seem to be more compatible with programs which extend modest amounts of aid to individuals somewhat higher on the socioeconomic scale than the very poor. A blue collar worker who puts in forty hours of hard work each week but whose wages do not provide the surplus necessary to cope with such problems as old age, illness, or layoffs would seem to be a more deserving recipient of aid than an unskilled, chronically unemployed member of the "underclass." As a matter of historical fact, it was just such programs (Social Security, unemployment insurance, etc.) which became the largest and most permanent features of the U.S. welfare state, but this occurred over the bitter opposition of many conservatives. Any attempts to broaden the base of benefits included in these original New Deal measures are resisted on the grounds that funds should be reserved only for those who are most in need.

The reason for this contradiction lies in the large amount of *resources* involved in offering even modest levels of benefits to the relatively better off members of the working and middle classes. Although these persons might be morally deserving, the broadening of aid to include them would involve the government in large scale reallocations of national wealth. Such reallocations enhance the power of the public sector and reverse market allocations in ways that are too extensive from the conservative point of view. Therefore, they have consistently argued for restricting federal programs in housing and other areas to those at the very bottom of the income scale, as a way to control the costs of such programs and to limit the political support which any given program enjoys.

THE LIBERAL VIEW. Although the prevailing cultural image of the poor has been negative, a number of strands in the U.S. cultural weave support the alleviation of poverty on moral or ethical grounds, and the contemporary liberal position has arisen, in part, from these strands. First, the Judeo-Christian belief in the ultimate dignity and worth of each human being, regardless of social rank, has led to constant efforts by church leaders to encourage the privileged to extend aid to the poor. Second, the American belief in democratic equality, while generally applied only to the political realm, has been extended by many to include notions of government-protected equality of opportunity and of a publicly guarranteed floor under market-generated inequality. Finally, though socialism has never enjoyed widespread support in the American working class, the notion of a fair share of society's wealth for those who help produce it has influenced the thinking of many of its leaders and their professional allies.

However, ethical arguments by themselves have rarely provided a sufficient basis for winning political coalitions in favor of social welfare programs. One reason for this is that beliefs supporting inequality have such a direct and powerful link to the immediate interest of the business, financial, and professional elites who have tended to dominate policy formulation in the United States. Moral suasion alone has been insufficient to dislodge this link, especially when guilt about the poverty of others can easily be assuaged by piecemeal, paternalistic, private charity.

Another reason is that working and middle class citizens who have supported various egalitarian reforms tend to have strongly ambivalent attitudes toward those below them on the economic scale. They often resent the taxes necessary to support social welfare programs, even when they agree with the ends of such programs in the abstract (Wilensky, 1975; Free and Cantril, 1967). In addition, they share with elites a strong belief in the work ethic, and they relate whatever gains they have made to the self-discipline required by their own very real struggles.

To overcome these sources of resistance and gain broader support for social welfare programs, advocates of such programs have, therefore, moved beyond moral suasion to strategies which appeal more directly to the interests and concerns of economic and political elites and of the mass of working and middle class citizens. They have tried to create an alternative set of beliefs by which these groups can link their interests to those of the poor. The result has been the development of what Lawrence Friedman (1968) calls "social cost" justifications. These arguments have in common an emphasis on the costs which the suffering of the poor imposes on the rest of society. As such, they represent a fundamental shift away from the older notion that poverty is beneficial to society.

Within this general classification, three distinct types of social cost justification may be discerned. The first stresses the long-term threat to the stability of the economic and political system posed by the sufferings of the poor. According to this view, the frustrations of the poor will lead them periodically to engage in violent, socially disruptive behavior and may make them receptive to the revolutionary appeals of radical counter-elites. Thus, those who benefit from the system must be willing to limit its most flagrant abuses, even if these spring "naturally" from the underlying structure of the system. Such an argument is particularly appealing in times of system crisis when calls for radical alternatives seem to be gaining momentum.

The second social cost argument emphasizes the immediate impact of the deprivations of the poor on other members of society. In the nineteenth century when infectious diseases such as cholera were still common, it was easy to show a direct link between pestilence bred in the slums and the health of the community as a whole. Later, as these threats receded, other themes were emphasized, such as reductions in crime and reductions in the costs of institutionalizing the victims of poverty. With regard to housing, an essentially aesthetic argument was often used. Slums were described as physically ugly, blighted areas of the community which were an offense to the sensibilities and pride of the whole. Getting rid of slums was seen as a way of cleaning up the community which was presumed to benefit slum dwellers as well, though in most cases they were simply displaced into other blighted areas.

The third social cost justification views the individual in poverty as a human resource. The individual's potential contribution to the productivity and well-being of the society as a whole is, in this view, wasted by poverty. Moreover, this wastage results not from individual character flaws but from material deprivation, a negative social environment (family, school, neighborhood, etc.) and psychological stress. All of these factors taken together have been referred to as the "culture of poverty," the effects of which may be counteracted by proper public intervention.

Radical critics of these social cost justifications, such as Piven and Cloward (1966; 1971; 1982), have pointed out that programs implemented with social costs as their rationale often contain strong elements of control and suppression of the poor behind a facade of enlightened humanitarianism. They ignore the structural causes of poverty within the overall system of labor utilization and treat the individudal characteristics of the poor as the primary causes of their status. Such a control element fits well within the basic appeal to the self interest of groups other than the poor which is at the heart of all social cost justifications. These approaches emphasize poverty as a problem within the larger social order with which it must deal in order to maintain itself, not the absolute value of the poor as human beings. Such a view also reinforces the status of those middle class professions which, as noted earlier, have arisen to take care of such problems for the society as a whole.

The social cost critiques of poverty just described form the core of the liberal justification of social welfare. As Savitch (1979) notes, mainstream liberalism in the United States has stopped short of advocating fundamental changes in the market system of allocation. This tendency toward moderate reform can be traced, in large part, to the fact that the needs of the poor are usually expressed not by the poor themselves but by more privileged members of society on their behalf. Liberal members of the politically active stratum have a stake in expanding services to the poor, but they also have a stake in the existing system of inequality which grants them their personal status, and they have close ties to those at the top of the system who provide the funds for research and service endeavors.

However, the historical record also shows that liberals have often been quite willing to expand social welfare and other forms of social engineering much further than is reflected in existing social welfare policies. Therefore, one must look at the political balance of forces between liberal and conservative coalitions to understand the limited nature of U.S. social welfare efforts, not just at the characteristics of liberals themselves.

The necessity of compromise puts both factions in the position of defending policy outcomes which they regard as less than optimal. This, after all, is the nature of politics. However, the compromise is, perhaps, more difficult and politically costly for liberals since it is they who are defending government action rather than nonintervention in social welfare matters. Liberal politicians usually have to fight hard to get any sort of program put in place, no matter how limited in scope or design. Yet, the very limits they must accept make the program vulnerable to valid criticisms from other liberal scholars, journalists, and policy advocates concerning its design, administrative procedures, comprehensiveness, or equity. The ultimate purpose of such critiques may be the improvement or expansion of the program in question, and, to the extent that the analysis encourages effective political demands for change on the part of clients and/or stimulates legislators and administrators to initiate improvements, it may have the desired effect. At the same time, in a political atmosphere of elite dissensus as to just what the overall role of the public sector in social welfare should be, such critiques may actually serve to undermine political support for existing programs, rather than generate pressures for expansion.

This may occur in at least two ways. First, conservatives may use such critiques to argue for the overall unworkability of the program and the consequent need to scrap it, or they may cite the problems of several programs in support of the even more global claim that government social welfare programs don't work. Second, while the constant critical analysis by liberals of programs whose overall intent they support is an important and necessary part of experimentation and improvement, it also serves to create division and uncertainty within their ranks, which makes programs more vulnerable to curtailment or elimination. In the face of a dual onslaught from the left and from the right, defenders of existing programs are left on rather barren intellectual and emotional ground. Statements such as "It may not be perfect but it's the best we could get," or, "We know there are problems but look at the program's successes," may be empirically accurate, but they hardly serve as clarion calls to political action on the program's behalf. (Mollenkopf, 1983, applies this argument in a thorough and sophisticated way in his treatment of urban liberalism.)

The above should not be construed as a suggestion that liberals stop making intellectually valid critiques of social welfare programs. To do so would not only be unethical but would surely invite even worse political disasters. Rather, it is to point out the precarious and ambivalent position in which liberals find themselves in their efforts toward greater government involvement in social welfare problems. As will be made abundantly clear in the following discussion of housing policy, our nation's seeming inability to arrive at coherent government policies in this area is not solely a result, as has often been suggested, of insufficient planning or information, but of the simultaneous existence of two intellectual and political struggles — one over *whether* government should get involved and the other over *how* public involvement should be organized and executed.

Housing as Community Development Policy

The second frame of reference within which housing policy has been viewed is that of community development policy. Community development, in its broadest sense, is the total process by which a geographic or political entity improves the quality of its physical structures, its economic life, and its social relationships; however, the major issues in this arena tend to revolve around *physical* improvements and/or their interaction with the other factors just mentioned.

Housing policy decisions are influenced by this environment because housing has traditionally been viewed, not just as an item of immediate consumption or as a service to particular families, but as a physical resource. As such, it occupies a large portion of the space available in the community and shapes the qualitative and quantitative allocation of that space. Each dwelling unit is also linked to a package of neighborhood and community services and amenities which, in addition to the physical condition of the unit itself, help determine the quality of life for several generations of families. Thus, urban housing programs have become embroiled in a larger debate over the shape and direction of local community growth.

Community development policy has been dominated by two distinct, but interrelated sets of issues. One set consists of issues pertaining to the role of local government vis-à-vis the private sector in the control of economic growth and physical development. The other set of issues relates to the changing distribution of power between federal, state, and local governments as they have assumed differing roles in the local community development process. The latter set is, of course, but one subset of a whole range of policy problems in the arena of intergovernmental relations, but community development issues have raised problems of intergovernmental roles more clearly and forcefully than many other issues.

Ideological divisions among political elites are not as clear with regard to community development issues as they are in social welfare issues. As shall be shown, community development policies tend to be pursued by different groups for different reasons. However, a clear division has emerged with regard to the proper direction community development should take. Most liberals and most conservatives have, since the New Deal, supported some kind of federal role in community development activities, but they have differed as to the nature of that role. These liberal/conservative differences are an important part of the environment in which housing policy has been formed.

COMMUNITY DEVELOPMENT: PUBLIC-PRIVATE RELATIONSHIPS. The urban community development process in the United States has, from the earliest days of settlement, been primarily in private hands. The rate at which cities have grown, the allocation of the physical space they occupy, and the distribution of the benefits of development among the population have largely been determined by private economic decisions based on market considerations (Chudacoff, 1981; Savitch, 1979). Nevertheless, public services and amenities have always been seen as a necessary element in this growth by key private actors.

In the mid-nineteenth century, many U.S. cities began to grow very rapidly. The massive influx of immigrants and the rapid pace of economic development required new investments in public services such as transportation, utilities, and police, even though the services expected of government were still much more limited than today. The initial response of many cities to the stress of growth was the development of political machines, whose leaders coordinated the development of public services through bribery and kickbacks, enriching themselves greatly in the process. This form of extralegal centralization enjoyed the support of business interests for a considerable period. However, as business itself began to change from the entrepreneurial to the professional managerial style, a new breed of managers and professionals became increasingly frustrated with the corrupt, personalistic style of machine rule. Tired of paying the financial price and eager to apply to government the same principles of scientific management to which they aspired in their private endeavors, they became key backers of the municipal reform movement which swept local politics during the early twentieth century.

The business and professional leaders who pushed for reform often received the support of middle class social reformers who wanted to improve the living conditions and opportunities of the urban poor. These reformers saw the bosses as essentially exploitative, in spite of their various charitable endeavors. Yet, the new reform leadership often proved even more insensitive to the needs of the poor and working classes than the bosses had been. Defenders of reform institutions spoke of a unified public interest for the whole community, to be determined by an informed citizenry and executed by competent, professional, public officials. In fact, the new institutions were often dominated by upper middle class and upper class groups who saw the public interest as closely identified with their own interest in economic growth. The concepts of minimum government and sound financial management which they advocated often meant an absence of services to the poor.

Lawrence Friedman (1968) has documented the attempt early housing reformers made to utilize this notion of a community interest in the shape of development. Jacob Riis and other early advocates of housing for the poor borrowed a term from biology — *blight* — to describe slum conditions. This term implied that slums were a disease which threatened the whole community, just as blight on one branch of a tree could soon spread its poison to the whole tree. Yet, in the hands of business-oriented elites, the concept soon came to focus on the physical existence of the slums, not the problems of the people inhabiting them. The goal of removing blight was used to justify physical destruction of the slums with little regard for the fate of their inhabitants.

These conflicting uses of the term *blight* highlighted the conflicting values which physical planning and other deliberate public efforts at community development would come to serve. In one sense, such efforts contradicted the laissez-faire notion of city growth. The forerunners of the modern planning profession, people like Frederic Law Olmstead and Daniel Burnham, dreamed of transforming the crowded hodgepodge of market-generated city growth into planned, orderly, convenient, aesthetically pleasing communities. In carving Central Park out of Manhattan's crowded street grid, Olmstead clearly went against the land uses that market forces would have dictated, in order to create open space and greenery for city dwellers. And other early planners optimistically predicted that physical improvements would alleviate the social problems of the poor. Thus, the professionals involved in physical planning seemed to share a common goal with those involved in expansion of social welfare programs; i.e., the need for conscious public modification of market outcomes in order to benefit society as a whole (Mohl, 1973).

In another sense, the kind of professionalization involved was quite different from the commitments to social reform which gradually evolved among other groups. Although both forms of planning contravene the pure market form of community growth (which allocates space to the highest bidder and rewards each citizen according to the market value of his or her labor) physical planning is a kind of market intervention which clearly reinforces the interests of the majority of economic elites. First, it fits their notion of "civic pride" in that planning can easily justify the creation of showy public facilities and open spaces which improve the community's image (i.e., attractiveness to new investment). Second, physical planning can be used to meet the need for some rational ordering of public services, facilities, and land use to support private economic development. Thus, zoning was transformed from a tool for the creation of orderly growth to a tool for excluding "undesirables" from certain neighborhoods, and for the strategic enhancement of property values; even transportation and utilites planning became the design of streets and sewers to serve areas already developed by private enterprise (Chudacoff, 1981). Social welfare programs, in contrast, present a more direct challenge to ideological justifications of inequality, and their long-term contribution to the stability of any given community is often not so readily apparent to many of its leaders.

Thus, a liberal/conservative split has come to be operative in community development policy over the scope and direction of such activities. Strict, laissez-faire conservatives have been reluctant to support any active government role, even in physical planning and redevelopment, but many otherwise conservative actors, who oppose social welfare measures, support such a governmental role as a useful and justifiable subsidy to private investors. These supporters believe that public community development programs should have as their predominant thrust the overall economic development of the community, even when that imposes costs on lower income persons. Liberals, too, have supported the use of public funds for physical planning and economic development, and in administering the nation's first major community development program, urban renewal, some politically liberal local leaders proved very insensitive to the needs of the disadvantaged. Nevertheless, the overall thrust of liberal action with regard to community development has been to urge that it directly address the needs of the poor, in addition to serving general economic development needs. As shall be shown in Chapters 7 and 8, this liberal/conservative struggle became very important in the later years of the urban renewal program, and it continued to shape the debate over the uses of Community Development Block Grant funds.

COMMUNITY DEVELOPMENT AND INTERGOVERNMENTAL RELATIONS. Debates over the role of local government in community development can be traced to the nineteenth century, but, prior to the Great Depression, most participants in these debates agreed that the federal government had little or no legitimate role to play in the process. During this crisis, in contrast, many cities were gripped by physical, and financial problems which far exceeded the capacity of local governments to respond. The federal government became involved because it was the only entity which could amass sufficient resources to deal with long lines of the unemployed or could provide needed public works when most city treasuries were nearly empty. Nevertheless, this increased federal role went against a long tradition of decentralization in U.S. politics. The defenders of this tradition, while not able to block federal involvement totally, were still strong enough to influence it profoundly.

The notion that state and local governments are closer to the people than the federal government has been a staple of U.S. political rhetoric throughout most of the country's history. However, it was James Madison who, in making his case for a strong federal government, first warned that smaller units of government might be more easily dominated by a single faction which could then guide governmental decisions exclusively in its own interest. Grant McConnell expanded this line of thought, arguing that privileged groups have a relatively easier time controlling the political decisions of smaller, decentralized units of government. The elite in each unit is smaller and more homogeneous, which facilitates communication and the formulation of common interests. Also, the unit is more likely to be dominated by one or two major economic activities, which control most of the resources for public action. Conversely, people whose resources are already small are weakened by their inability to join with large numbers of others in a common cause (McConnell, 1966).

Another reason why political decentralization tends to benefit economic elites, emphasized by Mollenkopf (1983) is the increased bargaining power which large economic entities have vis-à-vis government. Throughout the development of the U.S economy, the private sector has become more and more national and interdependent in scope, finally expanding beyond the nation's borders to acquire major international leverage. While even a large firm incurs substantial costs in moving a subsidiary operation of any size, the fact remains that economic units are very mobile in relation to units of government. This forces states and localities into competition with each other for economic development. In order to stimulate local economic growth, governments must strike a bargain with private sector entities which is favorable enough to attract and keep them. Of course, some parts of the bargain are not controllable by local government, such as climate, markets, and transportation; but this makes them even more eager to manipulate those they can control, such as taxes, subsidies, and regulations, to create a favorable business climate. This relatively weak bargaining position makes it very difficult for any locality to impose costs or regulations on the private sector, no matter how well such measures might serve the needs of local citizens. Only the federal government is in a position to impose strong, uniform regulations or obligations which firms cannot avoid by moving out of town or out of state.

It is, therefore, no accident that the lines of political division over the issue of centralization versus decentralization have closely paralleled the liberal/conservative split over the role of the government in altering market decisions. Even though the economic crisis of the 1930s shifted the American elite consensus to support some federal involvement, the liberal/conservative split soon reemerged in a slightly different form around issues concerning the extent and direction of such involvement. Conservatives continued to oppose programs which aided the poor, like public housing, but many became more willing to accept physical development aid which reinforced existing market tendencies, provided that such aid was administered locally, and so did not interfere with local elite prerogatives or alter program benefits in favor of the disadvantaged. Liberals, in contrast, supported both physical redevelopment *and* social welfare efforts. They were willing to accept greater federal planning, guidance, and financing of local efforts as a means to insure more equitable treatment for those disadvantaged by the market.

The Macroeconomic Frame of Reference

The third frame of reference which has influenced housing policy, along with virtually every other area of governmental activity, is that of macroeconomic policy. Since the Depression, and even more since World War II, the federal government has taken upon itself the responsibility of deliberate macroeconomic intervention, in order to minimize the peaks and valleys of prosperity and recession to which the market system is subject.

This larger environment affects housing policy in two ways. First, since virtually every actor in the system feels a strong stake in the outcomes of economic policy, the struggles between liberals and conservatives over the proper macroeconomic interventions help to set the tone and atmosphere for their struggles in more narrow policy areas. If the set of solutions offered by one group of policymakers is in popular favor or disfavor, then this tends to enhance or detract from their influence across the board. This aspect of the economic policy environment will be further discussed in the present chapter.

Second, the behavior of the economy as a whole, whether in response to its own internal dynamics or in response to conscious government interventions, has a direct and obvious impact on the housing sector of the private market. Long term economic trends, such as inflation, greatly affect the availability and cost of housing. Moreover, as these trends interact with broad social and demographic trends in urban communities, they create different problems for different segments of the population. These problems, in turn, have an influence on the kinds of federal housing policies which appeal to decisionmakers. This aspect of the impact of economic policy will be discussed in Chapter 3.

In sharp contrast to the economic crisis of the 1930s, the period from 1945 to 1970 was, in general, a time of unprecedented growth and stability in the U.S. economy. Many sectors of the economy were expanding, both in domestic and foreign production. Technological advances were rapid, and the real standard of living of most citizens improved. Both inflation and unemployment were present, but they appeared to be small and manageable factors.

This period was also an era of increased government responsibility for the management of the economy. During the Depression, John Maynard Keynes had suggested that deliberate management of aggregate demand by government was both possible and desirable, and that modest governmental deficits might serve as a useful economic stimulus. Fearful of a postwar return to economic stagnation, Congress enacted the Employment Act of 1946, which gave the federal government a formal mandate to stabilize cyclical economic swings with fiscal and monetary policy. The practice of fiscal policy was further guided by the formulation of the "Phillips Curve." This theoretical construct suggested a direct trade-off between inflation and unemployment which could be manipulated by government fiscal policy in order to fine tune the economy.

Since prosperity coincided with increased governmental economic management, it was easy for policymakers to convince themselves that the latter was the principal cause of the former. Specific fiscal interventions, such as the tax cut of 1964, were attempted, and they seemed to produce the desired results. This experience suggested that various techniques of federal intervention could, with further refinement, increasingly smooth out the troughs and peaks which had previously been endemic to the capitalist economy. The fact that some of the underlying causes of prosperity—expanding domestic and foreign markets, rapid technological changes, and cheap energy—were less under the control of government tended to be ignored in the atmosphere of confidence produced by these successful manipulations.

The belief that government can intervene positively to improve the workings of the market was earlier identified with the liberal ideology. Yet, in the realm of macroeconomic policy, a broad consensus covering a wide segment of the political spectrum seemed, in the late 1950s, to have developed behind the notion of countercyclical intervention by the federal government. Some conservatives protested the deficits of some years and increases in federal expenditures they considered excessive. However, these protests were often closely tied to their more typical concern with the substance of specific programs (particularly those aiding the poor.) This broad agreement on certain basic types of government intervention lent credence to the 'end of ideology' thesis expressed in different forms by several scholars, in which it was argued that issues of the governmental role which had stirred ideological debate in previous years would be reduced to technical issues concerning the means to accomplish such goals (Bell, 1962; Moynihan, 1967).

The general prosperity of the country, plus the apparent consensus behind the government's macroecnomic role, encouraged many liberals to believe, in the early 1960s, that the nation should use its wealth to solve some of the troubling social problems which remained. The smooth facade of the "affluent society" was still marred by the interrelated phenomena of racial inequality, chronic poverty, and the decay of many central cities. Therefore, the Kennedy and Johnson Administrations initiated a new series of social welfare measures more extensive than any since the New Deal. A sense of crisis and urgency was added to the situation by the growing racial conflict of the decade, and initially strong opposition in Congress was weakened by media reports of burning cities. As a result, the 1960s ended with a broad array of Great Society programs in place; such as the War on Poverty; Model Cities; the Civil Rights Acts of 1964 and 1968; the Voting Rights Act; and the Housing Acts of 1961, 1965, and 1968.

Before the full political effects of these measures, either positive or negative, could be felt, U.S. involvement in the Vietnam War produced a dark cloud on the political horizon of the Democratic leadership. The increasing frustration of this war slowed and blunted the Johnson Administration's efforts to use federal programs to rebuild the cities and aid the disadvantaged. Johnson diverted funds from domestic to military expenditures, and he began to use up his substantial political capital to defend the increasingly unpopular war. Disagreement over the war also divided Johnson's liberal political coalition and contributed to the Democrats' defeat in 1968.

Yet, despite its importance, the Vietnam War alone was not sufficient to derail the government's new social commitments. Higher levels of domestic expenditures continued during the entire conflict, and the moderately conservative Nixon Administration which took office in 1968 found these programs sufficiently popular with a Democratic Congress and with the public that it acceeded to their continued expansion during

Nixon's first four years. Thus, the political momentum of the Great Society programs carried them well into the early 1970s. It was only when a new set of problems came to the forefront of the national agenda that their progress began to be slowed and eventually derailed.

This new policy agenda of the 1970s was dominated by concerns for the health of the economy as a whole and new disagreements about the government's proper function in regulating it. The main concern was a phenomenon not anticipated by traditional models of the business cycle — a persistent combination of relatively high unemployment with high inflation which came to be called *stagflation*. Data provided by Best and Connolly show that the trade-off between modest levels of each which was predicted by the Phillip's Curve actually occurred in the 1960s. However, the unemployment/inflation combinations which occurred in the 1970s deviated strongly in the direction of simultaneously high levels for both (Best and Connolly, 1982, p. 159).

Discussion of this phenomenon often focuses on its proximate causes. Two events are most frequently mentioned as immediate precursors to the inflationary spiral. First, the Johnson Administration elected to avoid increasing the hostility toward the Vietnam War among his own liberal supporters by keeping to a minimum the replacement of social program expenditures with military expenditures. Johnson also delayed requesting additional taxes to finance the war for three years, until he could muster sufficient congressional support for such a politically risky move. The result was an increase in the federal deficit which proved difficult to overcome in later years. The second event was the rapid energy cost increases which hit in 1973–74. Though the political concerns of Arab oil producers were the immediate cause, their boycott was successful only because of a dramatic increase in the demand for energy in relation to supply (Szulc, 1978). Thus, their action signalled the end of an era of cheap energy, and, by increasing the costs of many key factors of production, it sent a ripple of inflation through the U.S. economy.

Nevertheless, in spite of the importance of these proximate causes of stagflation, many economists are convinced that the impact of these factors would not have been nearly as severe had not certain structural problems already existed in the U.S. economy. These problems bear some discussion, since their breadth and complexity contrasts with the simplistic analyses which, as shall be shown, were part of the political debate. Four problems stand out as most critical. First, Best and Connolly (1982) have called attention to the increasingly oligopolistic nature of the U.S. economy during the late 1960s. This affected inflation because firms controlling large market shares responded differently to reductions in demand than did competitive firms. Instead of lowering prices, these firms tended to curtail production, hoping to ride out demand delcines without sacrificing their profit margin on each unit. Their ability to influence prices through voluntary control of output also created chronic underutilization of capacity which contributed to unemployment.

Second, Best and Connolly emphasize the decline in the growth of the productivity of the average American worker during the 1970s. In earlier decades, rapid productivity increases enabled firms to grant wage increases out of reduced labor costs per unit. With productivity increases slowing down, wage increases were much more likely to stimulate price increases than had been the case before. Again, disagreement existed over the causes of lower productivity. Industry representatives tended, publicly at least, to blame new government regulations, but the problem was clearly much more complex than this. Some industries were allowing basic technologies to become obsolete while investing in mergers and other "nonproductive" uses of capital. In addition, business firms tried to satisfy worker discontent over alienating and unsafe working conditions with wage increases rather than structural changes, a strategy encouraged by the strictly economic orientation of labor unions.

A third factor contributing to stagflation, emphasized by Lester Thurow, was the changing structure of the labor market. In "classical" economic theory, a downturn in sales should lead to reductions in wages, rather than unemployment. However, in the modern economy, firms have a large stake in the training they have given each worker and in maintaining the cooperation of employees on the job. Therefore, they try to maintain or expand wages for those actually working, even if this requires layoffs. Unions have also supported this strategy, and nonunion firms, trying to compete for workers and avoid unionization, have tended to follow suit (Thurow, 1981).

A fourth structural factor, emphasized by Thurow and others, was the self-perpetuating quality of inflation. The persistance of high rates of inflation led both business and labor to incorporate anticipated inflation into their plans. Unions demanded compensation for past losses of real income and protection against future losses as well. Rising interest rates were also, in part, the result of investor anxieties about future inflation. And Congress responded to the concerns of the elderly by building into the Social Security system an automatic Cost of Living Adjustment (COLA) based on the Consumer Price Index.

The net result of all of these factors was to make the economy highly resistant to government attempts either to lower prices by cooling down economic expansion or to reduce unemployment by priming the economic pump. During the recessions of 1970–71 and 1974–75, unemployment rose sharply but prices merely leveled off. Once recovery from these downswings began, prices rose rapidly while unemployment stayed relatively high due to sluggish real growth. In addition, political fallout made it difficult to pursue either a stimulative or a contractionary policy consistently. In the 1960s, the inflation unemployment trade-off was acceptable in part because the levels of both were not considered unreasonable. In the 1970s, the fact that both were at much higher levels made either side of the trade-off harder to sell to various constituencies.

These difficulties also highlighted some of the problems inherent in utilizing fiscal policy to fine tune the economy. A major problem was the fact that spending and taxing decisions were shaped by many other forces besides fiscal policy considerations. Spending tended to be pushed upward by the demands of various groups for governmental assistance, while Congress was very reluctant to incur the wrath of taxpayers in general by raising taxes to pay for these demands. In fact, lawmakers were under constant pressure to lower tax rates in the face of inflation-induced 'bracket creep" and to provide additional tax breaks to finance new investment and other activities considered desirable. Thus, deficits, with their inherently stimulative effects, became a more or less permanent part of the federal budget during the 1970s, and they could not easily be manipulated out of existence in the name of fiscal restraint.

Ideological Responses to Economic Problems

The seemingly intractable economic difficulties of the 1970s contributed to a widely observed loss of public faith in the ability of government to take effective, positive action to deal with economic and social problems. However, it is unlikely that the atmosphere could have changed so strongly against governmental activism had it not been for the particular ways in which the liberal and conservative elite factions reacted to the growing discontent. Liberals, it appears, were neither willing nor able to develop a coherent response to these problems. Conservatives, in contrast, were able to construct from the crisis a fairly coherent critique of current government policies and thus to utilize the problems of the 1970s to their political advantage.

The conservative critique which evolved out of the experiences of the 1970s was based on principles espoused by conservatives since the New Deal, but they were revised and embellished to conform to new circumstances. The central premise of this critique was that the federal government (and the public sector in general) was the principal cause of the economic troubles of the era and that it was essential to reduce the role of government in the economy and the society in order to get the United States back on an expansive, inflation-free track. This premise had several complex corollaries.

First was the notion that high levels of government spending, and particularly of deficit spending, were the principal cause of inflation. Government borrowing, it was argued, drove up prices by pumping more dollars into the economy, especially when this borrowing was 'monetized' by the Federal Reserve. As expressed in conservative political rhetoric, this argument took only one of the many complex factors contributing to inflation and elevated it to center stage, ignoring the built-in features of the private market which also fueled rising prices. However, it provided a convenient means to attack social welfare measures already distasteful to conservatives.

A second element in the conservative attack on government was the notion that the level of taxation in the United States was becoming increasingly burdensome both to the consumer and to the investor. The taxes paid by many citizens had increased faster than inflation, both because government needed new revenues to pay higher costs and because bracket creep automatically pushed up tax rates. Thus, the notion of excessive taxation fell upon sympathetic ears. In addition, since the phenomenon of productivity decline was little understood, it was easy to blame losses in productivity on the disincentives built into the tax system. Linking taxation to their critique of social welfare programs, conservatives would wax eloquent on the way in which such programs represented a drain of dollars from more productive activities.

The two most visible manifestations of a popular tax revolt which appeared to support this notion occurred in the late 1970s. One was Proposition 13 in California. The passage of this measure was widely read by political elites as a popular rejection of the overall tax burden, and it stimulated tax ceilings in many other states. Another more philosophical manifestation of the tax revolt was the development of "supply side economics." This theory focused on the disincentives to private investment and production provided by taxation. On the basis of the Laffer Curve, it was argued that achieving an optimum level of taxation was essential for economic growth and that existing tax levels exceeded this optimum (Palmer and Sawhill, 1982).

A third component of the new conservative attack was the argument that government regulation was strangling the economy by increasing inflation and discouraging investment. As a result of legislation passed in the 1960s and early 1970s, the private sector found itself with new governmental constraints in areas of decision making which had previously been its exclusive preserves, such as environmental regulation, consumer protection, and Affirmative Action guidelines. These new measures were sometimes costly to businesses because of the delays they imposed and because firms were forced to internalize new costs (such as paying for the control of pollution which had previously been borne as a negative externality by the public at large). Thus, it was not surprising that many would blame these regulations for inflating prices and slowing down investment. Conservative spokespersons calculated the billions of dollars government regulations cost consumers, and drew up lists of plant closings due to environmental regulations. These compilations tended to ignore the fact that the most costly regulations were those which *supported* business profits, such as trucking and airline rate controls (Pechman, 1979). Nevertheless, they made appealing political rhetoric.

A fourth component of the conservative attack on government was the blanket assertion that "federal social programs don't work." In order to bolster the notion that the increased size of government was essentially a nonproductive and even counter-productive use of the nation's resources, it was necessary to show that many public programs were both wasteful and ineffective. Unfortunately, evaluations of various Great Society programs provided much ammunition for this charge. Many of them had been hastily conceived, underfunded, and then oversold to the public. Thus, evaluation research often turned up evidence of an impact on the problem which was much less than the public had been led to expect (Aaron, 1978). As noted in connection with social welfare policy, much of this evidence was gathered by liberals with an eye to the expansion or improvement of these programs, but the negative findings were seized upon by conservative critics as proof of the inherent unworkability of such programs and as demonstrative of the need to dismantle them.

A fifth and final component of the new conservative rhetoric was often used as an envelope in which to wrap the other components. This was the idea of 'limits'—the notion that individual citizens had to contain their demands on government and the economy in order to avoid long-term economic disaster. Ironically, some of this rhetoric was borrowed from environmentalists and other essentially liberal groups who had argued that limits on the material consumption of the affluent, or at least changes in the patterns of consumption to make it less wasteful of resources, would be necessary in order to maintain the long-term quality of life. Some conservatives turned this argument on its head, asserting that the less affluent segments of the population, the poor and working class, would have to place limits on their demands for government protection and redistribution of wealth in order to restore economic health.

Media commentators glibly labeled the 1970s the "decade of lowered expectations." By this, they meant that most Americans would have to settle for less improvement in their living conditions than they had come to expect in the era of postwar expansion.

The liberal response to this growing chorus of criticism was a complex one. On the one hand, as shall be shown in connection with the federal housing effort, many liberal spokespersons continued to defend specific programs and to argue that, though problems existed, blanket assertions of their unworkability or failure were not supported by the evidence. They argued for the government's continued role in cushioning the effects of market-generated inequality and in regulating threats to the consumer and to the environment to which the market mechanism was not responsive.

On the other hand, unlike conservatives, they did not arrive at a central premise or set of premises upon which to base either a defense of existing government activities or a call for an expanded level of government activity. For conservatives, the central premise was that "the government is the problem." For liberals to maintain the momentum of the Great Society and their credibility as stewards of the economy, they would have had to forcefully argue the premise that the chronic economic problems of the decade required a *more* active government role in planning investment decisions and in regulating prices and wages. They would have had to direct criticisms of inflation and stagnation away from the actions of government and toward basic decisions made in the private sector. They would have had to direct the implications of criticisms of the effectiveness of social programs toward the notion of improved achievement of the basic objectives of these programs and away from the notion that government was inherently incapable of achieving these objectives.

The fact that mainstream liberals did not develop such a coherent defense of the government's role can be attributed in part to their own basic adherence to central capitalist ideological premises. As indicated in Chapter 1, U.S. liberalism has been primarily a philosophy of pragmatic adjustment. The kind of response just mentioned would have carried liberals, not beyond capitalism, but toward a redefinition of the government's role in the economy. Government would not cease to have economic growth as its main goal but would attempt to accomplish this goal through much more active planning and intervention than had previously been accepted. The liberal mainstream had little enthusiasm for moving in this direction.

However, even if more liberals had possessed the enthusiasm and imagination to espouse such an approach, they would have found the political atmosphere of the 1970s very unreceptive to their ideas. Unlike the crisis of the 1930s, the critical problems of the 1970s had not proceeded to the point where the survival of the system appeared immediately in doubt. Had this been the case, a broad segment of political and economic elites, and of the public at large, might have been receptive to additional restrictions on private economic prerogatives. Instead, the chronic, low grade nature of stagflation made both elites and the general public receptive to the notion that a repeal of the government's role might be the way out. The fact that the restrictions and redistributions of the 1960s were too new to have been accepted as part of the normal course of doing business created an even greater receptivity to such an approach, since an attack on government was a convenient way to place the blame on activities already widely resented. Thus, in the complex relationship between the formulation and acceptance of new ideas by various segments of the elite, on the one hand, and the political atmosphere created by current problems which encourages or discourages such ideas, one set of alternatives was accepted and the other, consciously or unconsciously, rejected as impracticable.

The purpose of this discussion is not to argue that a more aggressive brand of liberalism would have been a more effective approach to solving the nation's problems than the conservative alternative of retrenchment which increasingly became the strategy of choice. A complete answer to that question is beyond the scope of this book. The main point to be made here is that, given liberals' inability to develop or sell such a positive defense of governmental activism, the 1970s saw them move increasingly to the defensive. One has only to compare the stirring calls to action made by Lyndon Johnson in the mid-1960s to the cautious call for lowered expectations made by Jimmy Carter in the late 1970s to see how far the movement in this direction had proceeded. In the 1960s, more doctrinaire conservatives had lamented the tendency of moderate Republicans toward "metooism," i.e., the offering of modified versions of liberal initiatives as their alternative program. In the 1970s, ironically, it was liberals who fell into the 'me too' role, as they argued for a lesser version of the governmental retrenchment which conservatives were advocating so strongly.

It took most of the 1970s for the trend toward retrenchment to take hold. In housing, as in other areas, the quantitative data show an overall upward trend in governmental expenditures and activity. However, the continuing inability of the federal government to manage the central problem of stagflation gradually undermined the confidence of decisionmakers and the public. Though social programs continued at higher levels of expenditure than in earlier decades, they were increasingly losing support. And, finally, the stage was set for the drastic reorientation of government activities which the Reagan Administration began to implement in the early 1980s.

CHAPTER 3

The Economic Context:
Housing Markets and Submarkets

While the main concern of this book is federal housing and community development policy during the critical decade of the 1970s these concrete policy decisions are more clearly understood in the context of the behavior of housing markets as a whole in the United States during this period. The first step in creating such a context is the examination of major demographic trends in urban areas during this period. There is never a single housing market in the United States but, rather, a variety of submarkets, which are created by the settlement patterns of various economic and racial groups. The second step is the examination of general trends in housing prices and housing availability, in particular the rapid inflation of housing costs which characterized much of the decade. The third step is an exploration of the impact of these overall market trends on the housing submarkets created by demographic change.

In Chapter 9, supplemental data for the early 1980s will be provided in conjunction with the discussion of Reagan's policies. There was essentially very little change in most indicators during the first years of the 1980s but those changes which are significant for future policy will be highlighted.

Demographic Change in the 1970s

In the 1960s, most urban politics texts, and many more sophisticated analyses of urban problems began with a recitation of key demographic facts about the post-World War II U.S. city. This recitation became a kind of litany which, like an oft repeated religious chant, set the mood for the discussion of whatever set of urban problems the author wished to address. As the 1970s unfolded, and as statisticians and other scholars began to catch up with the behavior of the populace, changes began to be

51

heard in this litany. Although a number of important trends continued, other trends altered the flow of urban change. In the discussion which follows, I will examine some of the major themes of the 1960s litany and suggest changes in this description of the urban United States which developments in the 1970s made necessary.

Suburbanization and White Flight

Two interrelated themes of the urban litany of the 1960s were the rapid growth of the suburbs and the racial patterns of settlement accompanying it. First, let us examine suburbanization. In the years following World War II, millions of Americans, in search (according to Daniel Elazar) of the American dream of a quasi-rural existence in smaller scale, socially homogeneous communities (and propelled by subsidies from the FHA and the Highway Trust Fund) deserted urban neighborhoods for the suburbs (Elazar, 1966). The result was rapid growth in urban fringe areas. Accompanying this residential movement was the movement of the commercial enterprises who needed suburban customers, and numerous industries seeking trained labor and cheap land for expansion. Data from the 1980 Census and from population surveys taken earlier indicate that the suburbanization trend continued to be strong in the 1970s. The *U.S. Statistical Abstract* (U.S. Bureau of the Census, 1981d) shows an increase in the population of all central cities in the United States of 6.5 percent from 1960 to 1970, a rate which declined to almost zero (0.1 percent) between 1970 and 1980. This was in contrast to a suburban growth rate of 26.8 percent from 1960 to 1970 and 18.2 percent from 1970 to 1980.

However, even this small positive central city growth rate creates too sanguine a picture, for it includes growth in smaller cities which became metropolitan areas during each decade, and it includes increases due to annexation. The more detailed analysis of changes occurring between 1970 and 1977 presented in Table 1 is suggestive of patterns for the whole decade.

This table reveals an absolute population decline of 4.6 percent in central cities which were part of SMSAs in 1970, with an even more precipitous decline among those located in metropolitan areas of one million or more.

Economic shifts to the suburbs also continued during the 1970s. According to HUD (1980d), employment in 10 major cities dropped from 50.8 percent of total SMSA employment in 1970 to 41.6 percent in 1976. Retail trade, in which 60 percent of the jobs were already suburban in 1970, continued its outward spread, and even activities in which central

TABLE 1

METROPOLITAN POPULATION, 1970–1977

Location	Population in 000's			Percentage Change		
	1970	*1974*	*1977*	*1970–74*	*1974–77*	*1970–77*
United States Total	199,819	207,949	212,366	4.1	2.2	6.4
SMSA's Designated as of 1970	137,058	142,043	143,107	3.6	0.7	4.4
Central Cities	62,876	61,650	59,993	– 1.9	– 2.7	– 4.6
Suburban Areas	74,182	80,394	83,114	8.4	3.4	12.0
Metropolitan Areas of 1 Million or More	79,489	81,059	82,367	2.0	1.6	3.6
Central Cities	34,322	33,012	31,898	– 3.8	– 3.4	– 7.1
Suburban Areas	45,166	48,047	50,469	6.4	5.0	11.7
Metropolitan Areas of Less Than 1 Million	57,570	60,985	60,739	5.9	– 0.4	5.5
Central Cities	28,554	28,638	28,095	0.3	– 1.9	– 1.6
Suburban Areas	29,016	32,347	32,644	11.5	0.9	12.5
Counties Designated Metropolitan Since 1970	8,373	9,243	9,980	10.4	8.0	19.2

Source: U.S. Department of Housing and Urban Development (HUD), 1980d, *The President's National Urban Policy Report*, GPO, 1980, pp. 1–11.

cities retained some advantage due to central location, such as wholesaling, service, and office employment, saw strong rival centers develop in outlying areas.

These intrametropolitan trends were, however, occurring in a somewhat different context in the 1970s than in earlier decades. Previously, suburban in-migration had occurred simultaneously with an increase in the total metropolitan population which was faster than that for the United States as a whole (16.6 percent versus 13.3 percent, from 1960 to 1970). Between 1970 and 1980, metropolitan growth slowed to a rate slightly below that of the total population (10.2 percent versus 11.4 percent). Meanwhile, nonmetropolitan areas, which had grown less than one-third as fast as metropolitan areas between 1960 and 1970, grew almost twice as fast as metropolitan areas between 1970 and 1980. These data indicate a significant slowing of metropolitan in-migration, although the vast majority of Americans continued to live in large urban areas.

The second, related theme of the urban litany of the 1960s was "white flight." The suburban exodus of the 1950s and 1960s was predominantly a movement of whites, coupled with and related to an influx of blacks and Hispanics into the central cities. These groups came to the city seeking enhanced economic opportunities, but economic and racial discrimination prevented them from following these opportunities to the suburbs. 1980 Census data suggest that, in the 1970s, suburbanization continued to be largely a white exodus. Between 1960 and 1970, the white population of all central cities remained constant (again reflecting the makeup of smaller metropolitan areas); however, between 1970 and 1980, the white population declined by 11.5 percent, despite smaller stable and growing areas. Meanwhile, the central city black population increased by 32.3 percent from 1960 to 1970 and by 13 percent from 1970 to 1980. By 1980, suburban areas were 6.1 percent black, an increase of only 1 percent since 1970, and a proportion only half as great as blacks' share of the national population (11.3 percent). The central cities, in contrast, were 22.5 percent black, or roughly twice the national proportion.

Nevertheless, significant changes occurred in black migration trends during the decade. First, an increasing number of blacks joined whites in fleeing the central city, with the result that the black suburban population increased proportionately much faster from 1970 to 1980 (42.7 percent) than did either the white suburban population (13.1 percent) or the black central city population (13.0 percent). This did not mean, of course, that suburban neighborhoods became racially integrated, for as Phillip Clay has shown, most black suburbanites were resegregated within outlying communities (Clay, 1979). Second, although blacks did not join whites in the 'back to the country' movement mentioned above, there was a marked downswing in the migration of blacks from nonmetropolitan areas to metropolitan areas. This is reflected in the dramatic reduction in black central city population growth revealed by the figures just cited.

Ironically, the 1980 Census shows that a phenomenon widely perceived as a challenge to the themes of suburbanization and white flight, gentrification, did not have a large impact on the urban population. Economic data do indicate an increase in central city housing renovation, and, as will be discussed in Chapter 8, the psychological impact of the transformation of deteriorating neighborhoods could be greater than the numbers would suggest (Laska and Spain, 1980). Nevertheless, the middle class whites who opted for urban living in the 1970s were still small in numbers, and the far more usual choice of the group was flight to the suburbs or to small towns (HUD, 1980d).

Regional Migration

The urban litany of the 1960s generally took little note of regional differences in urban growth or of patterns of interregional migration, except for the flow of blacks from the rural South to the urban Northeast and Midwest. By the mid-1970s, however, regional contrasts had become so striking as to demand inclusion in any complete description of urban demographic change. Most frequently noted, of course, was the shift of both economic activity and population from the older urban areas of the Northeast and North Central regions (the Frostbelt) to the cities of the South and Southwest (the Sunbelt). Census data show that, in the 1960s, many southern and western states, with population increases, ranging from 20 to 40 percent, were already growing faster than the Frostbelt, where population increases ranged from 5 to 19 percent. However, the contrast became even greater in the 1970s, when many Frostbelt states experienced zero growth or actual population decline, while the Sunbelt continued to grow rapidly. The HUD report cited above (1980d) also notes these trends, pointing out that between 1960 and 1970, the South and West accounted for 63 percent of the nation's population growth, while between 1970 and 1980, these regions accounted for 88.7 percent.

Increasing regional differences meant diversity in U.S. urban areas in the 1970s. Some diversity had always been there, but the changes of the 1970s made it a more central theme in urban growth. Looking back at suburbanization, for example, one finds that suburban population growth was even more rapid in the Sunbelt, whereas Frostbelt cities experienced a relative downswing in growth even at their urban fringes. Central city population and economic decline, too, were much more precipitous in the larger, older cities of the Northeast and North Central areas than in rapidly growing metropolises such as Houston or Phoenix, though even in the Sunbelt, central cities lagged behind their suburbs.

Urban Poverty

Yet another major theme of the 1960s urban litany was the impoverishment of the central cities. The black and Hispanic immigrants attracted to central cities after World War II faced a commercial and industrial sector with a declining need for unskilled workers, except in dead-end service jobs; and many firms were taking their remaining jobs to the suburbs. Thus, many remained in the center city, part of an unemployed or underemployed "lumpen proletariat" with few chances for escape to higher levels of material well-being. The economic instability of their existence, plus the not so subtle influence of the Aid to Families with Dependent Children (AFDC) program, led to the creation of a large number of families in which the sole breadwinner was female. The women responsible for these families faced the added barriers of sex discrimination and lack of child care when they sought to enter the workforce, with the result that poverty was exacerbated for the whole group.

Table 2 confirms the picture of the 1960s pattern just described and shows that, during the 1970s, this pattern changed for the worse. For the United States as a whole, the percentage of families below the poverty level declined slightly, but during this same period, the percentage of central city families in poverty rose from 12.2 to 14.3 percent. Meanwhile, the percentage of poor families in the suburbs remained at a much lower rate during this period, while poverty declined sharply in nonmetropolitan areas. Thus, the central cities held an even larger percentage of the nation's poor at the end of the decade than they had at the beginning (U.S. Bureau of the Census, 1980).

The continuing impact of racial and sexual inequality is also shown in Table 2. Though the percentage of black families in poverty in the nation as a whole declined, this proportion remained over four times as high as the proportion of whites in poverty. In addition, the proportion of central city blacks in poverty increased dramatically from 24.7 percent to 30.4 percent, while central city white poverty was increasing only slightly from 8.5 percent to 8.8 percent. If these data are looked at in conjunction with the decline in black nonmetropolitan poverty which the table shows (50.4 percent to 38.1 percent), and a small net shift in black population from nonmetropolitan to central city areas which may be inferred from the actual population numbers in the table, they tend to support the conclusion that continued in-migration of poor blacks was at least partially responsible for the increase in black, central city poverty. However, data from other sources indicate that an absolute decline in economic opportunities in central cities was also partially to blame. The HUD report cited above (HUD, 1980d) notes a marked concentration of blacks in Northeastern and North Central urban cores and the failure of blacks to join the exodus to the Sunbelt in numbers proportional to whites. As a result, the declining economies of these cities tended to reinforce the racial disadvantages in employment opportunities. In cities where the economic base was expanding, poverty rates for blacks, as well as for other groups were much lower.

In both 1970 and 1979, Table 2 shows an extremely high incidence of poverty among families in which the sole breadwinner was female. This high rate reflected both the unequal salaries commanded by working

TABLE 2

POVERTY STATUS OF FAMILIES, 1970 AND 1979

Area and Race	All Persons in Families		Persons in Families With Female Householder		
	Total Number (000's)	Percent Below Poverty Line	Total Number (000's)	Percent of All Families With Female Householder	Percent Below Poverty Line
1970					
U.S. Total	187,132	11.0	19,798	10.6	38.5
Black	20,996	32.4	6,350	30.2	59.0
White	164,021	8.1	13,223	8.1	28.6
Metropolitan Areas	119,860	8.5	13,491	11.3	35.2
Central Cities	50,544	12.2	8,228	16.3	45.5
Black	11,176	24.7	3,732	33.4	52.6
White	38,621	8.5	4,403	11.4	30.4
Outside Central Cities	69,316	5.8	5,263	7.6	27.9
Black	3,396	23.8	852	25.1	54.2
White	65,163	4.8	4,384	6.7	23.0
Nonmetropolitan Areas	67,272	15.3	6,307	9.4	45.5
Black	6,424	50.4	1,767	27.5	74.8
White	60,235	11.5	4,435	7.4	33.3
1979					
U.S. Total	191,418	10.1	26,283	13.7	34.8
Black	22,133	29.9	8,828	39.9	53.2
White	165,277	7.4	17,005	10.3	25.1
Metropolitan Areas	128,106	9.2	19,273	15.0	34.0
Central Cities	49,990	14.3	11,022	22.0	41.3
Black	12,122	30.4	5,450	45.0	53.6
White	36,398	8.8	5,397	14.8	28.7
Outside Central Cities	78,115	5.9	8,251	10.6	24.3
Black	4,793	19.8	1,523	33.2	41.6
White	71,696	5.0	6,583	9.2	20.3
Nonmetropolitan Areas	63,312	12.0	7,009	11.1	36.9
Black	5,218	38.1	1,855	35.5	61.4
White	57,183	9.5	5,025	8.8	27.6

Sources: U.S. Bureau of the Census, 1971b and 1981a.

women and the higher proportion of female householders who were not regularly in the labor force. A U.S. Census survey of 1979 family incomes reports that the median income for families in which the sole wage earner was a male was $17,750, while for those with a female as sole wage earner the median was $9927 (U.S. Bureau of the Census, 1981c, p. 81). Table 2 also shows that the number of female-headed families in the nation as a whole increased, with faster increases among central city blacks. Thus, in 1979, white and black female-headed families continued to account for a large amount of central city poverty.

A number of the variables mentioned in the foregoing analysis may be used to define housing submarkets — that is, geographic areas or groups of people which may be differentially affected by national trends in the supply and cost of housing. These variables include race, sex of breadwinner, central city/suburban residence, socioeconomic status, and region of the country. From income data alone, it is not difficult to infer that a black, female-headed family in the central city had a much more limited range of housing choices than a white suburban family with both a male and a female wage earner. But a full assessment of the impact which housing cost increases had on these groups requires more careful analysis. In the following pages, I will present an overview of national trends in housing costs and attempt to account for these trends. Then I will return to some of the groups defined by these demographic variables and discuss the impact of these trends.

Housing Costs

Rising housing costs were a major object of concern during the 1970s, both for government policymakers and for various segments of the public. Statements by public officials and journalists decried the increasing cost of middle class housing and darkly hinted at the loss of the 'American dream' of single family home ownership. Real estate prices became a prime topic of conversation at middle class social gatherings, either as a lament about high prices or as an expression of satisfaction from those who had 'bought cheap and sold dear'. Meanwhile, scholars were documenting a variety of severe impacts which increased housing costs were having on the poor, from steadily increasing rent burdens to loss of rental units as a result of condominium conversion and abandonment. Because of these concerns, the phenomenon of housing cost inflation tended to assume larger than life proportions — to be treated as *the* housing problem of the decade. In fact, more careful analysis have shown that the problem was, at least until the very end of the decade, not as severe as often portrayed, particularly for middle and upper middle class families.

The data on various aspects of housing costs are quite extensive and come from a variety of sources: the Census, HUD, the Federal Home Loan Bank Board, the Bureau of Labor Statistics (BOLS), and others. These sources vary with regard to the specific numbers they provide (see Grebler and Mittelbach, 1979, p. 182, for a partial comparison). Nevertheless, they are remarkably consistent in the trends they reveal. The Consumer Price Index (CPI) for housing is the most useful for the current analysis, because it is broken down into various cost components which may be compared to each other and to the CPI's for other consumer items. Figure 2 shows the changes in the CPI for housing from 1970 to 1980, along with changes in the indexes for food, clothing, and medical care. The change in the national median income, as recorded by the U.S. Census Bureau's *Annual Population Survey* is also shown.

Figure 2 records a rapid increase in housing costs, but it also shows that the national median income rose at nearly the same rate during this period, as did the indexes for food and medical care. Only clothing costs lagged behind those of the other necessities. Thus, housing costs were generally in line with other elements of inflation and with rising incomes for most of the 1970s. Only in the last two years of the decade did they begin to accelerate faster than income.

There were, of course, substantial differences in the situations of tenants and of homeowners; therefore, it is useful to break down general cost trends by tenure. Figure 3 shows some key elements of housing costs for homeowners. Since separate median income data for tenants and owners were not available prior to HUD's first Annual Housing Survey in 1973, the CPI measures here and in Figure 4 have been converted to a 1973 base.

The topmost line indicates the CPI for homeownership costs. Included in this index are the purchase price, the mortgage interest, other financing costs, taxes, and insurance. Though there is no separate index kept for purchase price alone, data from the Federal Home Loan Bank Board indicate that the rapid increase in purchase prices was the main driving force behind the large increase in homeownership costs. Their monthly reports on housing sales indicate that the average price of a conventionally financed, newly built home rose from $35,500 in 1970 to $83,000 in 1980, while the price of existing housing rose from $30,000 to $74,000 during the same period. The price indexes for interest and taxes show that these costs did not increase as rapidly as did purchase prices, at least until the very end of the decade. Nevertheless, the more modest increases in these factors interacted with the price increases to accelerate

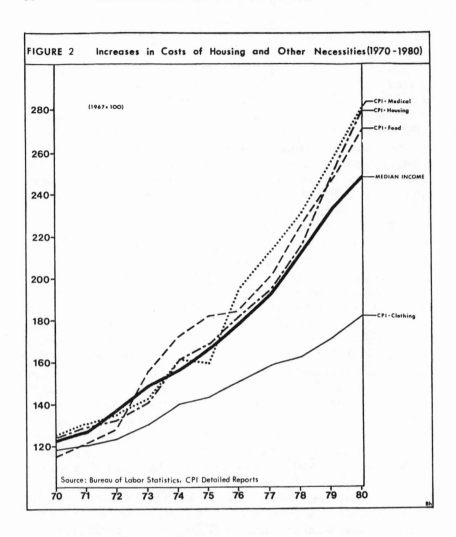

FIGURE 2   Increases in Costs of Housing and Other Necessities (1970-1980)

(1967 = 100)

CPI - Medical
CPI - Housing
CPI - Food
MEDIAN INCOME
CPI - Clothing

Source: Bureau of Labor Statistics, CPI Detailed Reports

the overall rate of inflation. In addition, there were equally rapid increases in fuel, utilities, and maintenance costs.

During this period, as Figure 2 showed, the median income for families and individuals also rose, but at a much slower pace than homeownership costs. One effect of this was to price many low and moderate income persons out of the market, a fact which is reflected on the more rapid increase in the median income for homeowners than for the population as a whole. Another effect was to make the cost burden greater on those who did purchase homes, for though homeowners were

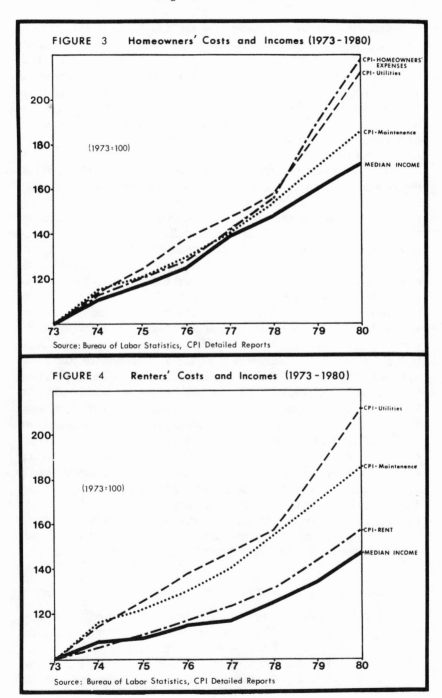

FIGURE 3   Homeowners' Costs and Incomes (1973-1980)

(1973=100)

CPI·HOMEOWNERS' EXPENSES
CPI·Utilities
CPI·Maintenence
MEDIAN INCOME

Source: Bureau of Labor Statistics, CPI Detailed Reports

FIGURE 4   Renters' Costs and Incomes (1973-1980)

(1973=100)

CPI·Utilities
CPI·Maintenence
CPI·RENT
MEDIAN INCOME

Source: Bureau of Labor Statistics, CPI Detailed Reports

a relatively higher income segment of the population in 1980 than in 1973, Figure 3 clearly shows that costs rose faster even than their incomes. Interestingly enough, data from the Annual Housing Surveys indicate that the percentage of income paid for housing by homeowners as a group stayed relatively constant; however, this average included those who purchased their homes at fixed mortgages up to 30 years ago. This reinforces a point made by several researchers; namely, that the burden of housing cost increases hit hardest those who were purchasing homes for the first time.

The cost picture for tenants was also unfavorable during the 1970s. Figure 4 shows changes in renter costs and incomes from 1973 to 1980. The CPI for rent does show a much slower rate of increase than any other element of housing costs, but fuel and utility costs, which are usually borne by tenants, increased rapidly. Moreover, as Figure 4 reveals, the median income for tenants rose even more slowly than rents and substantially less than fuel and utility costs. This led to a gradual increase in the percent of income tenants paid for their housing — from 24 percent in 1973 to 27 percent in 1980.

Ironically, the slow growth in rents imposed an indirect cost on tenants in the form of declining availability of rental units. Investors were paying increasingly high construction and financing costs, similar to those shown for homeowners in Figure 3. Maintenance costs, too, were escalating rapidly. These costs, in combination with slowly rising rents, made rental property much less attractive as an investment. This led, in turn, to a long term decline in the production of rental units, except where federal subsidies and tax breaks made the investment more profitable (HUD, 1980d, p. 5-14). In addition, existing rental units were withdrawn from the market in some cities. Condominium conversion was one well-publicized form of withdrawal of middle income rental units, though its numerical impact was significant only in large city markets such as Chicago (HUD, 1980a). On the lower end of the quality and income scale, there was also disinvestment through abandonment, particularly in central cities where rapid population decline was already weakening the market for lower quality units (HUD, 1980d, p. 5-17).

The Causes of Housing Cost Inflation

The inflation of housing costs was, of course, related to the rapid rates of inflation which plagued the entire U.S. economy during the 1970s. However, there were unique pressures on housing costs which bear closer analysis, since housing, as a major sector of the economy, contributed to as well as suffered from, the overall inflationary trends.

As is the case with any product, the price at which a given unit of housing was sold depended both on supply factors, such as the availability and cost of basic production elements, and the level of demand for that unit. Various analyses of housing prices in the 1970s suggest that, for most of the decade, there was a high level of demand for housing, particularly in the single family sales market. There were also significant increases in the costs of basic elements of housing production. It was the interaction of these two factors which produced a housing price spiral somewhat faster than the general rate of inflation.

Grebler and Mittelbach (1979), in their very thorough study of housing prices in the 1970s, suggest several reasons for the high level of demand for single family housing, particularly from 1975 on. First, the population bulge caused by the postwar Baby Boom was entering the 25-35 age bracket, a period in life when homeownership is frequently initiated. The increase in the absolute size of this age cohort helped counterbalance the fact that a declining percentage of them could afford single family housing. Second, the increase of women working outside the home made a second income available to a larger percentage of these families, and the Equal Credit Opportunity Act of 1975 put pressure on banks to take the wife's income more fully into account in determining loan eligibility. Third, the average size of the family unit was becoming smaller, as divorce rates increased and adult children less frequently remained in their parents' homes. Sternlieb notes that, between 1970 and 1976, the population grew by only 5 percent, whereas the number of family units grew by 16.6 percent (Sternlieb, 1980, p. 73). Only the most affluent of these new families could afford single family homes, but the rapid increase in the absolute size of this group kept demand strong.

In addition to these demographic trends, Grebler and Mittelbach cite important attitudinal dimensions of high housing demand, based on their extensive surveys of home buyers. In the classical free market situation, rising prices should reduce demand, but in the case of single family housing, rising prices had the opposite effect. People who had purchaed homes in prior years saw an opportunity to convert the rising value of their existing homes into cash which could be invested as equity in a newer home, the value of which would presumably rise even faster. Those who had not previously entered the market saw investment in a home as an effective hedge against inflation; and they feared that escalating prices would soon put a purchase totally out of their reach. For this reason, they were willing to sacrifice a relatively large share of their income to house payments.

Throughout most of the decade, this tendency was further encouraged by the housing industry's continued reliance on the fixed interest, long-term mortgage. Once a family had set a level mortgage payment, they could anticipate that it would decline as a percentage of their income. In addition, the federal tax deductions for interest and local property taxes which were available to homeowners were a further incentive for well-paid professionals to move into homeownership. The housing subsidy provided to middle and upper income property owners by these tax breaks amounted to $32.6 billion by 1981, or about five times the amount paid out by the federal government in housing subsidies to the poor (Palmer and Sawhill, 1982, p. 402).

Given the steady high demand generated by these various factors, it was not surprising to see periodic expressions of concern, in the media and elsewhere, about the ability of the housing industry to meet this demand. Much of this concern was directed at the supply of credit available to builders and purchasers of housing. Table 3 shows the level of housing starts and the average mortgage interest rate for each year between 1970 and 1980.

This table reveals sharp fluctuations in housing production, which followed the expansion and contraction of the economy as a whole. However, because housing is such a credit-dependent industry, increases

TABLE 3

INTEREST RATES AND HOUSING CONSTRUCTION STARTS: 1970–1980

| | Private Housing Starts (in thousands of units) | | |
Year	1-4 Unit Structures	5 + Unit Structures	Interest Rate on Conventional Mortgages
1970	897.7	535.9	8.27
1971	1271.3	780.9	7.59
1972	1450.5	906.2	7.45
1973	1250.3	795.0	7.78
1974	948.7	395.8	8.72
1975	956.2	204.3	8.75
1976	1248.3	289.2	8.88
1977	1563.4	403.3	8.82
1978	1544.7	462.5	9.34
1979	1316.1	429.0	10.60
1980	961.7	330.5	12.46

Sources: U.S. *Federal Home Loan Bank Board Journal*, January 1974; 1976; 1980; October, 1983.

or declines in credit availability associated with federal fiscal and monetary policies tended to make the peaks and valleys in housing production much sharper than those in other sectors of the economy. When the Federal Reserve restricted the money supply, interest rates rose, affecting both the builder who was borrowing for land purchases and short-term construction financing and the buyer who was entering into a long-term mortgage. In addition, higher interest rates on government securities and other investments caused "disintermediation" of funds from the fixed ceiling savings accounts at savings and loan associations, which are a major source of capital for the housing industry.

Housing starts reached a decade high of almost 2.4 million in 1972, which was followed by a rather precipitous decline to just over 1.1 million in 1975, during the 1974–75 recession. The credit crunch of 1973–74, caused in large part by the antiinflationary policy of the Fed (Federal Reserve) also contributed to the duration and sharpness of this decline. When the economy began to rebound in 1976, housing starts went up too. However, the slow but relentless increase in mortgage interest rates throughout the period (from 8.3 percent in 1970 to 9.3 percent in 1978) helped limit the housing recovery to a peak of 2 million in 1978. And the precipitous increase of interest rates in 1979 and 1980 corresponded with another sharp housing decline, which preceded the recession of 1980. By the early 1980s, interest rates were so high that the sheer cost of borrowing overcame the perennial eagerness of Americans to invest in housing, and activity in the housing sector came to a virtual standstill.

In spite of these sharp fluctuations in housing production, both the Sternlieb work and the Grebler and Mittelbach work conclude that production was able to keep up with the demand for new housing, particularly in the single family sector. No drastic, nationwide shortages of housing occurred, although there was some lag between demand and supply during the economic recovery of 1976–77. Nevertheless, the continuation of a high level of demand for most of the period meant that there was little slack in the market — that the production of new units was just able to keep pace with the growth in the number of families wanting them. Thus, builders had little incentive to lower prices, and inflationary expectations insured the buyer's willingness to pay the higher prices asked.

The steady high demand for housing which continued through most of the 1970s also reinforced a steady upward push in the costs of housing production factors, a trend which had been in evidence since World War II but was accelerated by the general inflationary trend of the decade. In the area of single family, owner occupied units, a big part of the per unit cost increase was due to an increase in the size and amenities of the typical house. Persons buying homes were purchasing more rooms per family member, and they were demanding more amenities such as appliances and central air conditioning. The size of renter occupied units did not increase — in fact, apartment sizes tended to become standardized at 3 to 5 rooms. Yet, the demand for amenities was also high in middle class, multifamily developments.

Single family units require the most materials and labor of any type of unit, and the fact that the size of each unit and the proportion of total units which were single family increased put strong upward pressure on both labor and material costs. However, two studies of housing costs by HUD conclude that these costs did not rise at the same rate as housing prices and, in fact, declined as a percentage of the total cost of producing a unit (HUD, 1978a; 1979d). Grebler and Mittelbach suggest that demand may have pulled these costs upward, rather than these cost factors having pushed up prices. This made housing somewhat of an exception to the cost push inflation which characterized much of the U.S. economy during this period.

Unlike materials and labor costs, land costs did increase as a percentage of total production costs during the 1970s. Again, demand-pull accounts for some of this increase, but the HUD report attributes it to other factors as well. First, many localities became more restrictive in zoning and land use requirements, for purposes as varied as preventing the influx of lower income renters (or *any* renters), reducing the strain on public services, or preventing the loss of agricultural land through "leapfrog" development. According to the HUD report on housing costs cited above, these restrictions created delays in approval of new sites and decreased the supply of available land. Second, localities became increasingly reluctant to impose the cost of new site development (streets, sewers, etc.) on their restive taxpayers, preferring instead to make developers directly finance a larger share of site improvement or to impose higher connection fees for new services. Ironically, many cities had, in older residential areas, relatively large supplies of vacant land with its infrastructure already in place, but developers were reluctant to utilize these areas due to fears of reduced marketability.

However, while making a logical case for the role of increased government fees and regulations in the increases in land development costs, the HUD report does not present comprehensive national data either on land costs or on the contribution of regulatory activity to these costs, for the good reason that such data are not readily available. Therefore, the report leaves the general impression that rising land costs contributed to housing cost inflation but does not give a precise indication of how great this contribution was. Grebler and Mittelbach conclude that, while governmental restrictions had sporadic local impacts, a significant overall impact on supply and cost has not been clearly demonstrated (Grebler and Mittelbach, 1979, pp. 112–115).

Housing Costs and Housing Submarkets

Having shown the general patterns of housing cost increases which occurred in the 1970s and having discussed some of the factors which helped to account for these increases, it is now possible to examine the impact of these cost increases on the housing submarkets discussed earlier. However, since the physical condition of the housing provided is one key variable which distinguishes housing submarkets, it is first necessary to look briefly at the data available on housing conditions.

Only two criteria of housing quality have survived through the last four decades of census-taking; the percentage of dwelling units "lacking some or all plumbing" and the number of overcrowded units. The incidence of both of these housing problems has declined markedly over the last 40 years and even more rapidly between 1970 and 1980, a trend which has suggested an overall improvement in housing quality. Yet, these two criteria have been recognized as inadequate indicators of structural conditions, even by those who have used them; and they are even less reflective of changes in neighborhood conditions which are a part of the total package of housing services.

To remedy the lack of detailed information on housing conditions, HUD and the U.S. Bureau of the Census began the Annual Housing Survey in 1973. As part of this survey, they asked a large national sample of households very detailed questions about their housing conditions: condition of (as well as the existence of) plumbing; condition of walls, ceilings and floors; frequency of breakdowns in plumbing, electricity and heat, etc. They also asked about neighborhood conditions: transportation, shopping, schools, crime, rodents, abandoned buildings, and other pertinent conditions. Taken together, these data provide a fairly complete picture of the incidence of housing problems in the United States as a whole and for various subgroups within the population; therefore, a comparison of conditions in 1973 and 1980 gives some idea of trends during the 1970s. For the purpose of assessing changes in housing conditions, in Tables 4 and 5 I have constructed an index of housing conditions based on the incidence of some of the more serious of these defects.

Table 4 presents a breakdown of key housing and income characteristics of central city and suburban residents. One trend which is

TABLE 4

HOUSING VALUES AND CHACTERISTICS FOR CENTRAL CITIES AND SUBURBS: 1973 AND 1980

Characteristics	Central Cities		Suburbs (Inside SMSA but outside central city)	
	Owners	Tenants	Owners	Tenants
All families and individuals				
1973	11,087	11,406	17,854	7,377
	(49.3%)	(50.7%)	(70.8%)	(29.2%)
1980	11,804	12,027	21,782	8,936
	(49.5%)	(50.5%)	(70.9%)	(29.1%)
Change	+6.5%	+5.4%	+22.0%	+21.1%
Median Income				
1973	$11,700	$6,900	$13,300	$8,800
1980	$19,600	$9,800	$12,400	$12,900
Change	+67.5%	+42.0%	+76.7%	+46.6%
Median Home Value or Rent				
1973	$22,300	$130	$29,500	$162
1980	$48,000	$234	$62,700	$283
Change	+115.2%	+80.0%	+112.5%	+74.7%
Percent of Tenants Paying > 25% of Income in Rent				
1973	–	43.6%	–	39.9%
1980	–	55.2%	–	51.4%
Change	–	+11.6%	–	+11.5%
Percentage of Units with Selected Dwelling and Neighborhood Defects				
1973	3.5%	9.0%	2.3%	5.2%
1980	2.7%	9.7%	1.5%	4.9%
Change	–22.9%	+7.8%	–34.8%	–5.8%

Sources: U.S. HUD and Census Bureau, *Annual Housing Survey*, Part C, 1973 and 1980.

TABLE 5

HOUSING VALUES AND CHACTERISTICS FOR FAMILIES WITH BLACK HOUSEHOLDERS IN CENTRAL CITIES AND SUBURBS: 1973 AND 1980

Characteristics	Central Cities		Suburbs (Inside SMSA but outside central city)	
	Owners	Tenants	Owners	Tenants
All families and individuals				
1973	1,581	2,787	597	491
	(36.2%)	(63.8%)	(55.9%)	(44.1%)
1980	1,866	3,208	858	837
	(36.8%)	(63.2%)	(50.6%)	(49.4%)
Change	+8.0%	+15.1%	+43.7%	+77.7%
Median Income				
1973	$9,600	$5,700	$9,600	$6,900
1980	$15,300	$8,100	$17,200	$10,700
Change	+59.4%	+42.1%	+79.2%	+55.1%
Median Home Value or Rent				
1973	$16,400	$111	$20,700	$135
1980	$32,800	$204	$43,600	$258
Change	+100.0%	+83.3%	+110.6%	+91.1%
Percent of Tenants Paying > 25% of Income in Rent				
1973	–	43.7%	–	41.4%
1980	–	57.1%	–	57.7%
Change	–	+13.4%	–	+16.3%
Percentage of Units with Selected Dwelling and Neighborhood Defects				
1973	8.4%	16.3%	8.2%	13.7%
1980	6.9%	16.7%	5.3%	11.0%
Change	–17.9%	+2.5%	–35.4%	–19.7%

Sources: U.S. HUD and Census Bureau, *Annual Housing Survey*, Part C, 1973 and 1980.

readily apparent from the first line in this table is the increase in the number of households in both central cities and suburbs. A comparison with Table 1 confirms the trend noted by Sternlieb, i.e., the much more rapid increase in the number of families than in the population. Another important trend confirmed by these data is that median incomes went up more slowly for both owners and tenants in the central city than in the suburbs, causing an increase in the already substantial income gap between the two areas.

At the same time, Table 4 shows that both purchase prices and rents went up FASTER in the central city than in the suburbs. For owners, increased house prices are both a blessing and a curse, in that they increase the payment burden but also increase the return on investment while the house is held (Sternlieb, 1980, p. 126). For tenants, the result is an increasing percentage of income devoted to rent, and Table 4 shows that this percentage started larger and rose faster for central city renters than for suburban renters. Absolute rent and price levels were lower in the central city than in the suburbs, but lower central city incomes appear to have negated the effect of this price break.

In addition, central city dwellers appeared to be getting a lesser quality dwelling for their money. For homeowners, in both the central city and the suburbs, the average incidence of housing and neighborhood defects was below 5 percent in 1973 and in 1980 but the incidence of defects was lower in the suburbs in 1973 and it declined much more rapidly there between 1973 and 1980 than in the central city. For tenants, the contrast in quality was more striking. Suburban tenants were twice as likely to have a dwelling with defects as suburban owners, but the percentage of defects they reported was still just above 5 percent in 1973 and it had declined to 4.9 percent by 1980. For central city tenants, the incidence of defects was nearly double that of suburban tenants in 1973 and, instead of declining between 1973 and 1980, it showed a modest increase. Therefore, in 1980, central city tenants as a group were paying 80 percent higher rents than in 1973 for structures with an incidence of defects greater than that in the earlier year. Clearly, this group did not benefit equally from the overall improvement in housing conditions which the nation enjoyed.

Another dimension is added to the analysis by looking at the racial composition of central city and suburban households. Table 5 presents a separate breakdown for black households, parallel to that presented in Table 4. Comparing Table 5 with Table 4, one finds that between 1973 and 1980, the proportion of central city owners who were black increased from 1,581,000 out of 11,087,000, or 14.3 percent, in 1973 to 1,866,000 out of 11,804,000, or 15.8 percent in 1980. Similarly, the proportion of central city tenants who were black increased from 24.4 percent in 1973 to 26.7 percent in 1980. This suggests that a portion of the overall increase in central city households was accounted for by a rapid increase in the number of black households. Nevertheless, it is interesting to note that even when black households are subtracted from the total, the remaining (largely white) households in central cities managed to increase slightly (4.5 percent for owners and 2.3 percent for tenants). This suggests that the smaller size of white households remaining in the city helped to compensate for the rather substantial loss of white population which occurred during the 1970s. Such a disparity is significant because it is often households, rather than population, which determine the perceived racial composition of neighborhoods.

Further comparison of the data in these two tables, shows that the median income of each category of blacks was significantly lower than the overall median for that category. This is in line with the population data reported above. The table also shows that median home values were lower for both central city and suburban black homeowners, with the former having the lowest values of any group. Median rents, too, were lower for central city and suburban black tenants; however, these rents increased more rapidly between 1973 and 1980 than the rents for the urban tenant population as a whole. As a result, a larger proportion of black tenants is both the central city and the suburbs were paying more than 25 percent of their incomes for rent. Furthermore, black tenants and owners reported a much higher incidence of housing and neighborhood defects than was reported by the population as a whole.

It is tempting to attribute the central city/suburban and black/white contrasts in the incidence of housing defects to the underlying variable of income, since median incomes decrease for both owners and tenants as one moves from the suburbs to the central city and from the population as a whole to blacks alone. To isolate the effects of income on housing and neighborhood quality, Figure 5 breaks urban households in 1980 into income groups.

Not surprisingly, there is a consistent decline in reports of defects as one moves up the income scale. What *is* noteworthy is that disparities in housing quality between central cities and suburbs, between owners and tenants, and between blacks and the population as a whole remained true regardless of income level. The effects of all these variables on housing quality were cumulative, in that black, central city tenants with incomes below $7,000 reported defects over 10 times as often as the typical suburban homeowner. Yet, even among the affluent, tenants reported more defects than owners, blacks more than whites, and central city residents more than suburbanites. Thus, a black central city tenant making

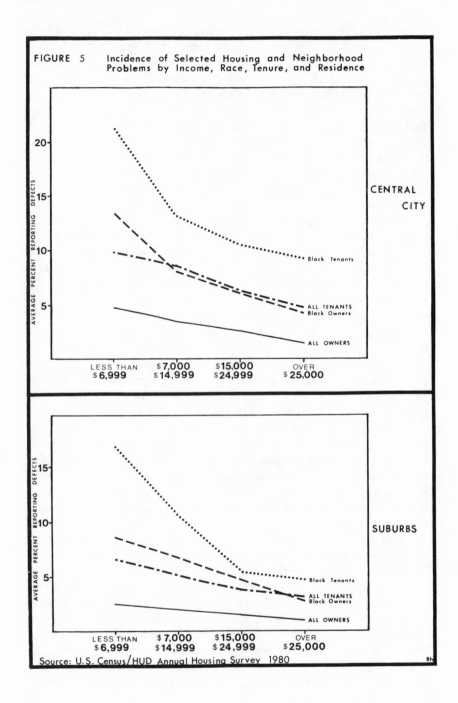

FIGURE 5   Incidence of Selected Housing and Neighborhood
Problems by Income, Race, Tenure, and Residence

CENTRAL CITY

SUBURBS

Source: U.S. Census/HUD Annual Housing Survey 1980

$25,000 a year still reported more defects than other tenants and owners making much less income and, presumably, paying less rent.

Conclusion: Housing Markets and Housing Needs

One of the important features of the housing policy debate in the 1970s was growing uncertainty and disagreement about the actual extent of housing deprivation in the United States. Disagreement about this issue has always been present, in part because of the ambiguity of available data and in part because the ideological perspective of the observer tends to influence how he or she views the degree of housing need. As was discussed in Chapter 2, there are deep divisions in American society concerning what it is that the poor deserve, with critics of social welfare programs often asserting that such programs are giving the poor more than they want or deserve. Obviously, one's estimate of need is subtly or not so subtly influenced by one's view of just deserts. However, the debate over the extent of deprivation seemed to intensify during the 1970s. Therefore, in concluding this chapter, it seems appropriate to suggest what the data presented may tell us about housing needs.

The two most salient trends during the 1970s were the overall increase in housing quality and the overall increase in housing costs. The upward shift in quality reflected the rising level of real incomes which occurred in spite of inflation, as well as the quite substantial quantities of new housing built during the decade. Since the qualitative shift occurred at virtually all levels of income and in virtually all social groups (except central city tenants), it was apparent that the poor were sharing in this general improvement, even if their housing was still inferior to that available to those with higher incomes.

This trend led a number of scholars to conclude that the chief housing problem of the poor was no longer one of substandard housing but one of living in standard housing for which they were paying too large a percentage of their incomes. Perhaps the most widely cited study supporting this conclusion was one produced for the Harvard-MIT Joint Center for Urban Studies by Bernard Frieden and Arthur Solomon (1977). This and other studies lent support to the argument that the federal government's housing subsidy strategy should shift from an emphasis on producing new units of standard housing for the poor to the more extensive use of cash subsidies which would enable them to purchase standard housing on the private market. As shall be shown in Chapter 5, there were many other reasons why alternatives to federally financed new construction were advocated, but this was a powerful argument in support of such a change. If, in fact, an across-the-board improvement in housing conditions had occurred, then low income people should be able to find adequate housing if their incomes were appropriately bolstered. As Henry Aaron observed, the housing problem was being redefined as an *income* problem (Aaron, 1981).

This argument dovetailed with increasing support by economists for Milton Freidman's assertion that in-kind housing subsidies were forcing the poor to consume housing at higher levels than they would if given an unconstrained cash grant. Many economic analyses begin with the assumption that consumers prefer unconstrained cash payments to in-kind subsidies because they allow greater freedom to choose what items to purchase. This, in itself, would tend to reduce the psychological value of housing production subsidies to consumers. However, the assumption that the poor would actually spend less was reinforced by data from low income tenant surveys (HUD, 1974a) and from the massive Experimental Housing Allowance Program which seemed to indicate that the poor, if given a cash subsidy, would spend only part of it on housing and most of it on other items of consumption. It was argued, therefore, that cash subsidies might be a more efficient way to provide the poor with housing than the construction of new units designated for their use.

It is beyond the scope of this work to exhaustively demonstrate the validity or invalidity of the arguments supporting cash housing subsidies. However, the data presented in this chapter do cast some doubt on the notion that the housing problems of the poor can be totally converted to an income problem. The case for skepticism may be made by looking at some of the major conclusions which emerge from the data just presented.

First, these data make it clear that the overall improvement in housing and neighborhood quality was not shared equally by all segments of the population. Though improvements occurred in almost all groups, blacks as a whole, central city residents as a whole, and lower income persons as a whole were still living in housing markedly inferior to that of the rest of the population: and, when these factors were combined, they produced as much as a *tenfold* variation in incidence of defects from the worst-off group (black, central city tenants with incomes under $7000) to the best-off group (white, suburban homeowners with incomes of $25,000 and up). The persistence of high levels of defects suggests that the increased availability of standard housing had not eliminated physical housing problems as an important dimension of housing need.

Second, doubt is cast on the notion of 'overconsumption' by the very fact that many low income people were paying large percentages of their incomes to obtain standard housing. Some commentators have suggested that this is a choice forced on the poor by the nation's strict building and health codes. However, it hardly seems plausible to explain the willingness of low income persons to regularly pay 30 to 50 percent of their incomes in rent, thereby sacrificing other needs, strictly by this 'forced choice' argument. The high levels of housing expenditure among the poor would seem to make a *prima facie* case for a strong demand for decent housing, regardless of the findings of a short-term, experimental program.

While both of the foregoing conclusions must be given weight in evaluating housing need, neither totally contradicts the notion that new housing strategies based on new definitions of housing need might be required. After all, even if certain groups remain behind in housing quality, it could be argued that the upward shift in standards would eventually bring them up to an adequate, minimum quality level. Also, even if many low income persons do spend a large percentage of income on housing, perhaps they should still be allowed to choose between this and other spending patterns.

Much more serious doubt is cast on the 'housing needs = income needs' argument by the cost and production trends outlined in the previous pages. To explore the issues raised by these cost trends, it is first necessary to outline the two basic ways housing reaches the poor. First, since low income persons generally cannot afford to buy or rent new, unsubsidized units, much of it must filter down to them, as middle and upper income persons leave older units for newer ones with better locations or amenities. Second, standard housing reaches the poor through federal subsidies which reduce the cost of such housing, either through direct governmental construction of units or through payments to private sector providers.

Some features of housing production and demand in the 1970s had a potentially positive impact on the filtering process. As has been shown, overall demand for new, owner occupied housing remained high. The rising costs of homeownership for middle and upper income groups were offset by rising incomes and by the attractiveness of housing as an investment, while the federal government continued to increase buying incentives with large tax breaks. This meant that rental housing was being left by an increasing percentage of these groups, thus potentially allowing these units to filter down to others.

However, other equally significant features of the 1970s did not bode well for the filtering process. The potential availability of rental units was offset by the fact that, as shown in Figure 4, the average costs of building and/or maintaining rental property were increasing much faster than the median income of tenants. The increasing unprofitability of building new units led to stable or declining levels of unsubsidized rental construction, thus restricting the total supply. As HUD's 1980 *National Housing Production Report* states, "Since there is some cause and effect relationship between housing construction and housing removal—in both the physical and economic sense—fluctuations in housing construction are closely allied with the rate at which housing units with deficiencies are eliminated from the housing inventory." (HUD, 1980c, Appendix B, p. 12). Moreover, increased operating costs provided a strong disincentive for landlords to make major investments in their existing properties or even keep up basic maintenance. The growth of condominium conversions in middle income housing and of abandonment in lower income housing were only the most salient symptoms of this problem. It is difficult to see how, under these circumstances, filtering could continue to provide housing of acceptable quality to lower income persons.

The other alternative, federally subsidized new construction, did provide a significant proportion of all rental housing constructed in the 1970s. In the subsidized housing construction boom of the early 1970s (to be described in detail in Chapter 5), subsidized units reached a high of 30 percent of new rental starts (HUD, 1974a). Through most of the rest of the decade the proportion ranged from 12 to 17 percent, although it was slightly higher after 1978, as unsubsidized production declined (HUD, 1980d). This small percentage indicates the importance of filtering as the largest provider of low income housing; however, the absence of even this small percentage of new units would have clearly meant a much less favorable market situation for those on the bottom. Even if, as some have suggested, the construction of subsidized housing does not increase the total supply of rental housing by an amount equivalent to the units constructed, such construction certainly redistributes this housing in the direction of the disadvantaged.

The needs of low income persons are not, of course, the only legitimate housing needs which exist, yet these seem to have been the needs most threatened by the problems of the decade. At various times, housing analysts expressed concern that rising costs and/or sluggish productivity might have a negative effect on the quantity and quality of housing available to middle and upper income groups. This constituted a major justification for the continuation of federal subsidies and regulations directed at middle income housing. However, in retrospect, the threats to the housing needs of the middle class were not as serious as initially thought, while the continued problems of lower income households were more serious than many claimed. In the following chapters, the long and complex policy debate over whether and how to assist this low income segment of the population will be described. The data and tentative conclusions presented in this chapter should provide a useful background for this discussion.

CHAPTER 4

The Emergence of Federal Housing Subsidies: 1934–1968

In this chapter and the two following chapters, the historical development of housing policies in the social welfare policy context will be examined. This historical terrain must be explored at three levels of generality. At the broadest level, housing policy developments must be placed in the context of the various shifts in the overall political climate which have occurred since the 1930s. It was suggested in Chapter 1 that ideology influences policy because it is a major element in this general climate and because the political climate shapes decisions in a wide range of policy arenas. In the following pages, shifts in the overall balance of forces between liberals and conservatives at the national level will be shown to correspond to major changes in the scope and direction of housing efforts. In particular, liberal and conservative attitudes toward social welfare policy will be shown to have had a major impact on housing programs.

Yet, simply establishing a correspondence between such ideological shifts and changes in housing policy is not sufficient to explain how liberal and conservative values shaped the types of housing programs which have emerged. One must also identify the issues and concerns central to the housing policy arena itself, and a relationship must be shown between the ways these issues have been handled and the overall political climate. This analysis of major housing policy issues will constitute the second level of generality at which housing policy decisions will be explored.

It will be shown that four central issues have been of primary concern in virtually every housing policy decision: the issue of the *quantity* of housing to be produced; the issue of the *quality* of the housing produced; the issue of the *cost* of the programs; and the issue of *equity* (i.e., the fairness of the programs in serving various income groups). Liberals and conservatives have taken conflicting positions on all of these issues, and housing policy outcomes have been shaped by compromises between these points of view based on the relative power of liberal and conservative coalitions at various points in time.

Finally, the history of housing policy is the history of specific programs. Congress does not enact 'philosophies' or "approaches' per se but rather programs which embody these broader ideas. As noted in Chapter 1, the problems encountered by specific programs often become feedback which is variously interpreted by liberals and conservatives and which is incorporated as ammunition in their political struggles. Moreover, new programs evolve as responses to the specific shortcomings of the programs preceding them, as well as in response to broader attitudinal shifts. Thus, the third level of generality at which housing policy must be explored consists of the unique problems encountered by each of the major housing efforts; FHA, public housing, Section 235 and 236, and Section 8.

While the principal focus of this book is the attitudes and alliances which produced fundamental changes in housing policy during the 1970s, a longer historical perspective is vital to an understanding of these more recent events. The present chapter attempts to provide such a perspective by examining major developments in housing policy from the Depression to 1968. Lawrence Friedman's classic study of government involvement in housing problems (1968) traces the debate over the governmental role even farther back, to the mid-nineteenth century, when reformers began to pressure local governments to do something about the sprawling, unsanitary tenements spawned by rapid urbanization. Friedman notes the continuity between the socal cost arguments then raised by Jacob Riis and other reformers and the arguments used in contemporary battles. Nevertheless, the debate over the federal government's role in housing for the poor did not begin in earnest until the Great Depression, for it was only then that liberals had enough national political power to initiate serious proposals for federal involvement. Furthermore, the history of two major housing initiatives stimulated by the Depression — the Federal Housing Administration's mortgage insurance program and the public housing program — played a major role in shaping later political struggles.

Figure 6 summarizes the periods and programs to be covered in this review of major housing initiatives up to the late 1960s.

The Creation and Transformation of FHA

As Figure 6 indicates, the Great Depression was a time of ascendancy for the liberal point of view. A broad consensus existed that positive government action was needed to respond to the multifaceted crisis in which the country found itself. The sense of emergency, of a need to *do something now*, enabled the federal government to expand into areas in which its intervention would previously have been overwhelmingly resisted. Both the Federal Housing Administration and the public housing program represented just such novel interventions and, while neither was without opposition, both were enacted by large congressional majorities.

The establishment of the Federal Housing Administraiton by the National Housing Act of 1934 clearly had as a large part of its rationale aid to families in need. The widepsread loss of jobs and income produced by the Depression led to astronomical foreclosure and tenant eviction rates, as both creditors and borrowers succumbed to the economic crisis. This, in turn, led to a rapid drop in housing construction which accelerated unemployment in the building trades. In 1933, Congres set up the Home Owners Loan Corporation (HOLC), an emergency measure which used government loans to rescue homeowners in imminent danger of foreclosure. However, the 1934 Act introduced federal regulation and support of the housing credit system through FHA mortgage insurance. Thus, it went beyond correction of immediate problems, and aimed at a fundamental restructuring of the way people borrowed money for home purchases. By introducing the long-term, low downpayment, fully amortized, level payment mortgage, in place of the short-term, high downpayment, balloon notes of earlier years, the FHA program greatly broadened the segment of the U.S. population which could afford to purchase a home. The working or middle class family who could obtain a modest but steady income, now found mortgage payments to be within their financial reach. It was these persons, whom Lawrence Friedman has called the "submerged middle class," who were most severely hurt by the housing credit situation and whom the FHA program helped rescue.

The FHA mortgage insurance program did not, however, address the problems of those too poor to purchase a home, and during the subsequent history of the FHA, this shift toward service to the white middle class was accentuated. After World War II, the program expanded to aid the housing industry in meeting the vast new demand generated by returning veterans; but the persons aided were largely white middle or working class families with enough income to purchase the new suburban tract housing springing up around most U.S. cities. Blacks were first officially and later unofficially segregated by the FHA program, and the spiral of decline which was beginning to affect many central city neighborhoods was actively encouraged by the FHA's refusal to underwrite mortgages in such areas. Thus, the FHA program was an important aid to the betterment of large numbers of people of modest means, but

FIGURE 6

Impact of Major Political Trends on Key Housing Programs
from 1930 to 1970: A Schematic Outline

Summary of Major Political Forces

TIME PERIOD	Executive	Legislative	Interest Groups
1930-40	From 1932 on, Roosevelt presidency put exec. in liberal control.	Strong consensus behind liberal programs, but residual philosophical opposition to govt. social welfare role reflected in modifications & restrictions on new programs.	Broad base of support for social welfare, since many groups of "market winners" were now in trouble.
1941-45	War concerns reduced pressure for social welfare programs across the board.		
1945-52	Presidency remained in liberal control. Truman pushed Fair Deal.	Conservatives much stronger than before the war. A Republican-Southern Democratic coalition opposed many programs. However, liberals still strong.	Housing industry united in opposition to public housing. Labor, liberal groups in support of new programs, but poor clientele lacked a direct voice.
1953-60	Eisenhower brought conservatives back into power. No attempt to repeal New Deal, but little expansion.	Conservative coalition opposed to s.w. initiatives but liberals strong enough to block major retrenchment.	Housing industry still united in opposition to public housing. Helped to organize local opposition to sites proposed by local govt.
1961-68	Liberals back in power and pushed for measures to aid blacks and quiet the cities.	Strength of liberals increased, esp. after 1964. Sense of "emergency" created by urban violence helped build support.	Housing industry split – NAHB began support for subsidies while realtors opposed. Poor gained limited voice through civil rights leaders, CAI activists, new urban groups and their "extra-legal" participation (riots).

Categories of Housing Programs

Programs for Housing/ Credit Industry and Middle Income Clients	Publicly Subsidized Private Housing for Low Income	Public Housing
Banking, savings & loan industry was reorganized & regulated. Secondary mortgage market set up (FNMA) FHA mortgage insurance program set up in 1934.	Rent vouchers proposed as alternative to public housing but rejected.	Initially part of public works program but this replaced by Housing Act of 1937.
Construction slowed due to materials shortages.		Program diverted to war housing.
Post war housing shortage enhanced FHA support. Agency played major role in suburban growth but perpetuated racial segregation and central city decay. VA program added.		1949 Act made large commitment to public housing but opponents nullified through appropriations cuts. Program faced rising costs.
Production fluctuated but FHA still had important role in middle income areas.	Commission appt. by Eisenhower recommended private sector approach but no follow-up.	Continued at low level of funding.
FHA under pressure to get involved in central city, low income areas.	Pressure for change in other programs led to first programs of this kind - Sec. 221d3, Sec. 235, Sec. 236.	Major expansion of program but alternatives sought.

many segments of the population were bypassed by its benefits (Semer, 1976; Bradford, 1979).

The FHA program was vast in scope, a factor which might have been expected to engender opposition from conservatives, in spite of the "respectability" of the middle income groups being served. However, the FHA became established during one housing crisis and it substantially broadened its clientele during another period of general housing shortages. The large degree of popular support it derived from its large clientele made it politically difficult to attack such a program. Therefore, while other housing proposals were being subjected to intense scrutiny and debate by the more conservative post-World War II Congresses, the FHA program remained relatively unscathed, and the inclusion of funding for this program in various broader housing proposals actually smoothed the way for their passage.

Of perhaps greater importance to the political acceptance of FHA than its popularity among the public was the fact that it was part of a package of programs developed during the Depression to bail out a group that in normal times would be major beneficiaries of market allocations—bankers and other investors. The near collapse of the banking system during the Depression led to quite substantial government intervention in a wide range of banking and investment problems. In the area of housing credit, federal intervention in the form of the Federal Home Loan Bank Board and the Federal Savings and Loan Insurance Corporation virtually created a new form of financial intermediary by molding a fragmented, locally based group of building and loan associations into a nation-wide, government insured and regulated system of savings and loans. In addition, the creation of a secondary mortgage market was encouraged by the establishment of the Federal National Mortgage Association (FNMA, or "Fannie Mae") in 1938. FHA mortgage insurance played a crucial role in the success of these new systems, since it provided sufficient security to permit the national flow of housing capital (Semer, 1976). Thus, the FHA was, in a very critical sense, a conservative program as this term has here been defined. Since it facilitated the profitable business transactions of a key group of private market participants, it was less likely to be viewed as excess government interference and was guaranteed political support by a very powerful interest group which at other times stood in opposition to various forms of governmental activism.

In a manner typical of programs which reinforce the position of market winners, the FHA, from the 1940s on, graduallly became closely identified with the industry which it served. Responsibility for the initial processing of FHA-insured mortgages was assumed by private savings and loans and by mortgage bankers, with the result that the concepts of sound underwriting prevalent in this segment of the banking industry became those which governed FHA lending (Bradford, 1979). The FHA policies of discrimination against blacks and against central city neighborhoods were, thus, reflections of widespread business practices, rather than any unique malevolence of the FHA toward blacks or the central city. In addition, Bradford suggests that the close association between the FHA and private lenders encouraged the development of a lax attitude toward supervision of their activities, which contributed to the problems later encountered by the FHA when it tried to expand into low income areas.

It should also be noted here that the new long-term mortgages created by FHA enhanced the value of income tax benefits which had been available to property owners ever since the inception of the income tax early in the twentieth century. These were, of course, the ability to deduct mortgage interest and local property taxes from taxable income. Such deductions gradually grew into a major "tax expenditure" on behalf of homeownership, one which was of relatively greater benefit to higher income persons because of their higher tax rates. Again, this large loss of federal revenue was not seriously questioned by either conservatives or liberals, because of its benefit to market winners.

Throughout the Eisenhower years, the presidency was basically in the control of moderate conservatives. Though their ability to shape policy was limited by the countervailing power of the liberals in Congress, the Eisenhower Administration succeeded in slowing the growth of federal involvement in social welfare problems. In the atmosphere of relative stability thus created, the FHA's role as an aid to private bankers in serving the middle class was not seriously questioned. However, the election of John F. Kennedy in 1960 signalled the return of liberals to power and the beginning of a gradual increase in pressure toward more governmental action to aid the disadvantaged. The FHA became the target of some of this pressure.

The liberalism of the 1960s was initially different in spirit from that of the New Deal. As noted in Chapter 2, the social welfare programs of the New Deal were undertaken to deal with a massive economic crisis, whereas the Kennedy-Johnson proposals were seen, at least initially, as modifications of an essentially prosperous and productive economic and social order, which would bring the disadvantaged into the mainstream. Nevertheless, the unfolding events of that decade led to a growing sense that such programs were needed as a response to a new crisis. According to Piven and Cloward (1971), Democratic leaders saw blacks, particularly the growing urban black population, as a pivotal element in the party's winning coalition and, therefore, felt obliged to respond to the demands of the civil rights movement. When the largely nonviolent protest of the early 1960s was augmented by the urban riots of 1965 to 1968, the Democrats' sense of urgency was intensified, and the focus of their efforts shifted from the abolition of legal segregation in the South to the economic concerns of the northern urban ghettoes. As a result, the Johnson Administration actively sought to create new programs for the urban poor and to modify or supplement existing programs so as to intensify their impact on this group.

The FHA, which had been widely accused of ignoring the needs of the inner city, became a logical target for their efforts. One way the agency became involved was through the use of its mortgage insurance to back subsidized rental housing programs such as, in 1961, the Section 221(d)(3) program and, in 1968, the Section 236 program. However, since these programs were, in part, a response to the problems of the public housing program as well, they will be discussed later in this chapter, after the history of that program has been reviewed. A second avenue of FHA involvement in the new priorities of the 1960s was the modification of its single family homeownership program in an attempt to meet the needs of central city and minority neighborhoods. This initiative bears some discussion at this point.

It began in the mid-1960s with FHA administrative rule changes aimed at altering insurance underwriting criteria to accommodate central city areas. One HUD directive stated that in dealing with these new "high risk" areas, FHA approved lenders should refrain from lending in "only those instances where a property has so deteriorated or is subject to such hazards . . . that the physical improvements are endangered or the liveability of the property or the health or safety of its occupants are seriously affected." (Quoted from HUD internal documents in Bradford, 1979, p. 326). In the Housing Act of 1968, these changes were given the legislative imprimatur by the addition of Section 223(e) to the National Housing Act of 1934 which "gave legislative sanction to waiving or relaxing FHA property standards to permit mortgage insurance for housing in blighted areas of central cities." (Semer, 1976, p. 23).

The FHA's role in insuring housing for the disadvantaged was further enhanced by the 1968 Act's creation of the Government National Mortgage Association (Ginnie Mae) to supplement the work of the Federal National Mortgage Association (Fannie Mae). The purpose of Ginnie Mae was to buy mortgages on higher risk low income housing projects at a higher price and to resell them at market rates, absorbing the loss as an additional government subsidy. It was split from Fannie Mae to avoid any threat to the marketability of the latter's mortgage-backed securities. Ginnie Mae soon became the major purchaser of mortgages for government subsidy programs.

Finally, the 1968 Act added Section 235, which provided a federal subsidy of mortgage payments to persons of modest income wishing to purchase their own homes. This subsidy covered the difference between the mortgage payment at the regular FHA interest rate and the same payment at 1 percent interest, or a payment comprising 20 percent of the purchaser's income, whichever was greater (Semer, 1976, p. 124). There were two specific attitudes, or perceptions, which contributed to the choice of homeownership programs as a vehicle to aid urban areas.

One was a growing awareness that the credit problems of property owners in urban areas were both a symptom and an important cause of housing and neighborhood decline. "Redlining" is now a standard term of opprobrium in the vocabulary of urban affairs, but the fact that property owners in certain areas could not easily obtain credit for purchase or property improvement because lending institutions had written off the area as high risk was just beginning to rise into public consciousness in the mid-1960s. Though the returning white gentry of the 1970s were to find that redlining was more than a racial problem, in the 1960s it was viewed primarily in those terms — as one more form of discrimination contributing to the despair and frustration of the black community. Therefore, the use of a federal credit mechanism directed at individual property owners presented itself as a logical response to the problem.

A second attitude was a widely held belief in the beneficial social effects of homeownership. As many authors have noted, the purchse of a single family home has always been a central part of the American Dream. However, proponents of homeownership for the poor went one step further than recognizing it as a legitimate aspiration. They argued, in addition, that the purchase of a home would instill in individuals a sense of personal pride which would counteract the culture of poverty, thereby improving not only the care which individuals devoted to their dwellings but their overall outlook on life. In the words of Wright Patman (Dem., Texas), chair of the House Banking and Currency Committee:

> Pride of ownership is a subtle but powerful force. Past experience has shown us that families offered decent homes at prices they can afford have demonstrated a new dignity, a new attitude toward their jobs. . . .
> By extending the opportunity for homeownership to low and moderate income families, we will give them a concrete incentive for striving to improve their own lives. . . . (CQ Almanac, 1968, p. 329).

Furthermore, it was felt that homeownership would create a greater sense of commitment to the neighborhood and the community as a whole which would lead to more responsible forms of participation. As various journalists more bluntly stated it, "People won't burn down houses that they own." Interestingly enough, this particular argument, though essentially a liberal social cost justification, was very appealing to many conservatives, and all 39 Republicans in the Senate cosponsored Senator Charles Percy's proposal for a homeownership provision in the 1968 Housing Act (McClaughry, 1975).

One other source of political support for the expansion of FHA activities into central city and minority areas needs to be mentioned here, although it will also be discussed in connection with subsidized rental housing. This was the growing tendency in the 1960s for key segments of the private housing industry to support active government intervention on behalf of the housing needs of the poor, especially where the private sector would be the provider of such housing. Government subsidies for privately produced housing services was not a new idea. It had been proposed in the 1930s as an alternative to public housing and had been explored thoroughly by a commission on housing appointed by Eisenhower in the early 1950s. Nevertheless, since the New Deal, homebuilders, realtors, and bankers had been more or less united in their opposition to any expansion of the government role in housing beyond the regulations and insurance programs already in place, particularly where that expansion involved sudsidies to the poor. They viewed the long-term potential threat of government competition and regulation as outweighing any short-term gains from federal subsidies. They concentrated their efforts on limiting the incursion already made by public housing, rather than risk a nominally private sector program which might ultimately increase the government's role (Freedman, 1969).

In the 1960s, the National Association of Real Estate Boards (NAREB), whose concerns tended to focus on the sale and rental of existing dwellings, and who thus saw government stimulated supply increases or subsidies as a threat to their market, continued to resist new subsidy programs. In contrast the National Association of Home Builders gradually became a strong supporter of such programs. They became, in fact, part of an alliance which also included the Housing and Home Finance Agency (HHFA—later to become HUD) and the pro-housing members of the House and Senate Banking and Currency Committees. This alliance followed the subgovernment pattern mentioned earlier, and it became an important source of support for governmental housing initiatives. The Kennedy and Johnson Administrations actively courted such support by emphasizing the need for a public-private partnership in solving housing problems, and they were supported in this stance by a number of moderate Republicans. The new FHA homeownership programs were seen as prime examples of such a partnership.

As a result of all these interests and attitudes, the FHA entered the 1970s at the helm of programs that had previously been foreign to its basic value orientations as an agency. Such an uneasy marriage contained great potential for problems, and the emergence of these problems in the first two years of the decade created an image of program failure which was to shape the policy debate which followed. The precise dimension of these problems will discussed in Chapter 5.

The Convoluted Fate of Public Housing

The public housing program, enacted by Congress as the Housing Act of 1937, emerged relatively late in the New Deal period. Though there was organized opposition to it from the beginning (led by NAREB), they were unable to block it, due to the wide congressional support engendered by the dual crisis in housing and in construction trades employment which still afflicted the country. (Semer, 1976). However, the program was unable to fully capitalize on its initial support because it had barely begun to produce units when World War II began. War needs diverted materials from housing construction, and the public housing that was built was mainly utilized for war industry workers, rather than the poor. In addition, NAREB and its allies succeeded in imposing budget cuts in the late 1930s and this curtailed production (Gelfand, 1975).

Because of the hiatus caused by the war, major political conflicts over the existence and expansion of the program did not fully emerge until after the war, when the liberal New Deal coalition had lost some of its strength. In 1946, Truman proposed a large new commitment of funds to the program as part of his comprehensive housing proposal, but the public housing provisions proved to be the most unpopular sections of the bill and barely escaped deletion from the final legislative product, the Housing Act of 1949. Even this commitment was later to be seriously undermined, as shall be shown.

The complex history of public housing can best be understood in terms of four basic issues which were the focus of debate and struggle between its opponents and proponents. These are: site selection, the target population, financial problems, and problems of administration and project design. In each of these areas, the political balance of forces created contradictory pressures which made it difficult for the program to meet its objectives. Moreover, some of these basic contradictions continued to affect the alternatives to public housing which were later initiated.

Site Selection

The issue of site selection arose early. The precursor to the public housing program, the Housing Division of the Public Works Administration, had been a centralized program, in which the federal government itself bought and developed the project sites. Because of the political appeal of decentralization and because of legal challenges to the federal government's right to use eminent domain for such a purpose, proponents of a more permanent public housing program opted for local control. Local housing authorities would be created by special legislation in each state, and these would develop and administer the federally financed projects. In addition local governments would be given a role in site selection because of a "cooperation agreement" which had to be signed between the public housing authority and the local government regarding payments in lieu of taxes for fire, police, and other public services.

This devolution of authority to local entities set the stage for the community battles over the siting of public housing projects which became a recurring feature of local politics over the next 40 years. Unfortunately, but not surprisingly given the negative attitudes toward the poor described earlier, middle class neighborhoods often greeted the introduction of public housing with the same enthusiasm as they might have greeted the introduction of bubonic plague; and such citizen's groups were in a position to generate more heat than most local politicians were willing to endure. In the years following World War II, local opposition was fanned by a vigorous national propaganda campaign carried out by NAREB and its allies. The enabling legislation in many states required that local participation in the program be subject to direct voter approval by referendum. These referenda gave opponents the opportunity to excite public fears. In Seattle, for example, opponents went so far as to publish a map purporting to show intended sites for public housing in middle class areas, even though the local housing authority had made no such decisions (Freedman, 1969). Even where referenda were not required, pressure was exerted on the local political structure through aldermen representing various areas, as in the case of Chicago so well documented by Meyerson and Banfield (1955).

Most localities managed to build some public housing, in spite of such opposition, but the pressure to locate new units in areas already occupied by the poor was overwhelming. Any large concentration of disadvantaged persons in a single development would have placed a certain stigma on it. However, the stigma associated with public housing was intensified by the construction of new projects in the midst of vast expanses of dilapidated housing which already bore the label of slums (Meehan, 1979). This stigma tended to be self-fulfilling, insofar as it influenced the behavior of the poor themselves. Families with dreams of upward mobility gradually came to avoid "the projects," even when the low rent would have been a great financial boon. This left a greater concentration of the most desperate, down-and-out poor who had no place else to go. In addition, those among the poor who responded to its pressures with sociopathic behavior tended to be attracted to the huge projects as fertile ground on which to practice criminal activity. Critics of public housing could then point to the deterioration of the quality of life in public housing as evidence that it should not have been built at all.

The Target Population

The nature of the target population to be served was a second major issue which created problems for the public housing program. In Great Britain and other Western countries, publicly owned housing served a rather broad segment of the population, albeit at the lower end of the income scale (McGuire, 1981). In the United States, in contrast, it was assumed from the beginning that only those of the very lowest incomes, persons so desperately poor as to have no chance of obtaining housing on the private market, should be served.

The 1937 Act limited income in two ways. The first was the stipulation that, with the exception of large families, tenant income could not exceed five times the rent charged. Coupled with a later restriction of rent levels to 20 percent below the prevailing local market rate for comparable housing, this requirement aimed at excluding persons of even modest means (Freedman, 1969, pp. 105-106). Second, it authorized the federal public housing agency to set specific dollar limits on income, to reflect the legislative intent that "only low income people" should be served. The limits set during the first 20 years of the program were, according to Freedman, so low as to insure that occupants were among the poorest persons in the United States (Freedman, 1969, p. 107). In 1959, these restrictions were removed, and limits were left to the discretion of local housing authorities (Mandelker, 1973). However, 1971 data from 74 cities, reported in U.S. Senate hearings, indicated that throughout the 1960s, local housing authorities' limits remained well below the median incomes in their communities (U.S. Congress, Senate Committee on Banking, Housing and Urban Affairs, 1971).

Such a policy satisfied a basic principle of vertical equity—namely, that those with the greatest need had the highest priority for help. This principle has been defended vigorously by liberals as the only fair way to distribute the typically slender resources allocated to social welfare programs. Nevertheless, the application of this particular principle has presented severe problems for the programs involved, problems amply illustrated by the history of public housing.

One problem was that the program which was the nation's major housing subsidy effort for 25 years was simply unable to serve a very large segment of the population with genuine housing needs. The program appeared grossly unfair to those families who worked hard to earn only slightly better incomes than public housing tenants, but who ended up occupying worse housing or paying much larger percentages of their income to secure decent quarters. A second, and related, problem was that strict income limits penalized modest efforts at upward mobility on the part of public housing tenants. During the 1940s and 1950s, most local public housing authorities evicted tenants whose incomes rose above the prescribed ceiling. Any laxity in pursuing this policy exposed the agencies to public criticism for letting "well off" people live in subsidized housing (Freedman, 1969, p. 107). However, the sudden eviction of a family whose income went up slightly often put them in much worse financial shape, since comparable private housing cost more. The projects themselves were hurt, too, in that it was just such upwardly mobile persons who provided stability and community leadership.

A third problem with strict income ceilings was that they contributed to a negative public image of public housing tenants. This problem was not as severe during the early years of the program, when the typical public housing tenant was a temporarily poor but otherwise respectable family who needed aid in difficult circumstances imposed by war or depression. Many housing authorities tried to maintain this respectability by designing other admissions standards so as to screen out all but these families. However, during the 1950s the composition of the American poor as a whole gradually shifted from the temporarily disadvantaged to a more permanently distressed underclass, and such a positive image became more difficult to maintain (Wolman, 1971, p. 31). For example, AFDC families, initially excluded from public housing by many communities, gradually came to be admitted and to comprise an increasing percentage of public housing tenants, just as they became an increasing proportion of the low income population. This helped reinforce public perceptions of the program as one more "dole" to those who were already receiving undeserved aid.

The overall effect of these three problems was to undermine political support for the program, but the restriction of the program to the very poor created another political problem as well, that of constituency. After World War II shook the nation out of its economic doldrums, the poor gradually became a minority of the population, a minority largely without the skills, resources, or inclination to exert political pressure on behalf of the programs from which they benefitted. As a result, the main interest group pushing for the public housing program consisted of the professional administrators responsible for it, acting through such organizations as the National Association of Housing and Redevelopment Officials (NAHRO). The support they could muster depended not on the political clout of their clients but on an appeal to social cost arguments. These were sufficient to keep the program from total extinction, but in the face of concerted ideological attacks from the private housing industry, they were hardly a political basis upon which it could thrive (Keith, 1973). That the direct participation of clientele groups could have made a difference is shown, in part, by the galvanizing effect which the extra-legal participation of the poor in the riots of 1965-68 had on this and other social welfare efforts.

The Cost Squeeze

Eugene Meehan has made the financial problems of the public housing program the centerpiece of his analysis of what he considers to be its widespread failure. He contends that over the greater part of its existence, the program was forced by financial starvation to provide a limited number of units and a declining quality of service to its clients (Meehan, 1977, 1979). While he may overstate the importance of this one factor in relation to the program's many other complex problems, he documents convincingly the important role played by lack of funds. There are several important ways in which funding levels were used to restrict the program.

The first and most obvious way was through the appropriation of funds for the construction of units. Over time, Congress developed a consistent pattern of appropriating funds for far less units than were authorized by the substantive legislation. The largest gap occurred in the 1950s. The Housing Act of 1949 authorized a major new commitment to the public housing program in the form of 810,000 units to be completed over the following six years, or 135,000 units per year. However, the actual appropriations in the ensuing years never exceeded a peak of 90,000 units—in Fiscal Year (FY) 1950—and reached a low point of zero in FY 1954. More typically, appropriations fluctuated around 25,000 units. (Freedman, 1969, pp. 19-32). As a result, by 1960, five years after the target date for completion of the 810,000 new units, less than one-quarter of these had been built (Freedman, 1969, p. 32).

This outcome resulted, in large part, from political configurations within Congress. The responsibility for substantive housing legislation was lodged in the housing subcommittees of the House Banking and Currency Committee and the Senate Banking and Currency Committee (later renamed the Senate Committee on Banking, Housing and Urban Affairs). These committees, as noted, attracted senators and representatives with an intense interest in housing, and they developed close ties with federal housing agencies, and with pro-housing lobbies such as NAHRO and the National Housing Conference. In contrast, the Independent Offices Subcommittee of the House Appropriations Committee, the group immediately responsible for housing appropriations during the 1950s and 1960s, contained a much greater proportion of conservative southern Democrats and conservative Republicans, many of whom were hostile to the whole concept of public housing. NAREB and other anti-public housing groups concentrated their lobbying on this more sympathetic center of power and helped encourage its use to prevent the achievement of the 1949 Act's ambitious goal.

Yet, the continued limitations on public housing funding cannot entirely be attributed to the skillful utilization of an alternative, specialized power center within Congress by its opponents. Throughout much of the 1950s public housing remained an unpopular program, subject to periodic dismantling attempts on the floor of the House and Senate, as well as in the Appropriations Committee. In addition, the presence or absence of presidential support had an appreciable impact on the level of effort. While Truman was president, he pushed for relatively large numbers of units (although the Korean War kept him from proposing the original annual goal of 135,000 units). Eisenhower, on the other hand, was cool to the program and, while never trying to abolish it, he consistently recommended low levels of funding. Finally, local community opposition affected national decisions, in that many of the units which were funded were subject to delay due to protracted battles over site selection. Although local officials, for the most part, desired more units as a means of reducing their slums and lobbied accordingly, these simmering local controversies had a dampening effect on congressional support.

The Kennedy Administration was much more enthusiastic about public housing, and, immediately upon taking office, proposed that 100,000 units be built by 1964. When Lyndon Johnson assumed the presidency, he further accelerated the program, proposing 60,000 units per year for four years in the Housing Act of 1965, and a total of 395,000 units over a three year period in the Housing Act of 1968. In contrast to the 1950s, in which production moved by fits and starts, the 1960s produced a strong executive branch drive toward a larger, smoother flow of units. Congress, too, seemed much more willing to appropriate funds without the long battles and vituperative rhetoric characteristic of earlier years. The aforementioned change in political environment due to the civil rights movement and urban riots, coupled with liberal control of the presidency and larger liberal majorities in Congress, accounted for this shift to a large degree. However, another rather paradoxical reason for the greater ease with which public housing expenditures made it through Congress was that the focus of debate over the proper federal role in housing had shifted to newer, more innovative programs such as rent supplements. Next to these, the public housing program seemed familiar and controllable. This point will be discussed more fully below.

Money considerations, in addition to limiting the quantity of public housing units built, greatly affected their quality. The 1937 Act provided federal support only for the capital costs of public housing. That is, federal funds paid only the principal and interest on bonds issued by local housing authorities to finance construction. Operation and maintenance costs were covered out of the rents charged, and any surplus rental income had to be immediately applied toward repayment of the debt (Meehan, 1979). During the program's early years, when most of the units were new and the tenants were often the working poor, authorities had little trouble in supporting their own operating and maintenance costs; however, during the 1950s and 1960s this became increasingly difficult. On the one hand, inflation increased these expenses, and the aging buildings required more repairs. On the other hand, tenant incomes were declining relative to the incomes of the rest of the population. Henry Aaron reports that between 1961 and 1970, the median family income of public housing tenants declined from 47.1 percent to 36.9 percent of the U.S. median family income (Aaron, 1972, p. 116).

By the late 1960s, according to Daniel Mandelker, many housing authorities were in serious financial difficulty (Mandelker, 1973, pp. 82-83). Nevertheless, though Congress was funding more units, they were much less willing to confront the issues of operating subsidies. A major reason was that local authorities' financial problems were widely perceived to be the result of inefficient or careless management, coupled with the alleged destructiveness of those who occupied them. Even though studies by the Urban Institute and the Rand Institute showed that price inflation, not poor management, was the main cause of the cost squeeze (Mandelker, 1973, p. 83), most members of Congress were reluctant to provide money which they felt would reduce local incentives to operate efficiently. When the cost problem was finally addressed, it was addressed obliquely through congressional response to a symptom of the problem, namely, the substantial rent increases to which many authorities had resorted in order to cover costs. These increases led to tenant unrest, culminating in rent strikes in such cities as Newark and St. Louis. Congress responded in 1969 with the Brooke Amendment, which restricted public housing rents to no more than 25 percent of tenant income. It also provided operating subsidies to cover local authority shortfalls and to pay off previously accumulated operating deficits (Mandelker, 1973). Thus was created one of the housing policy controversies of the 1970s, which will be examined further in Chapter 5.

Management and Design Issues

All three of the issues just described – site selection, target population, and costs – had an important impact on the quality and quantity of the services offered by public housing. However, the program stimulated another debate related to the quality of services it provided: a debate over the physical design of the structures and the quality of their management. Here, as in other areas, the program was caught between conflicting pressures from liberals for improvement and from conservatives for containment.

The issue of public housing design touched directly on a central problem which has affected all such programs – the problem of what level of housing quality should be enjoyed by those whom the government assists. The prevailing view among conservative critics and among many liberals as well was that the quarters provided by the government should be spartan. Anything more than the minimum quality necessary to maintain health would, in this view, weaken the incentive of the residents to better themselves and excite the resentment of nonsubsidized families. This viewpoint had a major influence on public housing, but its applications proved difficult and self-defeating.

To begin with, most citizens, and their elected representatives as well, tended to associate control over costs with control over amenities. It was believed that strict limits on the per unit cost of public housing would prevent local authorities from constructing units which were too luxurious for low income persons. In response to this perception, Congress placed extremely tight limits on "prototype costs" for public housing units, often setting them well below average construction costs for a particular area. However, in reality such costs were at least as much related to the quality of the basic elements of construction as to the extras which might make a unit luxurious (A 1982 HUD study of the costs of multifamily housing documents the relatively small impact which amenities have on per unit costs; HUD, 1982b, pp. 5–8). Therefore, the result of these limitations was, in many cases the use of cheap materials and shoddy construction in such basic elements as doors, windows, plumbing, and heating equipment. Such short-term savings were, of course, inimical not only to the quality of life of the tenants but to the taxpayers' long-term financial interest in obtaining durable housing units. Widespread negative perceptions of the poor obscured this problem, since the tenants themselves were blamed by the public and policymakers for the poor condition of the units.

Even where basic construction was sound, cost restrictions discouraged design features which were essential to the smooth functioning of families and of the projects as communities. Units with minimal floor space; elevators which stopped on every other floor; floor plans arranged to minimize costs but maximize security problems; a total absence of site planning or recreational facilities—all of these were seen as prudent cost-cutting measures. However, the long-term costs, both to the tenants and to the public, were clearly much larger than the dollars saved in the short run.

Beyond this, the absence of certain basic amenities was, to the residents, a symbol of the stigma attached to living in public housing. As Nathan Glazer and others have pointed out, one's concept of what level of housing services is minimal is a product of time and culture, and it is clear that the housing expectations of postwar Americans have far exceeded those of earlier generations or of their contemporaries in other cultures (Glazer, 1967). It is also true that individuals will generally aspire to the standard of living of those higher on the income scale and that the total equalizaton of housing quality with aspirations would be excessively costly. However, this having been said, there is another minimum quality line which is difficult to define precisely but which, if not met, leads the individual to put less value on his dwelling and, perhaps, on himself. The failure to meet such a standard can, as a result, contribute to the deterioration of life in the project. Common public housing design items like toilets without seats and cabinets or closets without doors would certainly fall into this category of stigmatizing deficiencies.

Yet another controversy concerning physical design which had a negative impact on elite and mass acceptance of public housing concerned the aesthetic contribution of public housing developments to the community as a whole. In sharp contrast to the widespread public sentiment in favor of spartan dwellings for the poor, a number of influential planners, architects, and social critics attacked public housing's lack of aesthetic quality as a blight on the community (Friedman, L., 1968). The concrete or brick monoliths which went up in larger cities and even the unadorned town house units in smaller cities were criticized not only for their drabness but for their lack of "human scale." Certainly, the vibrant community of Jane Jacobs' Greenwich Village (Jacobs, 1961), with its constant interactions and "eyes on the street" was the opposite of the massive impersonal housing blocks, where mothers had to send their children ten floors down to play, unsupervised, in barren, rubble strewn lots. Yet, these critiques were often made without taking into account reasonable and accurate expectations. On the one hand, middle class observers may have idealized the human and structural variety of older low income neighborhoods without taking into account their physical discomforts and lack of security. On the other hand, the expection that public housing provide low cost shelter for tens of thousands of people while at the same time meeting the criteria of a warm, personal, communal environment and/or making a major architectural statement was probably unreasonable.

Closely related to the physical deficiencies of public housing were widespread perceptions of serious local management difficulties. In the 1950s many local agencies tried to keep their projects respectable in the eyes of the community by screening out applicants they considered undesirable and by extensive intervention into the private lives of tenants. The eviction of female tenants for becoming pregnant out of wedlock was a standard policy in many localities, and tenants were often fined heavily for physical damage to the property (Steiner, 1971). In the 1960s, tenant groups challenged such regulations as paternalistic violations of individual privacy, and by the end of the decade, most housing authorities had loosened their "parietal" rules. At the same time, many other public housing managers were under fire for being too lax; i.e., for not responding vigorously to problems of physical damage, criminal behavior, or other social conflicts. Each of these criticisms was valid for some projects, and it was not impossible to find, in the same locality, strictness in some areas coupled with laxity in others. Nevertheless, the simultaneous existence of these two critiques was typical of the cross-pressures under which the program had to operate.

Because of the numerous criticisms of public housing management which arose during the 1960s, the decade saw the beginnings of various efforts at improvement. Existing managers received training, and tenant councils were set up to provide the opportunity for resident input. Also, a number of attempts to expand social services and recreation available to tenants were initiated. These experiments had varying levels of success, depending on the good faith which management undertook them, the ways in which the conflicts engendered by tenant participation were handled, and the adequacy of available funding. Overall, such efforts contributed to the atmosphere of uncertainty within the program which was to affect policy decisions in the 1970s.

The FHA and Public Housing: A Summary

In summary, it may be said that the nation's two oldest and largest housing programs entered the 1970s in a state of flux. The FHA, set up to serve the suburban middle class and the financial community, was embarking on a new and relatively untried venture into assistance for low income and central city areas. Public housing was undergoing rapid expansion in the number of units and, in one sense, enjoyed greater political support than at any time since its inception. Yet, in another sense, the program remained seriously troubled, for many of the problems which had plagued it all along continued unabated or intensified, while new demands arose from both tenants and the larger community. Thus, both these programs were to spawn controversies which would play a major role in the housing politics of the decade.

Before these new issues can be examined, it is necessary to look at another dimension of housing politics in the 1960s which was to have an important impact on the 1970s. This was the extensive experimentation with alternative ways to provide subsidies to low income tenants, through the use of private sector construction and leasing.

Subsidies and Supplements

As noted in connection with the Section 235 program, neither conservatives or liberals were very receptive to the idea of subsidies to the private sector for the provision of low income housing during the first 25 years of federal housing efforts. Conservatives feared the overall expansion of the government role in the housing market which might accompany federal subsidy dollars. Liberals were concerned that the private sector would be unable to provide the service as cheaply as the public sector, thus denying lower income persons the benefits of federal expenditures.

In addition to the ambivalent reactions to the concept of private sector subsidies from those representing various points on the political spectrum, one also has to look at the political dynamics of the housing policy struggle in the 1940s and 1950s to explain the absence of private sector subsidy programs. Public housing became an established program serving very low income persons, but it was under such severe attack that several moves in Congress to extinguish it very nearly succeeded. Therefore, liberal housing advocates concentrated their political efforts on maintaining a minimal level of activity in this existing program. In this way, the atmosphere of general distrust of federal involvement prevalent in the 1950s helped to discourage innovation of any kind. On the other side of the battle, conservatives discovered that they could not muster enough votes to kill the program altogether, and they gradually came to accept its existence on a limited scale. They found that its impact on the private market could be kept to a minimum: (1) by controlling appropriations; and, (2) by perpetuating local community struggles over site selection which would keep the poor concentrated and isolated. By the end of the 1950s, the program, though not particularly liked by either side, was at least a known quantity which both sides could accept.

In spite of these ideological and pragmatic factors, John F. Kennedy came into office in 1961 with a new agenda which encouraged him to push beyond the political equilibrium established around a 25,000 unit per year public housing program. On the one hand, his desire to improve housing conditions for the poor led him to push for expansion of the public housing program itself. On the other hand, there were several concerns motivating him to look at other forms of housing assistance.

First, qualitative criticisms of public housing from the left were becoming more intense in the late 1950s, thus encouraging Kennedy's advisors to seek alternatives to public ownership which might avoid such problems. Second, innovations in this area helped satisfy an urge which Kennedy's advisors displayed in many areas of policy—the urge to project an image of creativity and progress, in contrast to the stagnation which they attributed to the Eisenhower years. Third, they perceived a need to aid families whose incomes were too high for public housing but too low to obtain standard housing on the private market. According to Milton Semer, concern among housing policy analysts that this group was not being reached either by FHA or by public housing had been increasing during the late 1950s (Semer, 1976, p. 116). Fourth, Kennedy became president during an economic downturn which had hit the housing industry particularly hard, raising unemployment in the industry to as high as 20 percent. Expanding government involvement in housing construction was a way to stimulate this key element of the private economy.

Finally, the Kennedy Administration, and later the Johnson Administration, placed great emphasis on the principle of public-private cooperation in solving social problems. Without the Great Depression at hand to stimulate fears of total system collapse, it seemed necessary to move beyond this kind of threat as a social cost argument and to emphasize the direct gains which the private sector could realize from helping the poor. Not only would the stability and harmony of society as a whole be enhanced by governmental social activism, but various market winners could profitably expand their opportunities and help the disadvantaged at the same time. Such a commonality of interests would expand the political base of social welfare programs, thereby avoiding the pariah status which direct government handouts to the poor such as public housing and AFDC had endured. Such considerations overrode the liberal concerns about vertical equity mentioned above, and led to the pursuit of public-private partnerships as a major political strategy.

Kennedy's first successful initiative in this direction in the area of housing was the Section 221(d)(3) Below Market Interest Rate program, which was part of the Housing Act of 1961. This program enabled private lenders to originate mortgages on rental housing developments at a rate below the prevailing market rates. Then, they could sell these mortgages to Fannie Mae at a price based on market rates. The loss sustained in this transaction constituted a subsidy designed to reduce rents by reducing capital costs. Participation was also encouraged by the extension of liberal borrowing terms by FHA, and a Special Risk Fund was set up within FHA to underwrite these loans, so that the marketability of its conventional loans would not be jeopardized.

The Section 221(d)(3) program was explicitly directed at families with incomes too high for public housing but too low for standard private housing. In practice, the upper income ceiling was usually set at or near the median income for a particular geographical area, while the floor was the upper income limit for public housing eligibility. Another important feature of this program was that tenants were not to be evicted if their income rose above a certain fixed level, but could continue residence at higher rents.

In the first four years of its existence, approximately 90,000 units were committed under the program, yet, it remained vulnerable to attack on a number of grounds and thus did not establish a stable political foothold. First, the interest subsidies did not result in as large a reduction in rents as had been hoped, due in part to increases in interest rates during that period. In some cases, rents were only $20 a month lower than conventional FHA multifamily projects, with the result that only the upper range of moderate income families could be served. This, plus the lack of eviction with rising income (plus laxity of income verification by some project managers) combined to raise the median income of 221(d)(3) tenants to $5000 in 1965, a relatively high figure for that time. There were instances in which the media reported cases of allegedly "well-to-do" tenants living in these projects, reports which hurt the public's image of the program. In short, the program was caught on the opposite horn of the dilemma which had ensnared public housing. Public housing served a very low income group and as a result was stigmatized as a "dole" for the "undeserving." Section 221(d)(3) served a slightly higher income group, and it was attacked for giving aid to those who were too well off to deserve it.

A second political difficulty encountered by the program arose from the nature of its impact on the federal budget. Since the entire mortgage on each project was purchased by Fannie Mae, each development within a given year removed a relatively large sum of money from the federal coffers. Only a fraction of this amount would actually be lost to the government in the long run, since the loan was to be repaid by the developer out of rent receipts. However, the program's large initial outlays enabled its detractors to characterize it as "excesssively costly" and made it a target for strict funding limits.

To avoid the problem of budgetary impact, the Johnson Administration sought an alternative to the Section 221(d)(3) program in 1965. The alternative which they developed, called the *rent supplement* program, restructured the subsidy so that, instead of being applied indirectly, by the government's repurchase of the mortgage at a loss, it was applied directly to the tenant's rent. FHA would insure a market rate loan to finance the project which, along with other expenses, would determine an "economic rent" for the project. The difference between this figure and 20 percent of the eligible tenant's income would be paid as a direct federal subsidy. While costing the same, or possibly more, than the other type of subsidy, this approach had the advantage of limiting the program's yearly budgetary impact to the relatively small subsidy payments.

This new proposal became the target of an intense, often vituperative debate in Congress; however, the focus of this debate was not the budgetary impact of the program but other features. The major bone of contention was the income group to be served. Like Section 221(d)(3), this program was aimed at families in what Johnson Administration spokesmen referred to as the "20 percent gap" between public housing and private standard housing. Yet, the subsidy provided in the rent supplement proposal was somewhat deeper than that which the earlier program had provided, and it was far more direct and visible. While the change in subsidy method minimized budgetary impact, it converted the government's effort from an indirect stimulus to the construction of housing in a certain price range to what opponents could characterize as a subsidy to middle income families.

The debate on this aspect of the program split supporters of federal housing programs, as well as mobilizing opponents. The National Association of Housing and Redevelopment Officials (NAHRO) went on record against the program, calling it "administratively cumbersome and socially indefensible." (CQ Almanac, 1965, p. 361). This stance was clearly motivated by the self-interest of local public housing authorities in keeping their program in center stage, as well as an ideological objection to helping higher income groups. The proposal ultimately attracted such strong opposition that Johnson was forced to make a major modification in order to secure passage. Eligiblity requirements were amended so that, instead of serving the 20 percent gap, the subsidies were available only to those with incomes *at or below* public housing limits. Only by averting an expansion of federal activity into the moderate income area, and thereby allaying both conservative fears of government expansion and liberal fears of abandonment of the poor, could Johnson get his rent supplement program through Congress.

The rent supplement debate was also fanned by increasing fears that the federal government would force socioeconomic and/or racial integration on higher income areas. Rent supplements were seen by both proponents and opponents as a potentially more effective tool than public housing for achieving such integration. Higher income limits meant that subsidies could be extended to families who could afford to move into middle income areas, and, because it involved direct contracts between the HHFA and private builders, site selection would not require local government approval. By 1965, the federal government had become firmly identified with the cause of civil rights and with aid to the urban poor, as symbolized by the presence of black housing advocate, Robert Weaver, as head of HHFA. Congressman Paul Fino (Rep., N.Y.) expressed the fears of many opponents when he asserted that the bill was "without safeguards to prevent the housing administrator from moving the poorest people into the best housing." This position was echoed by Senator John Tower (Rep., Texas) who said that the program's goal was to "get low income, middle income, and high income groups all living together." Neither these nor other public statements explicitly mentioned the issue of racial integration, but *Congressional Quarterly* quotes one House member who characterized race as "a major subsurface issue" in the whole debate (Quotes are from the CQ Almanac, 1965, pp. 373-377, 246).

Though the rent supplement program was finally enacted, its actual implementation was very slow, in large part because opponents used their second line of defense, the appropriations process, to block implementation. Congress refused to appropriate funds in 1965, and in 1966, it cut Johnson's request in half. Also, a rider was attached to the 1966 appropriations bill which forced HHFA's successor, the new Department of Housing and Urban Development (HUD), to seek local government approval for rent supplement projects. (CQ Almanac, 1966, p. 245). This subjected the program to the same local site selection battles encountered by public housing. As it became clear that the program would remain small in scale, the Johnson Administration sought yet another alternative which would be more palatable to Congress and to the public.

The new plan was incorporated in Johnson's 1967 housing proposal and it eventually became law as the Section 236 program, a major part of the massive Housing Act of 1968. The Section 236 program again utilized annual subsidies to private lenders rather than direct or indirect government loans, in order to minimize yearly budgetary impact. But, in this program, the subsidies were not to be paid as direct rent supplements. Instead, the developer arranged a loan at market interest rates but was only required to pay 1 percent interest, the difference being made up by government payments to the lender. Furthermore, in an effort to avoid the virulent opposition which had greeted the income provisions of the rent supplement program, the new proposal buried its income limits in the subsidy mechanism. A "basic rent" was computed on the basis of the 1 percent mortgage rate, and no family paid less than this, regardless of income. (However, 20 percent of the units in each project were set aside for additional subsidy under the rent supplement program.) The upper income ceiling was set by a "fair market rent" which was calculated on the basis of prevalent rates for comparable units in the local community. No family for whom 25 percent of monthly income was less than or equal to the fair market rent was eligible (U.S. General Accounting Office, 1978).

However, Congress was, as Semer expresses it, "still not of a mood to turn the Department [HUD] loose to work in the general vineyard of 'low and moderate income' housing" (Semer, 1976, p. 126). As a result, the House and the Senate each came up with its own income ceiling, the former based on 130 percent of public housing limits and the latter based on 70 percent of the Section 221(d)(3) limits. The compromise enacted into law, in which some units were allocated according to one formula and some according to the other, was in Semer's view, complicated to the point of incomprehensibility, but Congress had once again expressed its desire to keep a strict income lid on such programs. In the end, the new program was enacted with much less controversy than the rent supplements program and was funded at a much higher level than any previous subsidy program. Also, the income limits, while low, were much more liberal than those of the rent supplement program.

To complete the picture of new subsidy efforts made in the 1960s, it is necessary to mention one other program which slipped through Congress quietly in 1961 – the Section 23 Leased Housing Program. This program enabled local public housing authorities to take advantage of vacancies in existing housing units. An agency could locate a vacant unit, select an eligible tenant from its waiting list, and determine the rent that the tenant would pay based on its usual criteria. Then, it could enter into a lease with the private landlord in which it agreed to pay the difference between the tenants rent payment and the private market rent for a comparable standard unit. This program avoided the controversy surrounding other ventures into private sector housing because it was clearly within the control of established agencies and because it remained relatively small in scale throughout the 1960s. It is significant primarily because, of all the housing programs enacted during that time, it was closest to the "housing allowance" concept which was to become popular in the 1970s, and thus, it served as a model for later ventures into this type of program.

Conclusion

I have attempted in this chapter to set the stage for the key housing policy decisions of the 1970s, by tracing the development of three major types of subsidy program; the FHA single family mortgage insurance program; the public housing program, and the collection of programs based on indirect and direct subsidies to private builders which were developed in the 1960s. By the end of that decade, all of these programs had, by one route or another, become important parts of the federal government's strategy for improving low income housing, and thus they form the background against which the housing policy decisions of the 1970s were made.

No single piece of legislation embodied the liberal commitments of the Johnson Administration more than the Housing Act of 1968. It reaffirmed the sweeping rhetorical goal of the Housing Act of 1949, "to provide a decent home and living environment for every American family," and it went beyond this to set specific numerical targets. The Act declared, ". . . that it [the goal] can be substantially achieved within the next decade by the construction or rehabilitation of 26 million housing units, six million of these for low and moderate income families" (HUD, 1976, p. 143). The authorizations included in the 1968 Act fell short of this goal in that they extended only three years, but all of the programs included in the bill were funded at levels unheard of in the previous 30 years of federal involvement. Looking at this legislation at that time, it was possible to conclude that the nation had finally made a serious commitment to the use of federal resources to improve housing conditions for lower income families.

Obviously, the actual course of events was quite different. After about four years of large scale expansion, the entire federal housing effort was brought to a halt by the Nixon Moratorium, amid charges that all the major new programs had been failures and amid calls for a totally new approach. In Chapter 5, I will show that much of the responsibility for this change of course lies with the Nixon Administration, which brought a conservative ideological perspective into the Executive Branch. But beyond this, the seeds of this rapid policy reversal lay in the unresolved nature of the underlying ideological and political disputes in which housing as a social welfare policy was embedded, disputes which had already been aired in connection with the policy developments of the 1950s and 1960s. In short, the ship was standing on the launching pad, with plenty of fuel and a seemingly clear flight path charted, but the captaincy had changed hands and the crew was still deeply divided on the basic direction it should take. Thus, it could be expected that the mission would dissolve into midcourse wrangling which would nearly halt the flight altogether.

CHAPTER 5

From Boom to Bust in Federal Housing Subsidies: 1969-1973

The Advent of Richard Nixon

Thomas Dye and Harmon Ziegler, in formulating their "elite theory" of U.S. politics (Dye and Ziegler, 1981), argue that a presidential election cannot be treated as a mandate for particular policy directions because: (1) voters are poorly informed about the issues and candidates' positions on the issues; and (2) voters choose candidates for a variety of complex reasons, of which only a small part are agreements or disagreements with specific policy stands. Even if one questions the applicability of this statement to all elections, there are certainly some in which the policy mandate has been extremely murky. One of these was the election of 1968. Voters were tired of the Vietnam War but hostile to the antiwar movement. They were not adverse to programs to aid the poor, but they wanted law and order restored in the cities, after three years of riots. The national turmoil which characterized the Johnson Administration's tenure seemed at one point to be driving millions of traditionally Democratic voters away from the party, either to Nixon or to the third party candidate, George Wallace. Yet, in the end, Wallace took votes equally from both parties, thus neutralizing his impact, while the Democratic candidate, Hubert Humphrey, gained majorities in most of the groups traditionally composing the New Deal Coalition, thereby rendering Nixon's victory margin razor thin (Converse, et al. 1969).

Dye and Ziegler go on to say that, while the popular will as to future policy options is obscure or incohate, elections do serve the function of bringing into power a new leadership group which usually has different plans for governing the country, or at the least, a different overall approach to solving its problems (Dye and Ziegler, 1981, pp. 210-213). In one sense, this was certainly the case in 1968. The group which assumed power when Nixon took office was distinctly different than the group which preceded it. Yet, in another sense, the division of power between liberals and conservatives was as complex as the voter's electoral decision, particularly with regard to social welfare policies such as housing subsidy programs.

A variety of perspectives were represented within the Nixon Administration. Some advisors, like Daniel Patrick Moynihan, Robert Finch, and George Romney, felt that the previous administration's commitment to solving the problems of the poor should be maintained, albeit with a distinctive stamp of having been reformed and stripped of excesses by the new administration. The key to future Republican electoral success was, they felt, to move toward the center — to portray themselves as more cautious and responsible liberals than the Democrats. Others, like John Mitchell, supported the notion of a 'new Republican majority', based on groups who wished to contain, if not totally reject, the demands of the poor. This majority would add to the traditional Republican core of conservatives many of the disaffected middle class who felt that their money and their values were being sacrificed to the demands of strident minorities. Nixon himself, according to several accounts, did not have a clearly articulated philosophy on domestic social programs and attached less importance to these issues than to foreign affairs (Evans and Novak, 1971; Safire, 1975). Therefore, the direction his administration took was greatly influenced by which group of advisors was able to gain his ear.

But the election of 1968 also left in place forces which strongly supported many of the Great Society programs. The election made only a slight dent in the Democratic majorities in both houses of Congress, thus leaving liberals with a strong legislative power base. In addition, interest groups with a stake in various programs retained considerable political clout. The governments of most large cities were not Republican strongholds, but many in the party did not want to write off this political base entirely; and local officials as a group, whether Democratic or Republican still commanded a respectful ear in Congress when speaking through such organizations as the National Conference of Mayors. There were also private sector interest groups who could be counted on the side of such programs. As noted in Chapter 4, the use of the private sector subsidy method had brought into the pro-housing camp such groups as the National Association of Home Builders and , somewhat less consistently, key banking lobbies such as the Mortgage Bankers Association. These were not groups Nixon could afford to totally ignore or alienate.

The result of these contradictory pressures was a Nixon Administration stance on social welfare policy which gradually shifted over his six years in office. Initially, following the lead of his more liberal staff members, Nixon made efforts to contain, control, and redirect, but not to reverse, major Democratic social welfare initiatives. Programs with the weakest support, such as the War on Poverty (which had alienated many in Congress with its efforts to organize the poor politically rather than simply give out benefits) were the first to be recommended for reorientation or reduction. Meanwhile, programs with greater support, such as housing subsidies, were continued and even expanded. Yet, as Nixon's term progressed, the liberals gradually lost influence and, one by one, departed the administration. This left a much more conservative group in control of domestic policy, a group inclined to use the political weaknesses displayed by various social welfare programs as opportunities to push for their curtailment. Particularly in the period between Nixon's overwhelming reelection victory in 1972 (which they interpreted as a mandate for a shift in policy in a conservative direction) and his total loss of political effectiveness in mid-1974 due to Watergate, the administration was more aggressive in pursuing reorganization measures and budget cuts which would reduce or redirect such programs.

These internal shifts in the Nixon team are stressed here because, in general, the failure of any goverment program to perform at an optimal level, or its generation of undesirable side effects, are not in themselves, sufficient conditions for a successful political attack on the program. As Wildavsky has pointed out, criteria for success or failure are usually ambiguous, judgments of efficacy are dependent on value perspectives, and many programs serve purposes other than their stated ones (Wildavsky, 1979). In addition, it is possible for decisionmakers to choose from a variety of responses to program deficiencies, ranging from minor administrative adjustments to total abolition. Therefore, in explaining instances such as housing subsidy programs, where concern about deficiencies led to severe program curtailment or abolition, one must also look for political actors with the motives and the ability to utilize the program's weaknesses to undermine its political support. Many of the Great Society programs displayed serious flaws, and the underlying ideology of the Nixon team led them to respond to those flaws, not with adjustments, but with major modifications or substitutions.

Another general aspect of Nixon's political strategy bears discussion before the particular problems of housing programs are brought into focus. This was his tendency to couch major efforts at retrenchment in the rhetoric of reform which had previously been associated with liberal initiatives. Even though Nixon's political strength grew as his term progressed (until Watergate exploded) and even though he intensified his efforts to change the direction set by the Great Society, the underlying political support for social welfare programs was sufficiently strong that he did not openly advocate, as Reagan has recently done, a full scale retreat from federal involvement. Instead, he continued to cast himself in the role of a reformer, one who wished to improve the fairness and effectiveness of federal efforts to help the disadvantaged. In an October 13, 1969 message to Congress, he declared that "this would be the watchword of the Administration: REFORM [caps in original]," and he went on to list eleven areas, ranging from the draft to revenue sharing to OEO, which he planned to reform (Nixon, 1971, p. 110-A). Most of these reforms were designed, in the long run, to lessen the public sector's active role on behalf of the disadvantaged, and they were often accompanied by reductions in funding. Such changes would, of course, be reforms from a conservative point of view, but Nixon was clearly appealing to liberals by suggesting that changes in the means, and not in the ends or the level of commitment to the ends were being sought. This blending of retrenchment with reformist rhetoric influenced the development of housing programs by encouraging an emphasis on new approaches to housing subsidies.

From Housing Boom to Growing Perceptions of Failure

Nixon's victory created great concern among housing proponents that Johnson's initiatives would quickly be abandonned (Keith, 1973). However, in keeping with the cautious strategy just described, Nixon sent just the opposite signal by appointing George Romney, a pro-urban, pro-housing Republican, as Secretary of Housing and Urban Development. Romney promised greater administrative efficiency with regard to the housing subsidy programs enacted in 1968 and then presided, for the next four years, over the most massive boom in the construction of federally subsidized housing which had ever occurred. Data on the production of units in the primarily urban housing programs run by HUD from 1969 to 1974 are presented in Figure 7. These show the extent of the boom and the relative contribution of each of the major subsidy programs either begun or accelerated by the Housing Act of 1968.

If a single time period can be identified during which the support for these programs began to unravel, it is probably the year 1971. As Figure 7 shows, this was the year in which production reached its peak, but it was also a year in which investigations by Congress and the media began to uncover problems in the Section 235 and 236 programs, and in which ongoing controversies over public housing intensified. Since each major

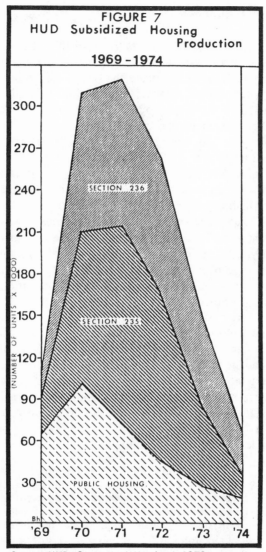

FIGURE 7
HUD Subsidized Housing Production
1969–1974

Source: HUD, Statistical Yearbook, 1979

program had its own path of development and decline, it is best to examine each one separately. Therefore, I will take up the history of the major housing subsidy programs where it left off in Chapter 4 — at the passage of the Housing Act of 1968.

The Section 235 Program

Cities Destroyed for Cash was the lurid title of one journalist's expose of the Section 235 program in Detroit. This book begins with figures purporting to demonstrate the program's failure on a national scale. Then, the author launches into the jucier details of the Detroit scandal, including the murder of an evil realtor by a conscience-stricken man who had helped her procure houses from inner city residents at rock-bottom prices in order to sell them at huge profits through the federal program (Boyer, 1973).

While most descriptions of the Section 235 program lacked the novelistic drama of this account, this expose accurately reflected the aura of scandal which began to envelop this program in 1971 and 1972. The *Wall Street Journal, Business Week, The National Observer*, and many other influential periodicals began carrying stories about FHA's troubles (McClaughry, 1975, p. 4), while several congressional investigations of the program were begun (U.S. Congress, House Committee on Banking and Currency, 1970; 1971b; Committee on Appropriations, 1972; Committee on Government Operations, 1971; 1972a; 1971b). Meanwhile, local grand juries handed down a series of indictments of builders, realtors, and FHA officials in Detroit, New York, Philadelphia, and several other large cities. Clearly, there were communities where these programs had gone awry and had served neither the interests of the general public nor their intended beneficiaries.

The pattern of abuse which emerged from these investigations is well summarized in this account of a home purchase under Section 235:

> In a typical case, a real estate operator would buy up a number of run-down or abandoned buildings in an inner city slum. He would make sufficient cosmetic repairs to make the building temporarily presentable. An FHA appraiser—often a fee appraiser—would inflate the appraisal value, occasionally for an illegal kickback. The operator would find an aspiring low income family with little knowledge of the responsibilities of home ownership. The bank would make the loan, knowing, of course, that FHA would step in in case of default. The operator would take his money and disappear. Later, the homeowner would discover that his home had many substandard conditions, conditions more expensive to correct than his limited budget permitted. Having only $200 in the deal, and facing huge expenses and protracted wrangling, the homeowner would abandon the property and disappear. And, another problem home went into the FHA inventory (McClaughry, 1975, p. 21).

This account delineates several key actors who influenced the outcome of the transaction; the FHA administrators, the prospective buyer, the realtor or builder, and the mortgage banker. All of these actors displayed attitudes or behavior which combined to make the results of the transaction less than favorable. In addition, the transaction was influenced by the condition of the inner city housing market in which it was taking place. Let us briefly explore each of these aspects of the problem.

The passage of the 1968 Act thrust the FHA into territory both unfamiliar and uncomfortable for its administrative staff. After years of underwriting mortgages for middle class buyers using the banker's criterion of economic soundness as a measure of risk, the FHA staff was suddenly asked to change both its criterion and its clientele. Backers of the 1968 Act were concerned that the economic soundness criterion erected an arbitrary barrier around inner city areas, since it was based as much on the location of a house as its physical condition. Their intent was that the FHA remove this barrier and bring its expertise to bear on inner city problems, with a reasonable relaxation of standards to reflect inner city conditions. However, at the level of implementation, many local FHA administrators heard a different message. In the words of a 1971 HUD Audit Report, "We were informed, both orally and in written comments [by local FHA officials] that the word was out from the Central Office to relax the inspection requirements." (U.S. Congress, House Committee on Banking and Currency, 1971b, p. 85). This tendency to interpret a lowering of standards as a philosophy of "anything goes" was exacerbated by the push from top HUD officials for high volume construction and rehabilitation of units, plus a lack of adequate staff in many field offices.

The result was, in some areas, a breakdown of the normal process of FHA review. Inspections of properties to be insured were not done or were done from the outside as a "windshield inspection." In a masterpiece of bureaucratic understatement, the HUD Audit Report cited above notes: "The conditions were so bad in some of the houses we inspected that the interior inspection by an appraiser prior to insurance is debatable." (p. 87). In addition, the determination of the value of houses was often done by private fee appraisers who were themselves local realtors, and their carelessly or deliberately inflated valuations were often accepted without review.

With FHA willing to relax its standards, there were numerous builders and real estate agents willing to exploit the situation for quick profits. After purchasing several houses at low prices from people leaving the area, these agents could easily find willing buyers among low income persons eager to improve their housing. The agents would use FHA backing to reassure the buyer of the quality of the house. Then, they would take advantage of FHA laxity, or, in some cases, actually bribe officials to look the other way while the house was sold in poor condition and/or at an inflated price.

They found their most fertile ground in neighborhoods which were changing racially or could be tipped toward racial change by skillful manipulaton. Block busting was, as Bradford points out, a technique which had been highly developed by unscrupulous inner city realtors long before the FHA programs were introduced. It depended for its success on whites who were afraid of property value loss due to integration and on blacks who, because they faced very restricted housing choices, were eager to open up new areas. However, the impact of block busting had, in the past, been limited in scope by the lack of available credit. Most banks would lend to blacks, if at all, only on the most unfavorable terms, and many blacks were forced to use less desirable forms of financing such as sales contracts and balloon notes.

The effect of the new FHA initiatives was to open a flood of credit to areas vulnerable to racial change. The presence of FHA mortgage insurance, plus the willingness of Fannie Mae to purchase federally insured mortgages made lending in these areas a virtually risk-free venture for mortgage bankers and savings and loan associations. They could get FHA approval on the structure, service the loan for a nice fee, and then immediately sell the mortgage to Fannie Mae. If the mortgage defaulted, FHA covered the loss and was left holding the property (Bradford, 1979).

The willingness of realtors to sell inferior units to low income persons at high profits can, in one sense, be explained by sheer greed, without reference to broader, more abstract value systems. Yet, in another sense, such behavior fits into the larger set of attitudes toward the poor which are prevalent in U.S. society. The fact that middle class persons often stereotype the poor as lazy, ignorant, unkempt, or destructive makes economic exploitation of them seem more ethically palatable to the entrepreneur. When challenged to justify their actions, such persons respond with statements such as "It's better than what they had," or, "these people don't care how it looks," or, "they'll just tear it up anyway." Where the entrepreneur is white and the client black, such stereotyping is often intensified, although black entrepreneurs may also exploit members of their own community. Interviews with local FHA officials conducted during HUD and congressional investigations show that they often shared similar attitudes toward their disadvantaged clients.

To reject these stereotypes, however, is not to suggest that the attitudes and lack of knowledge of buyers had no impact on the program.

By extending homeownership to lower income persons, the FHA was reaching many who had little knowledge of the meaning of homeownership or of the responsibilities it entailed. Typical of the problems cited by many authors is an account, given to this writer by a local government official, of a new Section 235 owner who went into the bank demanding that they fix the plumbing, as if the bank were the landlord rather than simply the mortgagee. Because of such problems, the FHA was justly criticized for a total absence of counseling of prospective home buyers or even a sense of responsibility for blatantly fraudulent representation of housing conditions by sellers to buyers. As the HUD Audit Report stated, "FHA personnel advocated, and continue to do so in certain areas, the caveat emptor concept." (p. 84). To its credit, HUD several times requested funding for a counseling program, but Congress refused to grant it until 1972, after the program had been tainted by scandal.

Yet, in spite of the importance of the attitudes of low income purchasers, the tendency of many accounts of the problems of Section 235 to focus on lack of buyer awareness becomes a subtle form of "blaming the victim" (Ryan, 1976) if it is not placed within the total social and economic context in which these transactions took place. Some accounts describe buyers who were aware of the shortcomings of houses they were buying but felt compelled to take advantage of what seemed to them a once in a lifetime opportunity for homeownership. Contrary to the abstract economic models of many market advocates, the poor are often unable, or perceive themselves as unable, to shop freely on the open market for the best possible product, even when given a cash subsidy to do so. Thus, they often take what they can get, even with full knowledge of its deficiencies.

Furthermore, the problems of many purchasers seem to have stemmed as much from financial overextension as from inadequate cultural background. The program not only subsidized interest but reduced the down payment to as low as $200, and this amount was often paid by the eager real estate speculator. Thus, the buyer had little financial stake in the property and was more inclined to equate home buying with renting. In addition, the procedures for determining the percentage of income to be paid for housing did not take into account maintenance expenses for which the owner would be responsibile, nor did the program allow for the accumulation of a maintenance reserve to deal with large, one time expenditures. Finally, the maintenance and liveability problems encountered by many buyers were the direct result of poor construction and thus were so costly that few homeowners could have easily paid for them. A staff report of the House Committee on Banking and Currency comments:

The staff did find cases where homeowners failed to take care of basic maintenance responsibilities, but in such cases the result was for the most part only poor housekeeping by middle class standards. However, no homeowner can be expected to cope with poor construction, cracked foundations, improper wiring, and a general failure of contractors to meet local building and maintenance requirements. A welfare mother with four or five children may well have a house that is in less than spotless condition, but they cannot be blamed because there is only one electrical outlet in the entire house and no . . . heating vents in any of the bedrooms on the second floor. . . .(U.S. Congress, House Banking and Currency Committee, 1971b, 106).

It is much easier to recite the well-documented catalog of Section 235 abuses than it is to establish a picture of the success or failure of the program as whole. Most critiques of the program, whether journalistic, governmental, or academic, were based on case studies of a few major cities. While this is understandable in light of the complexity of the data involved in analysing such a program, it is, nevertheless, hard to gain from a few cases an accurate picture of the program's national impact. In certain cities, such as Detroit and Philadelphia, the program generated massive corruption and had a clearly negative impact on some of the neighborhoods involved. Other cities operated the program in a manner beneficial to the low income people affected.

Because the response of many lower income families to problem units was, as noted, abandonment of the property, the rate of assignment or foreclosure of loans is a reasonably good indicator of the national incidence of the problems described above. Figure 8 shows the cumulative number of units assigned or in foreclosure from 1969 to 1979 in comparison to the total number of Section 235 units constructed during that period.

Figure 8 shows that over 90,000 units had been assigned or foreclosed in the program by 1979, or approximately 18 percent of the 500,000 units built. This rate was very high in comparison to the conventional FHA Section 203 program which had, since its inception, a cumulative foreclosure rate of less than 5 percent (HUD, 1979e). Clearly, some of the program's difficulties resulted in a much higher casualty rate than was typical for transactions in suburban and/or middle income areas. However, these rates of foreclosure and default do not suggest a program in a state of total crisis or collapse as was indicated in many contemporary accounts. Of all the loans made, over 80 percent *did not* end up in foreclosure, an indication that the majority of the program's clients were reasonably well served by the program. As Downs points

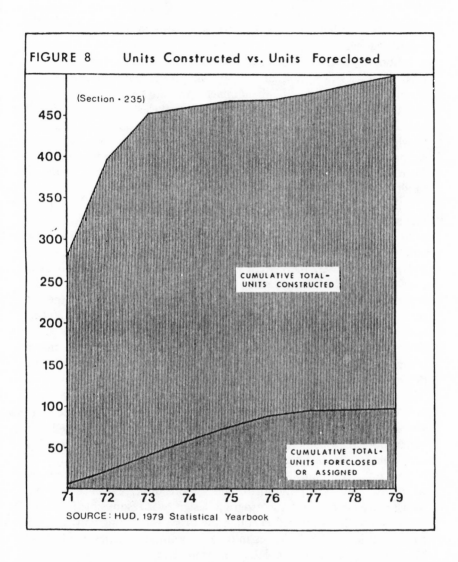

FIGURE 8   Units Constructed vs. Units Foreclosed

(Section · 235)

CUMULATIVE TOTAL-
UNITS CONSTRUCTED

CUMULATIVE TOTAL-
UNITS FORECLOSED
OR ASSIGNED

SOURCE: HUD, 1979 Statistical Yearbook

out, Section 235 was known from the beginning to be a high risk program, due to the marginal neighborhoods and low income families involved. Thus, high foreclosure rates should not have been surprising. He
also notes that the cost of such defaults was vastly overestimated by
Romney and others on the basis of the Detroit experience. He estimates a
net cost of $3000 per HUD acquired unit for handling and resale
(Downs, 1973, p. 65). For 90,000 units, this amounts to a cost of $270

million, a large but far from astronomical figure in relation to the total federal budget.

Looking at the impact of defaults strictly in terms of governmental financial losses does not, of course, take into account the social and psychological effects of abandonned dwellings and governmental callousness on particular communities. Nevertheless, even if one is less sanguine about the programs' failures than Downs, a question remains as to whether the program was fundamentally flawed or could have been substantially improved through changes in design and administration. There is some evidence that such modifications could have had favorable results.

First, another look at Figure 8 shows an interesting pattern in the rate of accumulation of foreclosures. The program began in 1969 and by 1970 had accumulated 1212 foreclosures on the approximatley 130,000 units which had been constructed. This rate began to accelerate rapidly in 1971, and by 1975, there were 76,102 foreclosures, or approximately 15,000 per year. However, after 1975, the rate declined rapidly. HUD reported 19,489 foreclosures between the beginning of 1976 and the end of 1979, for a yearly rate of about 4900. To put it another way, 80 percent of the program's foreclosures as of 1979 had occurred early in the life of the individual mortgages affected. This pattern suggests that a screening of the applicants was taking place through early foreclosure that could have taken place *before* the sale, since most structural or financial problems which could cause default within one or two years of sale should have been apparent at the outset. Once this early de facto screening of applicants occurred, the rate of foreclosure returned to a much more reasonable level, suggesting that most families had either been able to maintain their payments or sell to others who could.

Second, testimony before the various congressional committees which examined the program provides more direct evidence that administrative laxity, not basic program design, was responsible for much of the abuse that occurred. Though the task of changing conservative, business oriented FHA offices into social welfare agencies would have been difficult at best, top HUD officials made little or no effort to retrain local FHA staff to handle the program. Instead, they sent down a message equivalent to "Damn the torpedoes, full speed ahead." As Downs points out, existing FHA appraisal and inspection procedures contained sufficient safeguards to prevent gross abuse by private developers, had the staff been inclined to apply them properly (Downs, 1973, p. 51).

Beyond this, other features likely to result in even greater program success would not have been impracticable. Extensive counseling of potential buyers as to the responsibilities of homeownership would have minimized the role of buyer ignorance in the rates of default and abandonment, although this counseling would, in many cases, have had to be backed up by financial help with maintenance costs. In addition, as McClaughry's excellent analysis of the program suggests, (McClaughry, 1975), a conscious effort by the FHA to involve neighborhood groups in planning and executing the program might have at least curtailed, if not totally eliminated, block busting, shoddy construction, and abandonment. Such efforts would, it is true, have slowed down production, but they would have brought the program closer to meeting its objectives.

Evidence that such modifications could have made the program a success is provided by the testimony of Leonard Katz, a former FHA administrator from Milwaukee, Wisconsin. In Milwaukee, applicants were required to take three classes in home buying before being given a list of realtors to contact. For those program participants who were on welfare, an inspection of the home by the Welfare Department was required. If the purchaser lacked the $200 minimum downpayment, this was supplied by a grant from the St. Vincent dePaul Society. As a further safeguard, the buyer was required to personally inspect the property before purchase, and at the closing, he or she was represented by a lawyer from the Legal Aid program. Finally, the buyer was given a class in home maintenance by the University of Wisconsin Extension Service (U.S. Congress, House Committee on Government Operations, 1972, 162-171).

The extensive interagency cooperation involved in this approach required an administrative effort that, in one sense, was above and beyond the call of duty for an FHA official. Yet, this approach yielded concrete benefits for the agency as well as for the home buyers, since the Wisconsin foreclosure rate, as of early 1972, was 0.09 percent, or nine foreclosures out of 8500 mortgages insured (McClaughry, 1975, p. 25). Ironically, during much of the time this program was being implemented, Katz was being castigated by higher HUD officials for his office's low productivity, while the Detroit FHA Director, whose office would later produce the worst scandal in the country, was being praised for his "aggressive processing of inner city homes." (McClaughry, 1975, p. 26).

The fact that there was plenty of room for constructive change within the existing program structure was not ignored by program supporters. It was frequently raised in testimony by interest groups within the housing subgovernment, as in these opening lines from a Mortgage Bankers Association report to the Senate Appropriations Committee:

> When a human enterprise is going smoothly, headlines are not in order. . . . This journalistic axiom has attracted a lot of justified public exposure of the abuses that have occurred in the FHA Section 235 . . . program. . . . But, what about 235's successes? It is more constructive now to explore the causes of 235's success than to fan the ashes of its failures (U.S. Congress, Senate Appropriations Committee, 1971, p. 777).

The report then goes on to list many individual success stories and to laud the virtues of good counseling for prospective buyers. Other reports by congressional supporters of housing programs also emphasized the positive aspects of the program and took the Nixon Administration to task for most of its failures (See, for example, U.S. Congress, Joint Economic Committee, 1973).

This type of response by program supporters placed the Nixon team in a somewhat delicate position. On the one hand, the program's failures could be used as grounds for the type of disengagement to which Nixon was already inclined. Rather than making a genuine effort at improvement, it could gradually distance itself from the program, while claiming leadership in the search for alternatives. On the other hand, since virtually all Section 235 production had occured under the Nixon Administration, its spokesmen had to avoid criticizing the program in such a way as to direct more blame on their own administrative shortcomings. Thus, the testimony of George Romney over the first Nixon term contains negative appraisals of program performance, but it also contains various attempts to play down the extent of program abuse and to emphasize the steps being taken to improve the program. This ambivalent relationship toward the program created a further incentive for Nixon to couch his later attacks on the program in terms of reform rather than retrenchment. He could thus cast himself in the role of improving the tools of housing policy rather than throwing them away after failing to use them properly.

The Section 236 Program

The Section 236 rental housing program, which was the 1968 Act's counterpart to the Section 235 homeownership program, did not receive as much attention from Congress, from journalists, or from scholars as did Section 235. This was, in part, because its concept was not as novel as that of providing homeownership to the poor. Also, the failures of the program were generally less massive and visible than those of Secton 235. Nevertheless, the program's difficulties did receive attention which contributed to the loss of political support for subsidy efforts in general.

In early 1972, the Surveys and Investigations Staff of the House Appropriations Committee conducted an investigation of Section 236. They identified a number of problem areas in the program, which may serve as an outline for discussion. These problem areas may be divided into three groups: (1) problems of site selection; (2) problems related to the motivations and qualifications of sponsors; and, (3) problems of excessive costs and rents.

It was noted in Chapter 4 that one problem policymakers sought to avoid by going from public housing to private sector subsidies was lengthy local conflicts over site selection. In the Section 236 program, some conflict was avoided by the fact that builders could obtain their sites through private real estate transactions. However, the tendency toward concentration of units in low income or central city areas was not eliminated. Builders tended to see low income areas as their natural market and sought to locate new units accordingly. In addition, there were delays and restrictions on construction in higher income areas which could, under public pressure, be imposed by public bodies. Many suburban areas had zoning laws which virtually excluded any type of multifamily development; and, even where this was not the case, middle class citizens tended to see Section 236 projects in the same negative light as public housing (though tenant incomes were generally higher) and to utilize any available legal avenues to keep them out.

The concentration of Section 236 projects in central city and/or low income areas had a number of negative consequences. First, the projects sometimes inherited the negative reputation and the social problems of their surroundings, much as public housing had done earlier. Second, some cities experienced overbuilding of subsidized projects in relatively small geographic areas. If this did not directly create vacancies in new units, it often was the indirect cause of vacancies in older subsidized projects nearby, as eligible tenants sought out the greater amenities available in newer developments.

HUD regulations stipulated a careful check of marketability as part of the processing of Section 236 proposals, but its staff often lacked the detailed knowledge of local markets to make accurate assessments of demand. And, though the market mechanism will itself adjust supply and demand in the long run, it does permit many short-term problems of oversupply. If such an oversupply problem pertains to fast food restaurants on an urban commercial strip, then the failure of the last two built may not affect anyone but the investors. But, in the already volatile conditions of urban housing markets, the failure of a housing development may generate negative consequences for an entire neighborhood, as well as for project's owners and residents. Furthermore, when the entire program is under close, and often hostile, political scrutiny, then anything which increases the failure rate of projects can cloud the program's future.

Sponsors of Section 236 projects could be of three types—cooperatives; nonprofit organizations; or limited dividend, profit-making corporations or partnerships—with the last two types constituting the bulk of the developers. Nonprofit organizations accounted for roughly one-third of the starts. A typical pattern was that of one midwestern city in which a consortium of churches was formed to sponsore a Section 236 project. The intent of these organizations was altruistic—to improve housing opportunities for lower income persons. However, as shall be shown, these groups' lack of expertise in housing created serious problems with the units built under their sponsorship.

Limited dividend sponsors were, in contrast, investing in subsidized housing for profit. Their return on investment was formally limited to 6 percent, but there were numerous ways the various participants could increase their return. The complex relationships which developed in this situation bear some discussion, since these relationships affected not only the Section 236 program but also the Section 8 program which was to supercede it in 1974. (This discussion is drawn from the aforementioned House staff report; U.S. Congress, House, Committee on Appropriations, 1972; and from a Congressional Budget Office report on real estate tax shelters; U.S. Congress, Budget Office, 1977.)

As was also true for unsubsidized multifamily developments, the primary attraction of a Section 236 development to wealthy investors was not the return from rental income but the sheltering of other income from taxation. Mortgage interest and property taxes were, of course, deductible, but, in addition, tax law permitted the use of accelerated depreciation on the value of the property as a write-off against current income. The investor could, in other words, shelter current income by counting against it 'paper losses' in the value of the rental units.

These losses were, to some degree, recaptured for tax purposes upon sale of the property, because the difference between the actual sales price and the depreciated value claimed in prior years was subject to capital gains tax. However, the capital gains tax rate was much lower than the income tax rate for persons in the upper income brackets, and the difference between accelerated and straight line depreciation was not subject to recapture if the property was held for 16⅔ years or if the funds were reinvested in another subsidized housing project. In addition, the investor enjoyed the tax-free use of the sheltered income during the time the property was held. Finally, investors could, by putting up a certain percentage of the downpayment, claim that same percentage of the total cost of the development as a basis for figuring accelerated depreciation. For example, if a development cost $1,000,000, with a downpayment of $100,000, an investor could put up $20,000, or 20 percent of the downpayment, and claim 20 percent of the depreciation losses for the entire $1,000,000 project.

These tax benefits led to a variety of complex ownership arrangements under the general rubric of *tax syndication*. The developer himself usually did not have enough income to take full advantage of the tax benefits, so he would 'sell' them by setting up a limited partnership with other investors. In this arrangement, the developer served as general partner, with responsibility for the actual development process, while the liability of the others was limited to the money they invested. Since subsidized housing was considered a high risk investment, it would have been very hard to raise sufficient capital for Section 236 projects without the additional incentive of these tax benefits. However, the use of tax incentives for investors and the complex ownership patterns it engendered carried with it some disadvantages for the long-term viability of such projects.

To begin with, most of the tax benefits were realized in the first 10 to 15 years of the project's life; therefore, the temptation existed to use the project for these benefits and then sell it, without concern for its long-term survival. In addition, most of the partners had little knowledge or concern about housing management, and, since their financial risk was limited, they had little incentive to become effective watchdogs over the developer or his management agent. Finally, since income from rent was not the major source of return on the investment, investors had little incentive to pressure managers to "run a tight ship" in terms of operation, maintenance costs, or vacancy losses. Though investors did have an interest in avoiding the early collapse of a project, their 'arms length' relationship to it discouraged early detection and prevention of such a collapse.

A third problem area for Section 236 projects was that of cost and rent escalation. One source of cost escalation was the developers themselves, who had an obvious incentive to inflate construction costs in order to maximize subsidy payments. Higher profits could be inserted into development costs in a number of ways. One was through land acquisition. HUD based its mortgage amount on its own appraisal of the land, not the developer's actual cost, and the House Appropriations Committee staff found that the actual cost was often much lower than the appraised value. Another way to inflate costs was through fees and overhead charged by the developer to the limited partnership for design, general contracting services, setting up the tax syndication, or for management of the project by its own subsidiary.

HUD did, of course, attempt to regulate these costs, but a combination of lack of data on the local situation, general laxity in administration, and the shrewdness and determination of developers often made the regulations ineffective. Paradoxically, where HUD did enforce its regulations, the result was often delays in construction which themselves increased costs. The process was so complex that, in many parts of the country, a group of developers arose who specialized in subsidized housing construction. They developed the patience and expertise to negotiate the maze of HUD approval and to turn it to their advantage. The effects of such upward pressures on costs were reflected in a HUD estimate that Section 236 projects costs 10–20 percent more to build than comparable conventional projects, not including the additional tax expenditure due to sheltering of income (HUD, 1974a).

Problems also arose in connection with operating costs. These problems had two sources. One was the built-in incentive for developers to get HUD agreement on minimum estimates of operating costs for the purpose of project approval. As noted in Chapter 4, Congress had imposed upper income limits on eligibility for admission. Since tenants were to pay no more than the "basic rent" (the rent which would cover operating costs and profit plus financing at 1 percent interest), or 25 percent of their income, whichever was larger, these income limits put a ceiling on the initial rents that could be charged. Lower operating expense estimates could thus be used to insert higher construction costs in the original rents. However, once the project was rented, the enforcement of these limits tended to become much more lax. The management was required by HUD to periodically recertify tenant incomes, but in many cases, HUD did not verify or even spot check the data they provided. Meanwhile, managers could increase project income by requesting rent increases based on real operating expenses much larger than the original estimates.

In addition to whatever deliberate manipulation of cost data occurred, the real costs of maintenance and utilities began to increase rapidly in the early 1970s, in a manner which often invalidated the most honest of cost estimates. This was part of the larger, decade-long trend described in Chapter 3, in which the median income of tenant households increased much more slowly than the costs of rental housing. This trend created serious problems for all rental housing in the latter half of the decade, but its impact was especially severe on Section 236, which based its subsidy levels on costs rather than on a fixed percentage of tenant incomes. Steady upward pressure on costs and rents reduced the potential market of eligible tenants, prevented the most needy families from benefiting from the program, and created an additional incentive for project managers to skimp on maintenance and services.

As in the case of Section 235, it is easier to recite a list of problems than assess the total impact of these problems on the overall success or failure of the program. Again, the incidence of mortgage foreclosures is of some use as an indicator of the nationwide severity of program deficiencies. Figure 9 shows the cumulative total of units foreclosed or assigned in relation to the toal number of units constructed.

Figure 9 shows a relatively low rate of foreclosure in the first three years of the program, followed by a rapid increase in foreclosures from 1973 to 1976, when most of the units built under the program came into existence. In subsequent years, the number of foreclosures ceased its rapid increase, and moved upward only gradually, from about 83,000 in 1976 to just over 100,000 in 1979. As of that year, roughly 15 percent of the units built had ended up in foreclosure.

The strong surge in foreclosures early in the program's life reflects, in all probability, the initial problems of marketability and financing just discussed. These data conform to the pattern found in a 1978 General Accounting Office (GAO) report on the program; namely, that a very large percentage of the foreclosures occurred very early in the project's life, in some cases even before construction was completed. As in the Section 235 program, this early surge of foreclosures suggests that nonviable projects were being screened out by the foreclosure process. This, in turn, points to the inadequacy of HUD's preapproval screening process, which should have caught a larger percentage of these nonviable projects (U.S. GAO, 1978).

In one sense, this problem is very likely an inherent defect of such public-private programs. Evidence from many areas of public policy suggests the disadvantages in motivation and information control which regulating agencies suffer in relation to the industry they regulate, and the tendency for the regulatory body to be coopted by those it regulates. Also, as the 1978 GAO study pointed out, the very fact that investors were protected by government insurance made them more inclined to let a troubled project default rather than working out long-term payment arrangements as was often done when privately insured projects encountered financial difficulties. Yet, in another sense, this pattern of ear-

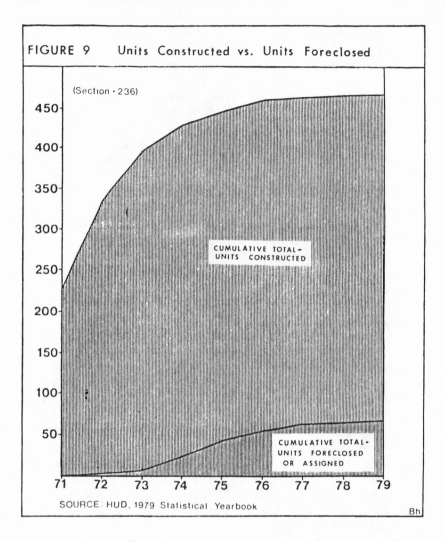

FIGURE 9   Units Constructed vs. Units Foreclosed

(Section · 236)

CUMULATIVE TOTAL-
UNITS CONSTRUCTED

CUMULATIVE TOTAL-
UNITS FORECLOSED
OR ASSIGNED

SOURCE: HUD, 1979 Statistical Yearbook

ly foreclosure suggests that, even within the inherent limitations of the public oversight process, a substantial reduction in the overall foreclosure rate of the program might have been achieved through tightening of administrative procedures. Moreover, even the foreclosures which did occur did not add up to the picture of massive and escalating financial disaster portrayed in the media during the early years of the program.

While providing a general picture of program outcomes, these data on overall foreclosure rates also conceal some important differences in rates of failure between various types of Section 236 projects. Table 6, taken from another GAO analysis of housing subsidy programs done in 1980, breaks down foreclosures according to project type.

This table shows that projects undertaken by nonprofit sponsors had over four times the rate of failure of those undertaken by for-profit groups. The GAO suggests that this was principally due to two factors: (1) These groups' lack of experience in housing finance or management; and, (2) undercapitalization of projects due to these groups' limited resources. Also notable is the fact that projects involving substantial rehabilitation had a much higher failure rate than new construction. This reflected the complex and tenuous situation in which rehabilitation projects found themselves. Since they were often located in declining neighborhoods, their marketability depended on improvements in the conditions of the entire area, an uncertain prospect and one over which sponsors had little control. Also, the fact that rehabilitated projects often cost nearly as much as new construction but could not command the same rents left them with a much more tenuous financial margin.

When these two problem categories are removed from the total, the failure rate for newly constructed Section 236 projects drops to just over 7 percent. According to the GAO, this was actually less than the rates for the FHA Section 207 market interest rate program (for middle income rental units) for a similar period (approximately 9 percent) and less than either the market rate or below market rate programs operated under Section 221(d)(3)—approximately 15 percent. It was still substantially

TABLE 6

**SECTION 236 CUMULATIVE ASSIGNMENT AND
FORECLOSURE RATES AS OF SEPTEMBER 30, 1977**

Type of Sponsor	New Construction		Substantial Rehabilitation	
	Family	Elderly	Family	Elderly
Limited dividend (for profit)	7.1%	1.7%	31.3%	13.6%
Nonprofit	32.6%	5.9%	65.1%	12.5%

Source: U.S. General Accounting Office, *Evaluation of Alternatives for Financing Low and Moderate Income Rental Housing*, PAD-80-13, 1980, p. 50.

higher than that for privately insured multifamily developments, which were just over 1 percent; however, considering that the Section 236 program was intitially designed to fund developments too risky for normal private sector investment, this higher rate should not have been surprising. In sum, had more caution been taken with nonprofit sponsors and with rehabilitation and had the tighter administrative controls mentioned above been implemented, the Section 236 could have been remarkably successful in terms of the long-term financial viability of its projects.

There were, nevertheless, other questions raised about this program which were not directly related to its numerical rate of failure and which did not necessarily arise in connection with the Section 235 program. The Section 235 program, to the extent that it was successful, conferred the substantial financial and psychological benefit of homeownership on low income persons, in addition to the benefits associated with occupying a "decent, safe and sanitary" dwelling. In this respect it had a distinct advantage over any other subsidy program which had been devised.

In contrast, the Section 236 program was essentially an alternative way to provide subsidized rental housing which could be fairly compared to earlier methods of achieving the same goal such as rent supplements or public housing. One point of comparison was vertical equity. Both liberals and conservatives criticized the program for not being designed to meet the needs of the lowest income tenants. This criticism was later confirmed by the 1978 GAO report, which found the 1975 median income of Section 236 tenants to be $5634, in contrast to the national median income of $11,400 and the public housing tenants' median income of $3531. However, the group in question clearly was not affluent and had legitimate housing needs which the private market could not meet. And, given the questions raised earlier about the image and political support problems of a governmental housing effort strictly for the poorest of the poor, one may legitimately ask whether vertical equity should be so strictly adhered to that moderate income persons must wait in line for federal subsidies until the housing needs of *ALL* of the very poor have been served. Nevertheless, this issue continued to be an important one for Section 236.

The other question raised about the Section 236 program was the cost of extensively subsidizing *NEW* construction of housing for lower income persons by the private sector. The program's attractiveness to private builders certainly contributed to its achievement, in a very short time, of a higher level of production than any other such program. Yet, in order to appeal to profit oriented firms, it had to funnel a substantial amount of public dollars into the pockets of wealthy entrepreneurs and investors. This proved to be a major weakness of the program in the eyes of both conservatives concerned with the size of public expenditures and liberals concerned with utilizing funds efficiently to serve the poor. As shall be shown in Chapter 6, it led to increased advocacy of programs relying on existing housing. Yet, the fact that new construction programs could add to the supply of low cost housing and the fact that they engendered a larger constituency for subsidized housing than did publicly owned housing continued to make them appealing. Therefore, the issue of new construction vs. the use of existing units would recur throughout the 1970s.

Public Housing

While the Section 235 and 236 programs were reaching new heights of production and also running into serious problems, the venerable public housing program also enjoyed an unprecedented construction boom, as is shown in Figure 7. However, this boom, too, coexisted with the continuation and exacerbation of many of the problems identified in Chapter 4. These continuing difficulties provided a rationale for the Nixon Administration's inclusion of public housing in its blanket attack on housing subsidy programs. The two sets of public housing problems with the most significant impact were those of financial management and those of site selection.

As discussed in Chapter 4, local public housing authorities had, throughout the 1960s, encountered rapidly rising operating costs. Since the federal subsidy covered only construction financing, these costs had to be paid out of rents, and as they escalated, local authorities had, in essence, only three choices: decrease maintenance and tenant services, increase rents, or both. Reductions in maintenance led, of course, to accelerated physical deterioration of public housing units. Rent increases put larger burdens on persons whose incomes were already low and stimulated rent strikes or other tenant protests in a number of cities.

Senator Edward Brooke, a liberal Republican and the only black elected to the Senate in the twentieth centry, joined the Senate Committee on Banking and Urban Affairs upon taking office in 1966. He soon became deeply concerned with the problems of public housing, and he spearheaded efforts to aid financially troubled local housing autorities with federal operating subsidies. At the same time, he wished to limit the rent burden these local authorities could impose on low income tenants. He succeeded in attaching to the Housing Act of 1969 an amendment which tied increased operating subsidies to the imposition of an upper limit on rents of 25 percent of tenant income.

The passage of the Brooke Amendment was followed by a protracted struggle between HUD, Congress, and various affected groups over how the new restrictions and subsidies were to be applied. According to Daniel Mandelker, top officials at HUD tended to hold local administrators responsible for their projects' financial problems, and thus, were very concerned that the new operating subsidies might encourage bad management practices at the local level. Therefore, they were inclined to put the most restrictive interpretation possible on the congressional intent with regard to distribution of operating subsidy funds. One result of this was that, in the first year after the Brooke Amendment was passed, HUD had spent only $33 million out of an appropriation of $75 million (Mitchell, 1974, p. 446).

Furthermore, according to Eugene Meehan, the entire process was carried out without consideration of the vast accumulation of deferred maintenance problems due to underfunding in previous years. Congress eventually enacted a modernization program to finance the correction of such problems, but it again was underfunded and did not allow localities enough flexibility in identifying and correcting their most serious physical deficiencies. This tendency to ignore accumulated problems, as well as a reluctance to respond to immediate financial problems was, according to Meehan, symptomatic of HUD's failure to carefully and objectively answer the most fundamental question of all—namely, how much does it really cost to provide minimum adequate housing services with a reasonable degree of efficiency? (Meehan, 1979).

The bottom line for most local authorities was that the funds they received were not sufficient to cover revenue losses caused by the Brooke Amendment, especially in light of continuing inflation. The program thus began in the 1970s with more new construction than ever before, but with many of its older units crumbling. Symbolic of this deterioration was the beginning, in 1972, of the demolition of St. Louis' vast Pruitt-Igoe project, which had been rendered uninhabitable by extreme physical deterioration. Pictures of the dynamiting of those buildings, which had been constructed a mere 15 years earlier, made the front pages of newspapers across the country and made an indelible impression on many who knew little else about the program. The media treated Pruitt-Igoe as a symbol of the alleged total failure of the public housing program, though thousands of other public housing units across the country continued, in spite of financial problems, to provide decent housing to their tenants. This new symbol added momentum to the push for new approaches to housing subsidies which Nixon was soon to initiate.

Problems related to site selection also continued to plague public housing in the early 1970s, and the issue which increasingly dominated this process was the racial composition and impact of public housing projects. Throughout most of its history, public housing had mirrored the racial segregation characteristic of all types of housing, but in the late 1960s, this pattern became increasingly unacceptable to groups of blacks and liberal whites who were striving for racial equality in all facets of American society. As the FHA had been attacked for perpetuating segregation, so, too, the public housing program was criticized for deliberately creating 'vertical ghettos'.

Throughout the 1950s and early 1960s, the Chicago city government had one of the most blatant policies of public housing segregation in the country. Each member of the City Council had de facto veto power over the location of public housing in his/her ward, with the result that virtually all of the units built were in predominately black areas (Lazin, 1976; Meyerson and Banfield, 1955). It was not surprising, therefore, that a major court challenge to the Chicago program was mounted by civil rights activists in the late 1960s. This challenge, often referred to as the *Gautreaux case* even though it was actually a series of cases, resulted in a federal court order charging the Chicago Housing Authority and the City Council with deliberate, racially motivated site selection practices. The court also set forth several steps to be taken to reverse this pattern (Mandelker, et al., 1981).

Court challenges in other cities were directed at the exclusion of public housing and other subsidized developments by white, suburban communities. Such challenges were successful when, as in the cases involving Lackawanna, Pennsylvania and Black Jack, Missouri, a clear intent to discriminate racially through zoning and other policies could be shown. Where this could not be shown, as in the *James vs. Valtierra* case, policies which had the indirect effeect of excluding low income (black) housing were upheld. In another case which had an indirect effect on public housing, *Shannon vs. HUD*, the U.S. Court of Appeals ruled that HUD had to take into account the impact of a project on the racial and economic composition of the neighborhood it was to be built in and that HUD should not cause further segregation by its site selection policies (Mandelker, et al., 1981, pp. 581-590). Partly as a result of these court cases, Nixon, in 1971, ordered all federal agencies with housing programs to actively promote equal housing opportunities, and, in conformity with this order, HUD issued a series of regulations designed to make racial concentration an important factor in site selection.

As the long history of civil rights legislation and litigation has shown, issuing court orders and federal policy guidelines banning segregation is relatively easy, while enforcing them vigorously is much harder, and actually obtaining integration as a result of enforcement is harder still. The difficulty of implementing court orders is shown by the events following the initial *Gautreaux* decision. Mayor Daley and the Chicago City Council responded to the decision with a policy of massive resistance reminiscent of the efforts of southern segregationists. The Council refused again and again to approve public housing sites in white areas which were offered by the Chicago Housing Authority and HUD in an effort to comply with the *Gautreaux* ruling. The result was a virtual suspension of public housing programs for several years until a further ruling was obtained which suspended the Illinois state law requiring local government approval for public housing sites and allowed the Chicago Housing Authority to proceed on its own.

As for HUD regulations, there was virtually no weapon HUD could wield over local communities to overcome determined opposition to racial or economic integration. Many were willing to forego participation in federal programs if this was to be the price. In some instances, HUD softened the regulations so as to minimize their impact. For example, the site selection criteria established by HUD as a result of the *Shannon* decision did not forbid low income housing in minority areas but rather required that "comparable" units be available to minorities in white areas (Mandelker, et al., 1981). This turned enforcement into a numbers game wherein the hypothetical possibility of a black person's moving into a white apartment complex was substituted for the actual development of new units in a nonminority area. But even in cases where pressure from HUD or the courts forced the location of new housing in middle income, white areas, the current residents could and often did vote with their feet, thereby tipping the surrounding area into a majority black status (Lazin, 1976).

The strength of white resistence to residential integration through federal housing programs, plus the fact that fears of racial integration seemed to increase the overall level of public and elite hostility to government housing efforts had long ago led many within the black community and its white allies to question the use of housing integration as the major strategy for improving black housing conditions. These questions continued to arise throughout the 1970s. When, for example, a federal court in one of the *Gautreaux* cases approved the cut off of funds to Chicago's Model Cities program as a way to force City Council to approve new public housing sites, many blacks protested that the integrationist strategy followed by Dorothy Gautreaux and her ACLU allies was actually hurting blacks more than it was helping them (Lazin, 1976). And, though the black power and black separatist movements played a key role in pushing an internal development strategy for black communities, they were not alone in the belief that segregated housing was better than no housing.

In the broader context of the development of federal housing programs, the constant struggle over the use public housing to achieve racial integration can be seen as one more source of division or ambivalence among liberal supporters. Basic liberal values permit genuine, plausible arguments to be made for housing integration as a primary or as a secondary strategy depending upon one's view of the best way to serve the long-term interests of blacks and other minorities in obtaining equality. Meanwhile, like other such divisions, it tended to strengthen conservative efforts to undermine the momentum of such programs and to keep them small and socially marginal. Though many factors in many programs set the stage for the Nixon Administration's attempt at retrenchment, the continued inability of public housing to resolve its basic dilemmas was certainly an important influence on this chain of events.

The Moratorium

Late in the fall of 1972, rumors began to circulate in the HUD bureaucracy and throughout Washington that Nixon was contemplating a moratorium on housing program activity. These rumors were taken so seriously that HUD Area Offices began to process Section 235 and 236 applications frantically, with the result that, as Nixon's new HUD Secretary James Lynn was later to comment ruefully, "more approvals . . . [were given] . . . in the three week period from December 15, 1972 to January 8, 1973 than in the entire fiscal year up to that time." (CQ Almanac, 1973b, p. 429). The fears that led to this last minute rush proved well founded. Choosing to take the battle into the camp of the enemy, the outgoing HUD Secretary, George Romney, announced the freeze in a January 8 speech to the Houston convention of the National Association of Home Builders. As outlined by Romney, the freeze included:

> A moratorium on all new commitments for subsidized housing programs, including . . . Section 235 and . . . Section 236.

> A hold on new commitments for water and sewer grants, open space land programs and public facilities loans until Congress establishes a

program of community development special revenue sharing of which thes programs would become a part.

A freeze beginning July 1 on all new commitments for urban renewal and Model Cities funding, also a part of the Administration's community development revenue sharing plan.

[A freeze on] . . . new commitments for similar, smaller Farmer's Home Administration programs in the Agriculture Department. (CQ Weekly Report, 1973a, p. 40).

So far, this chapter has described the major controversies and problems in existing federal housing programs which made them vulnerable to such a move and has outlined some of the general policy orientations of the Nixon Administration which led them to contemplate it. However, to convey the full political context of the moratorium, it is necessary to treat several other developments which played a direct role in bringing it about.

First, the importance of Nixon's massive reelection victory just prior to this decision must be emphasized. These were the heady days when Nixon's popular mandate seemed invincible — when it appeared that his approach had been strongly endorsed by all segments of American society. True, Congress remained in Democratic hands, but in the months before the Watergate poison began to seep into all aspects of Nixon's political life, it seemed that he had gained new strength with which to face down his opponents. Coupled with the gradual conservative shift within the Nixon Administration on domestic policy issues (symbolized, in the housing field, by George Romney's departure and his replacement by James Lynn) this new mandate could be expected to stimulate bold new moves in this area.

Second, the moratorium resulted from the impact on housing policy of another national policy debate — the debate over the proper role of federal, state, and local governments in the control and administration of domestic programs. Early in his first term, Nixon had set forth what he called the 'New Federalism' as a major facet of his approach to domestic policy. Basically, this involved two concepts. One was consolidation and simplification of the numerous federal categorical grant programs which had been initiated during the prior Democratic administrations. The other, related concept was devolution of control over program administration from the national level to the states and localities. As noted in Chapter 2, the advocacy of greater local control is a common stance among conservatives. However, the New Federalism had also struck a responsive chord among liberal local officials as well, because they saw the categorical grant-in-aid system as eroding their political and administrative control. These issues will be discussed more thoroughly in Chapters 7 and 8.

Many of Nixon's New Federalism proposals were destined, in the long run, to be enacted. In the short run, however, they had encountered rough sledding in Congress, because the congressional allies of many categorical programs feared loss of funds and loss of commitment to solving specific problems. The most recent struggle between Nixon and Congress in this area, occupying most of 1972, had been over the proposed Housing and Urban Development Act of 1972, which included both the consolidation of community development programs, such as urban renewal, into a block grant and the reorganization and consolidation of 50 existing federal housing programs. After passing the Senate in March, 1972, this massive bill had been buried by the House Rules Committee in September. Therefore, once the election was over, Nixon had an incentive to try a dramatic action which he hoped would break the deadlock over the community development revenue sharing issue.

A third major issue affecting the moratorium was the long struggle between Nixon and Congress over the executive impoundment of funds appropriated by the legislative branch. Nixon had tried impoundment on numerous occasions, succeeding in some cases, but having several others struck down by the judiciary. The Moratorium was, in effect, an impoundment of funds, but it was justified on the grounds that the programs as constituted could not be administered properly. Since these programs had serious and well publicized problems, Nixon's advisors felt he could make this action stick both in the political arena and in court. As it turned out, they were right on both counts.

In his January 8 speech, Romney laid out several arguments which were to serve as key elements of the administration's rationale throughout the Moratorium. He cited an "urgent need for a broad and extensive evaluation of the entire Rube Goldberg structure of our housing and community development statues and regulations." He went on to say that "While Section 235 and 236 programs appear to be working well in many parts of the country . . . they have too frequently been abused and made the vehicle of inordinate profits gained through shoddy construction, poor site location, and questionable financial arangements." As for public housing, he asserted that it, too, was "in crisis," because " . . . Some very fundamental mistakes have been made. . . .The public housing units began to fill up with welfare families and many who exhibited anti-social behavior. . . .Gradually, criminal elements, drug addicts, and other problem elements came to dominate the environment of these units . . . " (CQ Weekly Report, 1973d, p. 140).

Two months later, in his March 8 community development message to Congress, Nixon reiterated these themes. He announced that a team of researchers had been assembled within HUD to conduct a thorough study of all housing programs and to produce a report by the fall of 1973. Working with what the *National Journal* called "security precautions reminiscent of the Pentagon" this group quickly began its study, under the leaderhsip of Michael H. Moskow, HUD's Assistant Secretary for Policy Development and Research. The new HUD Secretary, James Lynn, was also heavily involved in the study (Phillips, 1973a, pp. 1256–57).

Meanwhile, housing proponents in Congress reacted with dismay to the Moratorium. Both pro-housing Democrats, such as Senator William Proxmire and pro-housing Republicans, such as Senators Charles Percy and Edward Brooke, were very critical. In addition, a national coalition of 49 organizations, including the NAHB, the National League of Cities, the NEA, the AFL-CIO, and the Mortgage Bankers Association called on Congress to delay confirmation of Lynn and other Nixon appointees until the freeze was lifted. Yet, when it came to action, Congress could not muster sufficient unity to take on the freeze directly. In May 1973, the House passed a resolution authorizing funds for basic housing and urban development programs. When this resolution reached the Senate, Proxmire attached an amendment ordering the president to end the freeze. The amended resolution passed the Senate and was accepted by House conferees, but with a veto of the entire bill certain, the full House voted to recommit the conference report, thereby forcing the passage of a new resolution without the anti-Moratorium provision. A number of other attempts to cancel the freeze during the 18 months it was in effect also met with failure.

Actions like the Moratorium ultimately intensified resentment against Nixon for attempting to create, in the then current phrase, an "Imperial Presidency," resentment which helped fuel reactions to Watergate. In the short run, however, it appeared to be a highly decisive and successful attempt by the executive branch to alter the course of housing and community development policy in a conservative direction, and it was given the judicial imprimatur by a favorable ruling in *Pennsylvania vs. Lynn*. Meanwhile, he used the hiatus in housing activity he had created to promote an alternative approach to the provision of housing subsidies to lower income persons. His proposals, and their impact on housing policy, will be discussed in Chapter 6.

New Directions in Housing Subsidies: 1973–1980

Housing Allowances—A New (Old) Idea

In September 1973, HUD completed its report. Under the title, *Housing in the Seventies*, it included what had been promised, a comprehensive review of the federal government's involvement in housing, focusing in particular on the housing problems of the poor. Though much of this report was couched in the technical language of policy analysis and though it contained many interesting compilations of hard data, it was clearly not an objective attempt at program assessment but a political document designed to achieve a certain end. One point it attempted to drive home was the alleged failure of previous housing subsidy programs, in order to legitimize Nixon's suspension of these programs. In making this point, virtually all the shortcomings mentioned in Chapter 5 were emphasized. Yet, the report was also designed to achieve a broader goal than criticism of existing programs. This was the justification of a new approach to addressing the housing problems of the poor, an approach involving much greater reliance on the concept of direct cash subsidies to housing consumers than had previously characterized federal housing efforts. Therefore, in order to fully understand the direction taken by this report, it is necessary to examine the concept of housing allowances and the genesis of support for this idea within the Nixon Administration.

The term *housing allowance* encompasses a range of possibilities, so it is best to begin with a brief description of the various permutations it may include. In its purest form, a housing allowance is simply a cash grant to a low income household (usually based on a percentage of income deemed appropriate by policymakers to be spent on housing) which enables them to rent or purchase a unit of better quality than they could afford unassisted. This approach presupposes that the main reason why the poor occupy substandard units is their lack of income to purchase standard housing and that a cash grant will enable them to shop in the private market for a unit that meets their needs. Given the increase in effective demand which is generated by these grants, it is anticipated that the market will respond with an adequate supply. Thus, even though the term *housing allowance* suggests the continued earmarking of the grant for housing purposes, the assumptions behind this approach are very similar to those underlying even broader programs of unconstrained cash grants to the poor, such as the negative income tax, assumptions which were highlighted in Chapter 2 as central to the social welfare policy debate.

Because of a number of concerns to be discussed later, not all proponents of the housing allowance concept favored it in its pure form. Most advocated some form of constraints or supplements to the basic cash grant. The most widely accepted constraint involved supervision of the landlord-tenant relationship by some public agency, in the form of an inspection of the unit to insure its standard condition and varying degrees of participation in the lease agreement. The principal supplement was the linkage of the cash grant to some program of new construction in an effort to insure that the available supply of lower income housing would increase along with the demand.

The housing allowance approach was proposed at various times during the first 35 years of federal housing efforts, but it was kept on the back burner for the reasons discussed in Chapters 4 and 5. Nevertheless, this approach has always had certain features making it attractice to both liberals and conservatives, features which encouraged this alternative to surface in the 1970s, when other approaches were beginning to acquire some tarnish.

The housing allowance involves less active interference in the production of housing by the private market than any other type of public subsidy, because the government's role is limited to making lower income people more effective consumers of the products offered by the private sector. Little or no direct government production or subsidy of production is involved. This makes it a particularly appealing argument for conservatives who wish to keep government activism on behalf of the poor at a minimum, as was suggested in the discussion of Milton Friedman's position in Chapter 2.

The authors of *Housing in the Seventies* transformed Friedman's argument into a seemingly more precise formulation, which they used to demonstrate the greater efficiency of cash housing grants. Utilizing survey data from public housing tenants, they attached a dollar value to the amount of housing which tenants said they would consume if they were given cash, and they established a ratio between this amount and the actual cost of each of the in-kind subsidies. They refered to this ratio as "Transfer Efficiency." The cash value of the subsidy invariably amounted to less than its actual costs, thus allowing the authors to discount the overall efficiency of the existing programs by ratios which were always less than one (HUD, 1974a, pp. 90–91). This result is not surprising, since most consumers will prefer a free to a constrained choice and since low income consumers may have low expectations as to the quality of housing they can consume. It is questionable, however, whether a hypothetical dollar figure derived from this expression of preference should have been treated as equivalent in precision to the actual dollar costs of in-kind subsidies and used as a standard of comparison. In addition, this formulation tended to play down the positive externalities which are generated for the neighborhood and the community by improved housing conditions.

While the appeal of the housing allowance concept to those holding the traditional conservative belief in minimum government is obvious, one might raise a question about the compatibility of this view with the operating ideology of most conservative political actors. Since this group has traditionally been supportive of programs which funnel government support to the activities of market winners, it might have been expected that the housing subgovernment would have found a sympathetic audience for its emphasis on producer subsidies as incentives to aid the poor. To a significant degree, such subsidies were a logical extension of the government regulation and support which had already been given to the housing industry as a whole. The extra expenditures resulting from high production costs and tax breaks could have been justified as stimulants to private investment and employment in the construction trades.

The lack of appeal of these programs to conservatives, and their subsequent attraction to housing allowances, derived, in large part, from the inability of backers to these subsidies to disassociate them from the negative connotations attached to the ultimate beneficiaries of their programs — the poor. Other programs which subsidize private sector activities usually serve some overall goal of economic growth or national security which is widely shared by economic and political elites. The subsidy serves a particular firm or industry but it is also compatible with an image of shared well-being in which the common interests of economic elites are identified with the public interest. In the case of housing subsidies, the funds aided certain segments of the housing industry, but the product ended up in the hands of a group viewed by conservatives as undeserving. Therefore, to the extent that projects failed financially or deteriorated physically, the money flowing into them came to be seen as waste even though it did provide a subsidy to the construction industry.

In addition, the housing programs based on producer subsidies violated another key conservative norm—the desire to keep low income housing programs confined to a relatively small number of people who can be labelled as *truly destitute*. The authors of *Housing in the Seventies* devoted a great deal of attention to the issues of horizontal and vertical equity, using arguments which were replays of those raised about moderate income housing in the early 1960s. Throughout the report they lamented that: (1) current programs served only a small segment of the eligible population; and that, (2) persons of moderate income were being served while some lower income people were not. Although critics of the report pointed out that it exaggerated the proportion of the low income population not served (U.S. Congress, Senate, 1974), these basic characterizations of the programs were correct. However, at least two responses could have been made to this lack of equity. One was to recommend expansion of both low and moderate income programs until the legitimate needs of both groups were met. Clearly, the authors of the report were not willing to accept the extensive reallocation of resources to housing from other purposes necessary to eliminate inequity in this fashion, since the report also criticized existing programs for their aggregate costs.

They recommended instead that existing resources be concentrated on the lowest income segment of the population and that these resources be spread out to serve as many of this group as possible. The authors clearly expected that housing allowances would do this. Since their data suggested that families want to spend less on housing than they are compelled to spend as a result of in-kind subsidies, the authors concluded that housing could be provided at a smaller per unit cost if the poor were allowed to shop. Also, a larger proportion of existing housing could be used, rather than directing subsidies at relatively more expensive new construction. In sum, the report argued for the housing allowance as a means of avoiding a drastic increase in the share of the pie going to low income housing while redistributing it more broadly among those with housing needs.

The appeal of the housing allowance concept was not, of course, limited to those conservatives who saw it as a way to control and reorient the government's role in low income housing. The typical liberal stance had been to push for expansion of the government's role in this area, but many liberals began, in the 1970s, to look more favorably on housing allowances. Both pragmatic political considerations and considerations of program effectiveness contributed to this shift. On the pragmatic side, the supplementation of public housing with subsidized private sector projects, while it made production somewhat less subject to political blockage at various levels of government, did not succeed in improving the overall level of political support for such programs as much as had been hoped. True, it had made political allies out of a key segment of the housing industry, but, for the reasons cited above, this did not seem to guarantee a more stable political niche. In addition, local community opposition, and the resultant concentration of projects in marginal or poor areas, was often as intense for Section 236 projects as for public housing. Regardless of private ownership and regardless of occupancy by a slightly higher income group than public housing, such projects were still seen by middle income neighborhoods as instruments of socioeconomic and/or racial integration. Finally, the argument that housing allowances would reduce per unit subsidy costs had an appeal to liberals as well as conservatives, in that it promised a larger impact from a limited amount of dollars.

Liberal views of program impact and effectiveness may be grouped around three issues: (1) the changing needs of low income households; (2) the benefits of deconcentrating the poor; and, (3) the philosophical issue of empowerment. With regard to the first issue, it was noted in Chapter 3 that a broad spectrum of housing policy analysts in the 1970s began to share the perception that the overall physical condition of the housing stock had improved greatly and that the central housing problem of the low income population was no longer one of residence in substandard dwellings but one of paying too large a percentrage of their income for standard dwellings. A logical conclusion to be drawn from this view was that housing subsidies should shift their emphasis from production to direct support for the housing costs of lower income persons. Thus, the notion of housing allowances became more appealing than it had in the 1960s, when most housing studies stressed the shortage of standard housing for the poor.

With regard to the second issue, liberal concern with the ghettoization and stigmatization of the poor through their concentration in large housing projects increased rather than decreased during the late 1960s and early 1970s. Public housing was seen, by many liberals as well as conservatives, as going from bad to worse, in spite of efforts to save it financially and administratively, and Nixon struck a responsive chord when he blamed this trend on the concentration of an even lower income segment of the population in these units. The appeal of the 'culture of poverty' concept was still strong among liberals and the multiple social problems created by the concentration of the poor in the projects were seen as generating this culture in its most pathological form. Moreover, some of the moderate income Section 236 developments seemed to spawn similar problems.

As a result, the concept of *deconcentrating* the poor through scattered site, small scale public housing developments became increasingly popular among housing reformers in the early 1970s. It was seen as a way to provide the poor with decent housing while avoiding the negative side effects of such efforts. In the prevailing view, the poor could blend into a middle class neighborhood in small numbers without arousing too much hostility and could learn from their middle class neighbors the virtues of responsible community behavior. They would also enjoy the improved public services which the political clout of their middle class neighbors could command.

The fact that the housing allowance concept went one step beyond the deconcentration of public housing by eliminating or reducing production subsidies was seen as a further enhancement of the assimilation process. Middle income neighborhoods had proved quite capable of detecting and resisting even the smaller, scattered site developments, and such developments raised fears of infiltration similar to those voiced in connection with rent supplements a few years earlier. Also, the direct juxtaposition of new, government-built housing for the poor with unsubsidized working class or middle class dwellings often enhanced the sense of inequity felt by the units' neighbors. Such problems were eventually to occur with housing allowances as well, but at the time it was believed that the low visibility of housing allowance units would substantially reduce the friction normally caused by low income housing.

With regard to the third issue, the idea of housing allowances had a certain congruence with a philosophical theme in liberal thinking which gained importance during the late 1960s and early 1970s – the concern for *empowerment* of the poor (Beer, 1978). Whereas the New Deal legacy had been one of government interventions on behalf of the poor, interventions which were usually engineered by white, middle class professionals, the 1960s saw attacks on these interventionist institutions themselves by political organizations representing the poor. (Piven and Cloward, 1971) Stimulated in part by the community action rhetoric of the War on Poverty and by the direct action strategies of the civil rights movement, many leaders in disadvantaged communities began to view the bureaucracies which handed out social welfare benefits as instruments of social control designed to keep poor clients 'in their places' while at the same time addressing their immediate material needs. They began to demand, and to a limited extent receive, representation in institutions making and implementing social welfare policies. On the ideological level, the concepts of *empowerment* and *debureaucratization* began to appear in liberal writings which had, prior to this time, tended to emphasize more paternalistic values of social engineering.

The relationship between empowerment and the housing allowance is a complex one. When the idea was first proposed, some writers on the left of the political spectrum denounced it as a means of throwing the poor back onto the tender mercies of the private landlord. Chester Hartman suggested in a 1974 article that housing allowances were a "hoax." By increasing the effective demand for housing in the restricted market available to lower income persons, such allowances would, he argued, enable landlords to charge higher rents for existing units without substantially improving them and would give them more leverage in negotiating and enforcing lease provisions. Such a change would, therefore, restrict rather than enhance the ability of the poor to control their housing conditions. In contrast, keeping low income housing as a visible program in the public sector would ultimately give the poor more leverage over its administration, especially as advisory and participatory mechanisms continued to evolve (Hartman and Keating, 1974).

Nevertheless, the concept of allowing the poor to choose their own housing and to apportion their incomes between housing and other goods as they wished was still very compatible with the overall liberal concern with empowerment, especially as data on increased supplies of standard housing began to reduce fears of a low income market crunch. The other side to the increasing emphasis on trusting the poor to make their own decisions was an increasing distrust of the ability of public officials to make intelligent decisions for them. Conservatives had always distrusted the competence of the public sector and now some in the liberal camp were beginning to share that distrust.

Housing in the Seventies was not the first place where the idea of housing allowances emerged into serious consideration as a policy option. As early as 1968, the Kaiser Committee appointed by President Johnson had recommended that an experimental program of housing allowances be initiated. According to Raymond Struyk's account, Harold Finger and Malcolm Peabody, members of Nixon's HUD team who were appointed shortly after the Kaiser report was released, picked up this recommendation and pushed it within the Nixon Administration. In proposing the legislation that was to become the Housing Act of 1970, Nixon included general research funds which were intended to cover such a study. An amendment by Senator Edward Brooke went further, specifically mandating that such an experiment be done, and Brooke's proposal was included in the final bill (Struyk and Bendick, 1981).

This legislation marked the beginning of the Experimental Housing Allowance Program (EHAP), one of the longest, most complex, and most expensive experimental programs ever launched by the federal government. EHAP was really not one experiment, but three different experiments, set up in different communities throughout the United States to test various aspects of the housing allowance concept. As summarized by Struyk, these three were:

> The Demand Experiment, in which the responses of low income clients to alternative payment formulas, levels of payments, and minimum housing standards were measured in terms of participation levels, mobility, and level of housing consumption.
>
> The Supply Experiment, in which the response of housing markets in two communities to rapid demand increases due to large scale participation in the program were tested.
>
> The Administrative Agency Experiment, in which the impact of various administrative structures and various levels of client services was tested in a number of locations (Struyk and Bendick, 1981, p. 8).

This might seem a logical point at which to summarize the findings of these complex experiments. However, in terms of the history of Nixon's policy initiatives, these findings are not immediately relevant, since the EHAP study was barely underway in 1973 when the Moratorium was declared and *Housing in the Seventies* was written. Nixon did not wait for the results of EHAP before launching his policy initiative, and, with policy making racing ahead of experimentation, the immediate impact of the EHAP study stemmed more from the simple fact that it was being done. The existence of such a large and systematic experimental program gave the housing allowance concept a respectability and plausibility which it might not otherwise have had. Moreover, Nixon first touted the housing proposal which was to become Section 8 as a further experiment, thus linking it to EHAP.

One other element of the total environment in which Nixon's proposals were spawned — the Section 23 program — needs attention before I proceed with a full discussion of these proposals and their results. As mentioned in the Chapter 4, Section 23 was instituted without fanfare in 1961, as a means for local public housing authorities to gain additional units without stimulating the hostile community reactions which new, large projects engendered. Because of the commitment of the Kennedy,

Johnson, and early Nixon Administrations to production subsidies, the program remained fairly small throughout its first 12 years. However, when the Moratorium was declared and housing allowances were being considered, Nixon's team looked with new interest on this program. Section 23 was not a pure housing allowance program, since the local housing authority, not the tenant, secured and leased the unit. Yet, it did involve cash payments to private landlords, and Nixon asserted in this September 1973 housing message that the program " . . . can be administered in a way which carries out some of the principles of direct cash assistance." (CQ Weekly Report, 1973b, 2523). Consequently, he lifted the freeze on this program and authorized HUD to process applications for an additional 200,000 units. He and his advisors obviously saw it as a tried and true program which could lend further credibility to their new proposals.

The Section 8 Program

The Creation of Section 8

Although Nixon endorsed the housing allowance concept in his September, 1973 message, he also stated his intention to continue suspension of all programs except Section 23 while studying the problem further. However, in late 1973 and early 1974, he came under increasing pressure to do something about housing. The president of the NAHB, George Martin, complained bitterly in Senate testimony that "Under . . . [Nixon's] . . . plan, all that low and moderate income groups have to console them is the hope that 2 or 3 years in the future some type of housing allowance may be instituted on a gradual basis to help them obtain decent housing." (CQ Weekly Report, 1973c, 2969). This complaint fell on sympathetic ears in Congress. By late 1973, Watergate revelations were eroding Nixon's postelection strength. And, though Senator Proxmire lamented that (presumably due to Watergate) "I just don't know how you can get the attention of the country on this," the Watergate pressure benefitted housing proponents by gradually softening Nixon's stand, as he became eager to earn congressional good will in any way possible.

Therefore, the Nixon Administration lent its support to an "omnibus housing and community development bill" which slowly made its way through Congress during the first half of 1974. This bill contained the major provisions of Nixon's earlier proposal, the Better Communities Act, which consolidated various community development programs into a block grant (to be discussed in Chapter 7). It also contained a housing proposal in which Sections 235 and 236 would be rapidly phased out and replaced by an expanded version of the Section 23 program.

The House passed a version of the omnibus bill on June 20, 1974, which closely resembled Nixon's proposal. However, the Senate version, passed earlier, differed substantially from the administration's request. Under the strong influence of the pro-housing senators on its Banking and Urban Affairs Committee and the pro-housing lobby headed by the NAHB, the Senate had voted to reinstate the Section 235 and 236 programs with $500 million in new funds. Evidently referring to committee studies critical of *Housing in the Seventies*, the committee chair, Senator John Sparkman (Dem., Ala.), asserted that "much of the highly publicized criticism levelled at the subsidy programs did not stand up under deep scrutiny" and the "the two subsidy programs had been revised to meet legitimate complaints." (CQ Weekly Report, 1974d, 621).

In the summer of 1974, the imminent threat of impeachment led Nixon to rescind the Moratorium, in one of several last ditch attempts to salvage his presidency. The upcoming impeachment proceedings also spurred more rapid action on the omnibus housing bill by the House-Senate conference committee, since its members felt that the Congress' preoccupation with the Senate trial would kill the bill for that session. A compromise was reached between House and Senate conferees on August 6, 1974, two days before Nixon's resignation. With regard to housing subsidies, the conference committee report followed the House bill in adopting the administration's expanded version of the Section 23 program (Section 8 of the new law); however, House conferees agreed to continue Section 235 and Section 236, albeit with drastically reduced levels of new funding. To partially make up for this reduced new funding, the bill specifically authorized HUD to spend $400 million in prior contract authority which the Moratorium had left unused. On that same day, August 6, the administration announced that the compromise was acceptable. Nine days later, both Houses cleared the conference version, and it was signed into law as the Housing and Community Development Act of 1974 by the new President, Gerald Ford.

This new act was a large and complex piece of legislation. The impact of the community development aspects of it on housing policy will be explored in Chapter 8, while our present focus will be on Section 8 of the new act, which set a new course in housing subsidies. This new program, was, in fact, three programs in one—the New Construction program, the Substantial Rehabilitation program, and the Existing Housing program. A fourth, the Moderate Rehabilitation program, was added in 1978. Substantial Rehabilitation closely resembled New Construction,

Moderate Rehabilitation resembled the Section 8 Existing program, and both were rather small in scale. Therefore, this discussion will deal mainly with the two larger programs. It will begin with an outline of their common elements, and proceed to a description of the unique features of each subprogram.

What both subprograms had in common was an emphasis on the direct subsidy of the tenant's rent as the basis for aid to low income households. The widely accepted figure of 25 percent of income was chosen as a reasonable rent burden, although large families could pay as little as 15 percent. The subsidy for each household was the difference between this percentage of income and an "economic rent" for the unit which HUD determined to be reasonable based on building costs, age, and amenities; however, the economic rent could not exceed the Fair Market Rent (FMR) for that particular size and type of unit in the project's geographical area, a figure determined by HUD on the basis of rents of comparable units in the locality. FMRs ran substantially higher for New Construction than for units in the Existing Housing program. HUD officials were also given the authority to set the rents in a given project as much as 20 percent higher than the FMR, if they felt conditions warranted it.

Since Section 8 was intended to replace both low and moderate income subsidy programs, eligibility requirements were fairly broad. The income maximum was set at 80 percent of the locality's median income for a family of four, with higher limits permitted for larger families. Further requirements were designed to avoid two extremes — the exclusion of very low income persons from the program (which many felt had occurred with Section 236) and the undue concentration of lower income people in projects (which was one of the widely perceived shortcomings of public housing). On the one hand, the law required that 30 percent of those assisted nationally must have incomes of less than 50 percent of their local community's median income. On the other hand, the top limits were set high enough to include some of those previously considered to be moderate income, and new construction projects in which only a portion of the units were subsidized were to be given priority over projects consisting entirely of subsidized units (U.S. Congress, House Committe on Appropriations, 1977, 28–30; Mandelker, et al., 1981).

The total number of Section 8 units of all types in any given locality was determined initially by the level of congressional appropriation. Then successive allocations were made from the HUD Central Office to regional offices and from regional offices to area offices. The area office then had two further determinations to make. First, they arrived at the total number of units to be allocated to a given geographical area. Second, the proportions of the units which would be designated for new construction, rehabilitation, or existing housing were determined, based on the Housing Assistance Plan submittted by each locality.

The requirement of the Housing Assistance Plan (HAP) was another of the innovative features of the 1974 Act. Designed by congressional housing advocate Thomas Ashley and his staff, it was intended as a vehicle by which local governments would take direct and active responsibility for planning their community's housing needs, thereby becoming more aware of the integral role of housing in the community development process. It was also hoped that this decentralization would make the program more responsibe to the complex differences between local housing markets. In preparing their HAPs, localities were to gather data on the number, type, and condition of the housing units in their community, and they were to determine the groups in the low income population (e.g., families, the elderly, the handicapped, etc.) which were most in need of assistance. Based on these data they were to project housing needs for a three year period, tabulate the extent to which housing currently under development would meet those needs, and request federally assisted units on the basis of remaining needs. HUD would, in turn, base its future requests for funds on HAP data (Struyk, 1979).

The HAP process had a significant impact on the Section 8 program; however, each plan was actually submitted as a part of each locality's Community Development Block Grant (CDBG) application. For this reason, and because the HAP process raised issues of federal-local relationships which will be discussed more fully in Chapters 7 and 8, it seems appropriate to postpone a more complete discussion of its influence until the CDBG process has been examined.

Around the basic core of requirements just described, the two subprograms varied according to their distinct purposes. The New Construction program resembled the Section 236 program in that HUD reviewed and approved plans and cost data from each project and signed a long-term subsidy agreement based on its approval. This program also came to resemble Section 236 in the indirect subsidies which were associated with it. It was initially anticipated that the HUD approval and rent subsidy contract would be sufficient guarantees of project soundness to attract private mortgage money. However, private lenders proved reluctant to get involved on this basis alone, and the program was increasingly linked to other forms of government subsidy and guarantees. The traditional Ginnie Mae writedown of mortgage costs (the Tandem Plan) was frequently used, as was an FHA insurance program originally designed for unsubsidized units in high risk areas, Section 221(d)(4)

(Mandelker, 1981, p. 185). In addition, two newer forms of subsidy were brought into play to support the program.

One form of subsidy took advantage of the ability of local housing authorities to issue tax exempt bonds. These authorities could themselves be developers of Section 8 New Construction units, thus directly utilizing this form of lower cost financing. In addition, the use of tax exempt bonds (authorized for public housing under Section 11b of the 1937 Housing Act) was extended to private developers by the 1974 Act. Under this provision, the local authority usually formed a special entity to issue the bonds, and the proceeds were then lent to the private developer. Though not backed by the "full faith and credit" of the public entity, these bonds were seen by private developers as a relatively safe, inexpensive source of funds and were used with some frequency in Section 8 projects (HUD, 1978d, p. 178).

Another form of subsidy for Section 8 New Construction came from state housing and community development agencies. Created by state law to promote housing development, these agencies were empowered to issue tax exempt bonds to finance various types of housing, especially for lower income persons. In the early 1970s, states which already had such agencies utilized them to further subsidize Section 236 projects. However, the Section 8 regulations actively encouraged state agency participation, and a number of states without such agencies were enticed to create them by the prospect of easier participation in Section 8. Among other inducements, HUD regulations created a special allocation of units for state agency financed projects, permitted streamlined processing of applications for such projects, and allowed a 40 year Housing Assistance Payments contract (to match state agency bond terms).

Finally, the indirect tax subsidies resulting from accelerated depreciation and the deductibility of mortgage interest continued to be available to Section 8 developers. Tax syndication was pushed vigorously, as it had been earlier, and many of the same specialized developers who had put together investment packages for Section 236 projects continued to do so for Section 8 projects. A 1978 HUD survey of 100 Section 8 developers revealed that 69 of them had been involved in some previous HUD subsidy program, and that nearly all of them planned to sell the tax benefits from their projects (HUD, 1978d, p. 168, 180). In the end, the main differences between Section 8 New Construction and Section 236 were that the subsidy was couched in terms of a direct rent payment to tenants and that it was a somewhat deeper subsidy than the earlier program had provided. It is one of the ironies of federal housing policy that these very features, which had made Johnson's rent supplement program so unpopular in the mid-1960s that he substituted indirect subsidy arrangements, now *contributed* to the Section 8 program's appeal in the changed climate of 10 years later.

The Section 8 Existing Housing program more closely resembled the 'pure' housing allowance concept, except that local housing agencies retained a substantial degree of administrative control. Such agencies applied to HUD for a certain number of units and, if approved, signed an Annual Contributions Contract permitting them to subsidize these units. Applications were then accepted from tenants, who had to be certified as eligible under the income guidelines. Eligible tenants then had 60 days to find a unit which met their needs and to secure the cooperation of the landlord, or they could request to remain in their current unit. In practice, agencies usually maintained lists of suitable units from which tenants were encouraged to choose. Once the unit was selected it had to be inspected to determine compliance with minimum housing quality standards before occupancy was permitted. Having approved the unit, the agency then signed a Housing Assistance Payments contract with the landlord for up to 15 years. The tenant also signed an agency approved lease with the landlord (Mandelker, et al., 1981).

The Impact of Section 8

In spite of the enactment of this new legislation in 1974, the years 1974 and 1975 proved to be the nadir of subsidized housing production for the entire decade. This is clearly shown in Figure 10.

There were enough authorized units already "in the pipeline" to keep the moratorium from totally stopping the Section 235 and 236 programs, but the lack of new applications during that 18 month period was reflected in the very low levels of construction starts during the following two and one half years. Meanwhile, the Section 8 program was very slow in starting. It took over a year for HUD to develop and promulgate regulations and for local agencies and developers to gain a clear enough understanding of the new rules to apply in large numbers. Thus, Section 8 did not begin to make a major contribution until 1976.

However, Figure 10 also shows that, once the initial 'glitches' were worked out, both the New Construction and the Existing Housing programs took off rather quickly. The Existing Housing program went into high gear first, since the approval process was much simpler than for new construction. Yet, production of new units began to rise rapidly after 1977, so that the New Construction program contributed an increasingly large proportion of the total units subsidized. The Substantial and Moderate Rehabilitation programs began to have a visible role in

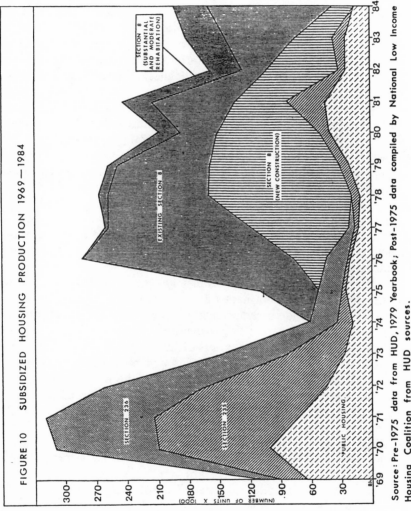

FIGURE 10   SUBSIDIZED HOUSING PRODUCTION 1969—1984

Source: Pre-1975 data from HUD, 1979 Yearbook; Post-1975 data compiled by National Low Income Housing Coalition from HUD sources.

1977, but did not contribute large numbers of units. Overall production continued at high levels into the early 1980s when Reagan's budget cuts and program changes began to have an impact.

This upsurge in subsidized housing construction took place in an atmosphere of relatively low conflict surrounding housing policy. The Carter Administration, which took office in 1977, did not display the desire for large new social welfare initiatives that previous Democratic administrations had shown. His advisors were, in many cases, staunch liberals; yet, they were not vigorous in proposing new governmental interventions on behalf of the poor. Items such as energy and controlling inflation ranked ahead of these on Carter's policy agenda, and his desire to lower federal deficits limited his willingness to propose funds for such purposes.

Furthermore, Carter proved unsuccessful in pushing through many of the modest proposals he did make. His welfare reform proposal made little headway in Congress and was finally scrapped. He did succeed in enacting changes in CDBG funding rules and the new Urban Development Action Grant program; but several other parts of his urban package were defeated, and this discouraged further initiatives. Some of the responsibilty for these failures must be laid at the feet of Carter and his advisors. As Edwards (1980) has documented, they displayed a notable lack of skill in dealing with Congress and on many occasions allowed potential support to dissipate through bad timing, bad communication, and poor personal relations with members of Congress.

However, Carter's difficulties may also be attributed to the nature of the times. As noted in Chapter 2, the optimism of the early 1960s had been replaced by widespread perceptions of economic stagnation and the notion that the nation was going to have to accept limits. In keeping with this mood, some former supporters of liberal programs moved toward the conservative view that government was becoming too large, too powerful, and too expensive. One indication of this mood with regard to housing was Congress' failure to reestablish housing production goals upon the expiration of the ten year goals set in the Housing Act of 1968. Because the goal of six million federally assisted units had not been reached, there was pessimism that a new goal could actually influence policy and a desire not to commit the nation to large new efforts in an era of limits (CQ Weekly Reports, 1978b).

Nevertheless, in spite of Carter's lack of successful initiatives, in spite of widely shared concerns about budget deficits, and in spite of Congress' disinterest in new social welfare commitments, the housing programs in existence reached high levels of production relative to previous years. The attention given to other issues helped to insulate these programs from scrutiny and debate, and the housing subgovernment, finding after initial skepticism that many aspects of the Section 8 program were very congenial to its constituents, continued to push for higher funding levels. It was only when Carter's ambivalent and unenthusiastic support was replaced by a new administration which was ideologically committed to major retrenchment that these programs, too, came under attack.

Because of the relative lack of controversy in housing programs during this period, evaluative studies of Section 8 are relatively scarce in comparison to the extensive evaluations and critiques which were directed at the programs of the early 1970s. However, available data permit a fairly detailed picture of Section 8 to be drawn. In addition, large amounts of data from EHAP became available during the late 1970s, data which have been compared to ongoing, operational programs. All of these evaluation efforts are politically significant because some of their results have since been used by the Reagan Administration to justify proposals for a large reduction and redirection of federal housing subsidies for the poor. In looking at these evaluations, I will focus on three key sets of issues — issues of cost and risk, issues relating to the population served by the programs, and issues related to the geographical distribution of the housing produced.

SECTION 8 NEW CONSTRUCTION. With regard to Section 8 New Construction, the attention of policy analysts has naturally turned to the issue of cost, since this part of the program most closely resembles earlier construction subsidies believed by many to be too costly. The estimation of the relative costs of Section 8 and other programs is a complex process for a number of reasons. First, the actual construction and operating costs must be accurately determined from data which vary widely within program types as well as between them. Second, the actual proportion of the toal costs the government pays out in subsidies varies, depending on the clientele served and on the extent of indirect subsidies resulting from tax shelters. Third, costs must be calculated for the entire 20 to 30 years life cycle of a typical project, a process which, when dealing with projects which are less than ten years old, relies as much on estimates as on hard data.

However, two recent government studies of Section 8 program costs, one by the General Accounting Office (GAO) in 1980 and one by HUD in 1982, found Section 8 New Construction to be comparable in costs and efficiency to the Section 236 program. The two studies also reached similar conclusions concerning the relative costs of various forms of Section 8 financing (Ginnie Mae Tandem, Section 11b, or state housing finance agencies). There was a variation of less than 3 percent in construction and operating costs among various types of Section 8 New Construction, but a larger variation in the subsidy costs to the federal government. Projects run by state housing finance agencies cost more in indirect subsidies because of the additional federal taxes foregone on the bonds they issued, a point which led the GAO report to question the cost effectiveness of this method of financing. Units built under the Section 236 program were found to have been slightly more costly than Section 8 units (in constant dollars). However, because of the somewhat higher income group served by Section 236, the level of federal subsidy was lower.

Another issue of importance in the evaluation of the Section 8 New Construction and Substantial Rehabilitation programs was the risk of project failure. Since this issue had a major impact on the fate of the Section 235 and 236 programs, it is legitimate to ask whether the new units constructed under Section 8 suffered similar problems. Due to the variety of financing mechanisms used in this program, there is no single readily available, source of data on foreclosures, such as exists with regard to the earlier, largely FHA-insured programs. Nevertheless, the GAO report cited above shows some striking differences in the development patterns of Section 8 and Section 236 which suggest that the newer program may suffer fewer problems in this regard.

Table 7 contrasts the Section 8 New and Substantial Rehabilitation programs with Section 236 by type of sponsor and by the proportions of family and elderly units.

TABLE 7

CHARACTERISTICS OF SECTION 8 AND SECTION 236 PROJECTS

Type of Sponsor	Percent of Total Units in New Construction		Percent of Total Units in Substantial Rehabilitation	
Limited dividend (for profit)	Family	Elderly	Family	Elderly
Section 236	62.0%	4.0%	9.0%	0.8%
Section 8	39.2%	45.7%	3.5%	0.4%
Nonprofit				
Section 236	15.0%	5.0%	3.5%	0.4%
Section 8	1.3%	4.5%	–	0.3%

Source: General Accounting Office, *Evaluation of Alternatives for Financing Low and Moderate Income Rental Housing*, PAD-80-13, 180.

If the data in Table 7 are compared with the data on relative foreclosure rates of various types of Section 236 projects presented in Table 6, it becomes clear that the distribution of projects shifted away from the higher risk categories to those with much lower risks of failure. The category with the lowest foreclosure rate, new construction for the elderly by for-profit sponsors, rose from 4 percent of Section 236 projects to 45.7 percent of Section 8 projects. In addition, in spite of the new emphasis being placed on rehabilitation as a housing strategy in the late 1970s, a smaller percentage of Section 8 projects involved rehabilitation than had Section 236 developments. Since rehabilitation projects had also shown a much higher foreclosure rate, this trend also suggests a lower probability of Section 8 failure.

Other factors are mentioned by the GAO as minimizing the risks of Section 8 financial failure. The caution with which state housing finance agencies approached the loans they made was a factor for those projects in which they participated. To a greater extent than federal agencies, state housing agencies were dependent upon a good financial track record for the continued saleability of their bonds. This made them scrutinize the projects they financed very closely.

Second, financial failure was discouraged by the flexibility of the Section 8 subsidy mechanism. In Section 236, the subsidy was attached to financing costs. Though operating subsidies were eventually made available, these were seen by Congress as an excessive additional cost and were only reluctantly granted, just as had been the case for public housing. Also, rising rents in Section 236 projects could force out the lower income tenants who originally occupied the units, thus reducing the market for the units. In Section 8, the subsidy was tied to the rents paid by the tenant, and the FMRs were expected to rise with inflation. Thus, the subsidy mechanism was set up to absorb cost increases and keep projects afloat. However, this flexibility also had a disadvantage in that rising costs contributed to political criticism of the program as too costly. Why subsidized housing rents should be expected to be immune from the same inflationary pressures affecting all other prices is not clear, but any social welfare program with rising costs seems to violate some conservatives' incremental criterion, regardless of the justification for the increases.

Besides the issues of cost and risk, a second broad set of issues has been raised in connection with Section 8 New Construction—those relating to the population served. The underlying irony of the risk reduction data just presented is that risk reduction was achieved in part by shifting the nature of the population served in ways that were subject to question on equity grounds.

The first and most obvious shift was away from family units toward units for the elderly. Table 7, based on 1977 data shows that just over 50 percent of new Section 8 units had been constructed for the elderly. By 1979, according the the HUD *Statistical Yearbook*, this proportion had risen to 74 percent. Many low income elderly persons had a genuine need for improved housing and could benefit from special security systems and other amenities often included in new Section 8 projects. Nevertheless, the elderly were greatly overrepresented in Section 8 units. According to the 1980 GAO report, the elderly represented only 23 percent of the total income-eligible population (U.S. GAO, 1980, p. 77). Therefore, the dominance of Section 8 New Construction by elderly units can better be explained by the obvious attractions they had for both builders and local officials than by need. First, the public tended to regard the elderly as the deserving poor and thus to be less hostile to housing for them than to family housing. Second, they were perceived as less likely to engage in antisocial behavior than families containing disadvantaged youth. This perception reduced neighborhood resistance to the development of such units and lessened the developer's sense of financial risk in erecting them.

The geographic location of new Section 8 units also affected the population served. Here again, the program shifted its emphasis away from high risk, inner city developments and toward construction in suburban and nonmetropolitan areas. The 1982 HUD study cited above found that, whereas 56.5 percent of Section 236 developments were located in central cities (with 19.8 percent in suburbs and 23.7 percent outside SMSA's), the central city percentage of Section 8 developments varied from a low of 18.8 percent for state agency financed projects to a high of 33.7 percent for GNMA Tandem financed projects (HUD, 1982, p. 4–28). While there were often legitimate and pressing housing needs in small communities, this trend also represented a movement away from the largest concentrations of the poor, which were still to be found in the larger central cities.

The disproportion of elderly and noncentral city units in the program also clearly had a negative impact on its ability to serve minorities. A 1981 HUD study of the program's clientele found both blacks and Hispanics to be underrepresented. The concentration on elderly units contributed to this underrepresentation because a much smaller percentage of the elderly poor (23 percent) than of nonelderly poor (39 percent) are in these groups; but even among the elderly poor, minorities were underrepresented, constituting only 11 percent of those served. Both blacks and Hispanics who did participate were often able to move into neighborhoods with less minority concentration, shifting on the average from areas that were 54 percent minority to areas with 35 percent minority residence. Nevertheless, this advantage for a few participants was counteracted for these groups as a whole by the location of most projects outside central cities, since the HUD study also found that program participation was heavily influenced by the geographical proximity of a project (HUD, 1981).

The impact of program characteristics on the income distribution of those served is more ambiguous. The inclusion of large numbers of elderly tended to drive the income level of those served downward, since a larger number of elderly than nonelderly persons fit into HUD's Very Low Income category (less than 50 percent of the median). Thus, the 1981 HUD study found that very low income persons were disproportionately represented among program beneficiaries. Yet, the 1980 GAO study found that Section 8 assistance was not as concentrated in the very low income brackets as public housing. According to their data, families with incomes at 75 percent of the official poverty line were over five times as likely to benefit from public housing as were families above the poverty line, whereas Section 8 benefits were much more evenly distributed between the very poor and the "near poor." (U.S. GAO, 1980, pp. 82–83).

In attempting to evaluate the total picture of the population served by Section 8 New Construction, one encounters the same complex trade-offs which have bedeviled federal housing policy since the 1930s. This program was explicitly designed to give administrators the flexibility to serve a fairly wide range of low income persons, from the destitute to the working poor. The GAO data suggest that this goal was met, while the HUD results suggest a marked, though not drastic, shift toward the lower end of the income scale. Either way, the results seem to violate one major criterion for policy success. Concentration on the lowest income persons satisfies the strictest principle of vertical equity which, stated simply, is to serve the neediest first. On the other hand, public housing suffered both administratively and politically from its concentration on an exclusively low income population, and it seemed unfair to penalize upward mobility by excluding people from participation when their incomes reached a certain level. In addition, Section 8 achieved its stress on very low income persons by concentrating on the elderly. Therefore, a shift away from the elderly would have meant a raising of the overall income level of Section 8 tenants. Though seemingly in violation of vertical equity, such a move might have actually made the program more fair by restoring the original flexibility to deal with the housing needs of working poor families closer to the eligibility cut off.

Another trade-off was that between financial risk and service to those most in need. On the one hand, risk and failure are labels which subject such programs to political attack by opponents who attribute these to poor administration or the inherent shortcomings of nonmarket approaches. Yet, in reducing its risk factors. the Section 8 New Construction program moved away from large segments of the eligible population. Its projects, so far, appear to have a better track record than either public housing or the earlier subsidy programs in terms of management and financial soundness, but they have achieved this by serving more of those considered 'safe', i.e., the "safe" elderly white poor in suburban communities.

SECTION 8 EXISTING HOUSING. The Existing Housing program, based as it was on units already in place, involved lower costs and less financial risk than the New Construction program. The typically lower rents of older, existing units meant that the Fair Market Rents were set much lower. As a result, according to a 1982 Congressional Budget Office study, the annual per unit subsidy was less than half that of the New Construction program (U.S. Congress, Budget Office, 1982, p. 39). Also, because the units were already in place, the federal government did not have to share the financial risks of new construction in order to induce participation. However, in spite of these lower costs, some analyses of this program have raised questions about its cost effectiveness. These questions revolve around the complex relationship between rent levels, housing quality, and tenant needs. They can best be understood as a logical sequence in which each successive question generates the next.

The first question is whether or not the program induced increases in the rents of existing housing. One facet of this question is the issue raised by Hartman and others when the housing allowance was first proposed — does the increase in real demand due to the subsidy push rents upward in areas where lower income persons are concentrated? The conclusion of both the EHAP study and of various analyses of Section Existing Housing was that this did not prove to be a serious problem. In most areas, the concentration of these units was simply not large enough to have an appreciable impact on the aggregate demand for housing, yet even where large numbers of units were concentrated in relatively modest sized communities, such as in the EHAP supply experiment, the introduction of the units was gradual enough not to have a major effect.

A second facet of this question is whether rents for participating units were pushed upward by the program. A 1978 HUD evaluation based on a sample of participating households found that, while the subsidy reduced the *tenants'* average rent burden from 40 percent to 22 percent of income, the total rents paid *on behalf of* program beneficiaries went up substantially. Many tenants moved to more expensive quarters, causing the average total rent to be 70 percent greater than their rent prior to program participation. Those who stayed in the same units had a smaller, but nonetheless significant increase of 28 percent. Since the subsidy was based on the difference between a fixed 25 percent of the tenant's income and the rent the landlord actually charged, the landlord an incentive to raise the rent to the FMR ceiling, while the tenant had no incentive to resist such an increase. Thus, the study found that the actual rents charged averaged from 92 to 96 percent of the FMR for the area, depending on unit size (HUD, 1978, p. 33).

A second question, flowing from the first, is whether or not the increase in rents actually improved housing conditions for the program's beneficiaries. The conclusion of the HUD study was that, while some of the increase could be attributed simply to the landlord's taking advantage of the FMR ceiling, much of the increase was related to improvement in the quality of the housing services received. Thirty-seven percent of all units received at least minor repairs in order to participate in the program, and movers reported their new units to be in better condition than the ones previously occupied. Moreover, tenants frequently reported that the subsidy enabled them to relieve overcrowding by moving to larger units or by separating families sharing the same quarters; and most who moved reported that they experienced better neighborhood environments.

The fact that housing quality improved for program participants raises, in turn, a third question, which harks back to earlier arguments about the overconsumption which allegedly results from in-kind subsidies. Was, in fact, the Section 8 Existing Housing program paying for overconsumption of housing by a few beneficiaries while leaving a large number of eligible families without subsidies altogether? Clearly, this program served only a fraction of those eligible, so the heart of the question is really whether or not the level of housing services provided constituted overconsumption, in relation to some more limited level of services which could be more broadly distributed within exisitng resource constraints. Expressed in this fashion, the question can, in turn, be divided into two parts: (1) Was there overconsumption relative to some reasonable objective standard of housing consumption; and, (2) was there overconsumption relative to the level of housing services the recipient would have chosen if given a less constrained form of subsidy.

The first part of the overconsumption question was raised in a 1979 study by Olsen and Rasmussen. Building upon another study by Follain (1979), the authors argue that Fair Market Rents gradually moved beyond the levels of rent required to obtain units meeting the absolute minimum standards set by HUD. Due to increases in the FMR greater than the CPI, it gradually became enough to purchase a unit in somewhat better condition than the minimum. The authors go on to suggest tighter controls on the FMR so that the same amount of federal dollars will serve more households. However, their analysis did not take into account a fundamental problem associated with program implementation, namely, the variation in the quality of units selected on both sides of whatever physical standard is used. In such a program it is virtually inevitable that substandard units will slip in through administrative laxity and/or through the inability of particular tenants to find units of the prescribed minimum quality. The 1981 HUD study found that, even with current FMRs, roughly 50 percent of the units sampled fell below the HUD minimum standard on at least one of its criteria. Therefore, if one wishes to assure that most tenants receive units at or above the minimum quality standards, it would seem poor policy to set a rent standard which will just barely purchase the minimum unit.

The second part of the overconsumption question raises a more serious difficulty for the program, in light of the long philosophical and political debate over the value of in-kind subsidies to their recipients. The findings of the EHAP study, which were disseminated in the late 1970s, brought this question into clear focus. In EHAP's Demand Experiment, less constrained subsidy mechanisms were used than those incorporated in Section 8. Though there were several variations, the basic design involved a direct cash payment to the tenant, not the landlord. The amount of this payment was based on the difference between a percentage of the tenant's income and some rent level determined to be appropriate on the basis of comparable units in the area. However, unlike Section 8, the tenant did not acutally have to pay this amount of rent to get the full subsidy payment but could choose how much of it to spend on improved housing and how much to allocate to other items of consumption. Given such a choice, EHAP participants usually chose to spend only a small portion of their grant on improved housing and to spend the rest on other items of consumption. Both tenants and landlords would make only the minimum repairs needed to comply with the program's physical standards, and if the extent of these repairs was too great, both tended to withdraw from the program rather than comply (Struyk and Bendick, 1981). Thus, the study suggested that tenants might be satisfied with lower housing quality standards than were set for them by middle class professionals and that subsidy levels could be lowered without too much sacrifice in the perceived well-being of low income households.

Such a conclusion fit well with the conservative perception of the inappropriateness of active federal intervention on behalf of low income persons. It seemed to suggest that the priority on high quality new and rehabilitated units and even on forced consumption of higher rent used housing was one shared by HUD officials, builders, and other housing advocates but not by the potential clients of their programs. As a result, this argument became a central feature of the 1982 report of the Commission on Housing appointed by Ronald Reagan. (U.S. President's Commission on Housing, 1982) It was used to support his proposal that a new "housing voucher" program, following the Demand Experiment model, be substituted for both the Section 8 New Construction and Existing Housing programs. This proposal will be discussed in more detail in the final chapter of this book.

Before ending this discussion of the Section 8 Existing Program, it is necessary to examine the population served, in order to compare the impact of this program with that of Section 8 New Construction. A general conclusion supported by all the evaluations done so far is that the Existing Housing program served a much more representative cross-section of the low income population than new Section 8 construction. According to the 1981 HUD study, the households served were 26 percent elderly and 44 percent minority, proportions much closer to those in the eligible population than those of new construction projects. In addition, both the 1978 and 1981 HUD studies concluded that this program came much closer to balancing the desire of some minority and/or low income persons to move into available units in higher income, nonminority areas with the desire of others to have the program accessible in areas where they already lived. The 1978 study points out that, while only a small portion of participating families moved out of the area in which they currently lived, the probability of moving to a new area was strongly correlated with the extent of searching in those areas. The authors further concluded that moving or not moving into new areas was, to a significant degree, a matter of individual choice, although it was also recognized that units were not available in better neighborhoods for all who might want to take advantage of them, especially in the case of minority households.

A FOOTNOTE - THE SURVIVAL OF PUBLIC HOUSING. While the Section 8 program was, in terms of numbers, the dominant subsidized housing program of the late 1970s, our picture of this period would not be complete without taking note of the continued support enjoyed by public housing. Figure 10 shows a modest, but nonetheless constant level of public housing starts in the late 1970s. A portion of this was accounted for by units authorized earlier, but data provided by the National Low Income Housing Coalition show that Congress continued to make new reservations of 35,000 to 50,000 units per year through the last Carter budget, 1981 (National Low Income Housing Coalition, 1983a, p. 12). Also, Congress continued to appropriate substantial funds for operating subsidies and for modernization of existing public housing units.

Why this continued support for public housing? Several reasons seem to be of central importance. First, for all its faults, public housing was a tried and true program that could be counted on to produce units for low income persons. It had a constituency of local housing authorities — represented by NAHRO — which continued to press for more units. In the period of uncertainty following Nixon's moratorium, when it seemed to many that Section 8 would never get moving, Congress decided to revive public housing and made a new appropriation for FY 1977. Out of frustration, they turned back to an established process of housing production (CQ Weekly Report, 1976a).

Second, many housing advocates recognized that public housing served a segment of the low income population which it was difficult to induce the private sector to serve, even with deep subsidies. As has been shown, Section 8 New Construction drifted more and more toward serving predominantly the elderly. This meant that relatively few new units were made available to low income families by this program. The Section 8 Existing Housing program served a better cross section, but, according to Sternlieb (Sternlieb, et al., 1980), there had been a general tendency during this period for privately constructed units to move toward a standard size of two, or at the most three, bedroom units. This meant that large, low income families were finding it increasingly difficult to find units in the subsidized or unsubsidized private market. In addition, both programs ameliorated but did not eliminate the market disadvantage suffered by minorities. For all these reasons, public housing remained the housing of last resort for some of the poorest and most desperate families.

A third basis for support was the efficiency argument which could still be plausibly advanced on behalf of public housing. One argument for investing in housing owned by the public sector was that the asset purchased remained in the public domain, thereby allowing the initial investment to produce services to the intended target groups over a long period of time. In contrast, there was no absolute guarantee that new private housing built with public subsidies would remain available for low income housing, and subsidies to existing units involved simply the purchasing of a service, not a tangible public asset. The value of the assets already produced by the public housing program was tacitly recognized by Congress through its continued approval of operating and modernization subsidies for the over one million units still in operation, although objections to the alleged excessive cost of these subsidies continued to be raised by some members of Congress.

Another efficiency argument was advanced in the 1980 GAO report cited earlier. GAO analysts argued that when costs related to the size and type of unit were held constant, the long-term subsidy costs for public housing units were less than for new, privately constructed units. Indirect tax subsidies, though included in public housing via the use of local tax exempt bonds were not as extensive as in privately built units. Also, the subsidy level in public housing was not as heavily influenced by rising rent levels in the private market.

Anyone who has raised house plants is familiar with the specimen which looks ragged most of the time but never seems to die. This seems an apt analogy for the public housing program. The standard treatment of public housing in the media, and in academic texts on urban policy and politics as well, suggests that it was the failure of this program which led to the development of new subsidy programs from 1968 on. Yet, for the reasons stated above, public housing continued to have its defenders, and the program's continued funding suggests that they were listened to by a majority in Congress. In addition, those who studied public housing more closely and comprehensively tended to find that its failure was far from total. For example, a 1983 study by the Congressional Budget Office found that approximately 15 percent of public housing units could be classified as seriously "troubled" while most of the rest provided the poor with affordable housing which was in relatively good condition (U.S. Congress, Budget Office, 1983, pp. 15–16). While not an environment which many middle class persons would find desirable, it was providing a necessary service to the very poor in a reasonably adequate fashion. Perhaps public housing will outlive both its detractors and its substitutes.

An Overview of Housing Subsidies for the Poor

In concluding the discussion of housing subsidy programs which has occupied this and the two previous chapters, it is appropriate to recapitulate some of the major themes apparent in the long struggle over public efforts to meet the housing needs of the disadvantaged. The basic pattern I have tried to set forth is one in which various programmatic alternatives rise and fall in response to conflicting perceptions of their success or failure and in response to conflicting political pressures. The broad liberal and conservative ideological orientations of political decisionmakers have acted as filters through which these programs have been perceived, and the ascendancy of either liberal or conservative leadership has heavily influenced the course of policy. At the same time, the most politically successful programs have been those with characteristics which have made them at least palatable — if not entirely desirable — to a broad spectrum of opinion within the politically active elite. Moreover, the efforts of groups with strong, direct interests in the production of subsidized housing have played an important role in keeping programs alive and moving, in the face of apathy or even hostility from the executive branch or Congress as a whole.

Common links between the various programs within this complex political milieu may be found in certain basic problems all of them have tried to solve, in one way or another. The four most prominent problems in housing policy have been those of *supply*, *quality*, *cost*, and *equity*. Each program had made its claim to deal with these problems; political leaders have evaluated those claims in light of their own ideological perceptions and interests; and the program has expanded, contracted, or disappeared according to its ability to convince a broad spectrum of leaders of its capacity to deal with them. At times, programs have been designed to deal primarily with one problem, only to have others emerge in implementation which opponents have used as weapons to weaken or abolish the program.

The emergence of the first major subsidy program, public housing, occurred in response to the widely shared perception of an acute need for a *supply* of good housing for lower income persons, although considerations of the need for construction jobs also played an important role. The private housing industry, of course, saw this program as a threat to their own profitable provision of low income housing (however inadequate by objective standards) and opposed it vigorously. They were supported by others who, on ideological grounds, opposed the notion of any basic need being supplied by the government; and this combined opposition was successful in keeping the government's role very small throughout most of the program's history.

Yet, viewing the history of public housing from another angle, it was precisely the ability of the program to supply standard housing to very low income people who could obtain it in no other way that kept the program alive. Supporters were always able to muster a congressional majority behind the notion that the trickle of units to this group should not, for humanitarian or social cost reasons, be cut off entirely. As has been noted, Congress could not bring itself to abolish the public housing program entirely, even with a major move underway to shift the federal government's approach away from the notion of newly constructed, government supplied units.

The supply issue did, however, play a major role in the development of alternative housing subsidy methods in the 1960s. As liberals who were dissatisfied with the trickle of publicly built units, the Kennedy and Johnson Administrations pushed private construction programs which attempted to get around the crystallized opposition to public housing and to build a political base of support for such programs within the private housing industry itself. They succeeded in building such support, and this, combined with the intense pressures for improvement in the lot of the poor which emerged in the 1960s, catapulted the new subsidy programs (Section 235 and 236) to heights of production never before achieved. In the mid-1970s, opponents of these programs began to capitalize on a changed political climate and on other problems encountered by these programs, and their output was curtailed. But, when a slightly more sympathetic, though by no means enthusiastically committed, administration took office, the underlying support for the private subsidy approach was such that it enjoyed a resurgence under the Section 8 New Construction program. Therefore, it may be said that this means of adding units to the supply of low income housing was politically successful, at least until stronger ideological opposition emerged in the Reagan Administration.

Nevertheless, while public housing and the private market subsidy programs continued to provide a large number of units, the supply issue reemerged in another guise which helped to undermine political support for the construction of new subsidized units. The steady improvement in housing conditions which occurred during the 1970s caused many scholars to conclude that the cost, rather than the supply of standard housing was the principal problem for low income households. This made a convincing argument for changing to housing allowances which could utilize existing standard housing to shelter the poor. Thus, the Section 8 Existing program was created and began to provide an increasing number of units in the late 1970s. However, this change of direction in housing programs was also popular among conservatives because it fit their ideological predisposition to minimize the government's role in productive activities. As a result, proponents of cashing out housing subsidies tended to minimize the real problem of supply existing in specific communities and among the lowest income groups in the population.

The *quality* issue has also been a common dilemma faced by all housing subsidy programs. The manifestly low quality of many public housing units, in both physical and social terms, undermined support for the program among liberals as well as conservatives and stimulated the search for alternatives. Though the problems inherent in concentrating large numbers of the poor under one roof lowered the quality of life in public housing, these problems tended to obscure the self-fulfilling prophecy which conservative political pressure imposed on the program. Opponents succeeded in limiting funding for construction and upkeep to such minimal levels that both the initial quality of the units and their long-term maintenance were seriously compromised. Although many local agencies succeeded in providing decent units in spite of these limitations, opponents could point to the abyssmal failure of some projects (like Pruitt-Igoe) as "proof" either that the poor did not "deserve" good units because they would destroy them or that the public sector was inherently incapable of building and maintaining good housing.

Quality problems arose again in connection with private sector subsidy programs in the early 1970s. A combination of private sector greed and public sector administrative laxity produced well publicized disasters in the Section 235 and Section 236 programs, though, as has been shown, both programs successfully provided thousands of decent units. Again, those philosophically opposed to low income housing subsidies seized on these failures to justify a massive disengagement from such activities. These activities continued to command sufficient political support that the disengagement was neither total nor permanent, but the qualitative problems which did emerge contributed to the redesign and reorientation of subsequent efforts.

None of the above should be construed as an argument that serious problems are not inherent in the use of the public sector or a public-private mix to produce such units. The federal bureaucracy has a very difficult time maintaining consistent quality standards in thousands of public housing units without introducing excessively rigid restrictions on the local housing authorities who actually administer the program. These local agencies, too, are subject to bureaucratic inertia and rigidity in operating these units, especially when their staffs share the negative views of poor clients which are prevalent in the society as a whole. Good management of public housing is possible, but it takes an intense level of commitment and effort.

In publicly subsidized private units, the ability of federal and local housing agencies to maintain quality control was further weakened by the fact that the government itself did not actually own the units. Many private entities found that sound management of subsidized units was both possible and profitable, but many others sought to extract profits from government programs through minimal investment in housing quality. Public agencies were often no match for the ingenuity and determination of private firms trying to cut costs or evade regulations, and the fact that much of the return came from tax breaks rather than rental income did nothing to encourage responsible management.

Nevertheless, I believe that the experience of subsidized housing programs supports the argument made earlier; namely, that the constant lack of consensus over *whether* such programs should be undertaken made it very difficult for these programs to evolve in positive directions. A vigorous and constructive debate over how each program could best achieve this quality would have contributed greatly to qualitative improvements in all programs. However, the fact that issues of means were inextricably intertwined with the debate over ends prevented such growth from occurring. With the qualitative failures of programs being used as cudgels to destroy them, the policy pattern became one of drift and uncertainty. Programs were abolished and new ones implemented before the knowledge accumulated through operational experience could be fed back into the system. And even where the knowledge was available, the resources and commitment to utilize it were often absent.

The debate over *costs* also affected virtually all the housing subsidy programs which were attempted. As has been shown, both the cost per unit (efficiency) and the aggregate cost of the federal effort were brought into play as arguments for and against various programs. In some respects, the debate over unit costs depended as much on perception and distribution of costs as on hard data. For example, it cost the federal government less in the long run to lend money directly to developers than to pay interest subsidies, but the former approach was scrapped because its immediate budgetary impact was greater. Similarly, the move to private investors was designed to leverage private capital with public funds, thus reducing the public investment required, but by the time the direct and indirect subsidies were added up, it cost the federal treasury about as much per unit as did direct government construction.

Yet there were genuine issues of efficiency raised in this debate, as well as merely perceptual ones. As just noted, strict per unit cost limitations on public housing kept the program from functioning properly. In this sense, concern over short-term cost savings and over symbolic issues of how well the poor should live resulted in long-term inefficiencies. At the other end of the cost spectrum, the cost of subsidizing the private sector to produce new housing for the poor was clearly running high, especially when indirect tax expenditures were included. This led some analysts to conclude that public housing might have been the best solution after all, and it led even more to advocate the use of existing housing as a less costly alternative. Critics of new construction for the poor also raised the efficiency issue of forced overconsumption of housing by the poor. EHAP seemed to suggest that the poor would accept lower quality housing is given a cash subsidy. However, advocates of this position did not counter satisfactorily arguments that: (1) new units generated positive externalities for the whole community; (2) new units were needed to keep the market for low income housing from becoming too tight; or, (3) that the expedient choice of the poor to spend the cash in the experimental situation might not represent their genuine, long-term housing aspirations.

With regard to the aggregate costs of housing subsidy programs, I have argued that the debate has been carried out in incremental terms. Conservative critics have, at various times, attacked the 'massive' commitment of federal funds for housing or 'drastic' increases in funding levels, without giving a good answer to the question "massive in relation to what?" Liberals, while periodically lamenting the low level of effort in relation to the problem, have tacitly accepted the notion that expenditures must not deviate too greatly from present expectations. This is, in large part, because they have not had the political power to significantly increase that level, except in times of national turmoil like the Depression or the mid-1960s.

Figure 11 shows Office of Management and the Budget (OMB) estimates of all housing subsidy payments as a percentage of total federal outlays from 1962 to 1985. Since federal subsidy commitments are usually for long periods of time (15 to 40 years) the various federal efforts over the last 20 years have had a *cumulative* impact on outlays, with the result that they have risen quite dramatically. There are two ways to look at these data. From an incremental perspective, one sees an almost tenfold rise in expenditures. Critics of these programs have used this increase as *prima facie* evidence that the federal government's role is becoming too extensive.

However, another way to look at these data is in relation to the total level of federal activities and the total productive output of the society. Note that the vertical scale of Figure 11 is measured in *tenths of a percent*, and that the share of federal outlays consumed by housing subsidies has been well under 1 percent throughout most of this period, with a peak of 1.2 percent in 1983. Whether or not one agrees with the wisdom of these expenditures, it is difficult to justify the label *massive* for an expenditure of 1 percent of the budget on so important a part of the quality of life as housing. Moreover, if one compares these outlays to the total Gross National Product (GNP), which has been just over four times the federal budget in recent years, then they appear even more miniscule.

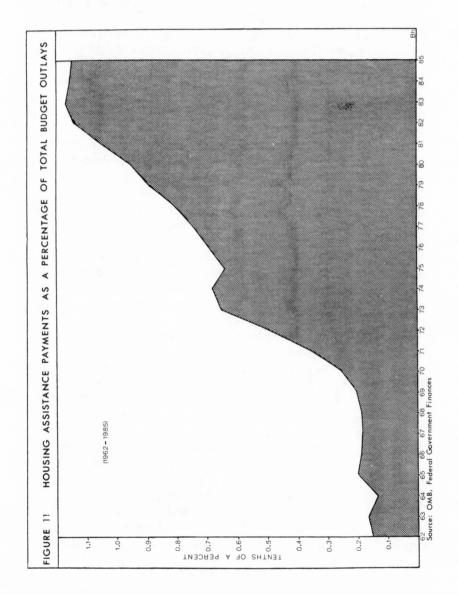

FIGURE 11   HOUSING ASSISTANCE PAYMENTS AS A PERCENTAGE OF TOTAL BUDGET OUTLAYS

(1962 – 1985)

Source: OMB, Federal Government Finances

Given the many competing demands on government, it is, perhaps, inevitable that expenditures in any one area will be judged in incremental terms. Yet, a rational picture of the appropriate level of expenditures simply cannot be obtained outside the context of the *need* which the society has for the activity and the total amount of resources which the public sector, and the whole society, is consuming. Political actors have disagreed over the extent of the need for housing, but most have agreed that it is fairly substantial. Deciding how much is too much cannot be done without assessing the extent of this need and weighing it against other needs the public sector is called upon to address. Looking at increments outside this context is virtually meaningless unless one is trying to use dollar figures to generate opposition to the *substantive purpose* of the program. This is precisely what opponents of federal housing efforts have done.

The fourth issue which has arisen repeatedly in the debate over housing subsidy programs is that of *equity*. The central question of equity is the question of what groups in the population should be served by housing subsidies. Most decisionmakers have supported the eminently fair and rational conclusion that the most desperately poor should be served first, and given limited resources, that programs should concentrate their expenditures on this group. However, as has been shown, the widespread agreement on this principle has concealed some fundamental problems.

First, it further obscures the question of what portion of the population really needs housing assistance. Clearly, people with very low incomes cannot afford to obtain standar housing on the private market, but how far up the income scale one extends this criterion of need depends on how one defines such concepts as 'standard housing' and 'ability to pay' and on how one measures both income and housing conditions. At vaious times in the history of housing policy, liberals have asserted that moderate income people need subsidies, as in the debate over the 20 percent gap between public housing and standard private housing in the early 1960s. Conservatives have bitterly resisted the extension of subsidies to this group, and liberals have usually had to retreat on this issue. This standoff obscures somewhat the questions which remain about the extent of housing deprivation—or, conversely, the existent of deprivation of other necessities due to large housing expenditures.

Secondly, the use of the criterion of "serve the poorest first due to limited resources" tends subtly to reinforce the notion that resources really are too limited to help anyone else. By stressing this criterion, conservative critics of social welfare policy can appear to be pursuing vertical equity in federal policy while, in fact, their principal concerns is the limitation of the amount of resources devoted to these purposes. The United States, despite its recent economic difficulties, is still a tremendously wealthy and productive society. Because of this, considerable discretion exists as to the allocation of our resources to various purposes. Thus, the assertion that the nation cannot afford to carry out a certain activity usually may be reduced, on closer examination, to an assertion that we should choose to spend resources for some other purpose. Given the small percentage of GNP spent on housing subsidies for the poor, the argument that the nation cannot afford to spend more seems implausible. The real issue is whether or not housing expenditures for the poor or near-poor or moderate income persons constitute a valid use of the national welath. The focus of the housing subsidy debate on whether subsidy funds should be spent on the very poor *or* the less poor tends to obscure the alternative choice of spending money on *both.*

Finally, the equity debate has tended to conceal a deeper struggle over the political consequences of expenditures for various groups. Extensions of the welfare state to large numbers of working and middle class persons have tended to be politically irreversible, since the votes of these persons can represent a genuine threat to political leaders who oppose their needs. Those who oppose the welfare state have generally been aware of this and so have fought programs involving additional mass entitlements, even though the recipients might be more deserving in terms of the traditional capitalist value of hard work. By limiting subsidized housing to the very poor, the political support for such programs is also limited. By buying into this limitation, whether out of caution or necessity, liberals have helped maintain the politically marginal status of these programs.

Can one justify housing as an entitlement for which graduated support should be given up to some point on the income scale where families could genuinely afford housing on the private market? This author's inclination is to say yes, although extensive research would be needed to demonstrate this conclusively. The point of the present discussion is not to argue for the proposition that this is a genuine unmet need but to argue that the dynamics of the political debate in the 1970s and before have discouraged honest inquiry into this question. When the debate revolves around which small portion of the need should be met, then questions of vertical equity become harrowing, and political support is lost among those whose needs are ignored. To return to the central concept stressed by Bachrach and Baratz (1962), only when the decisions that have been made are viewed in light of the "non-decisions" just described can the complex and tortuous path of housing policy be understood.

CHAPTER 7

The Growth of the Federal Role
in Community Development

Introduction

In this chapter and Chapter 8, the major federal initiatives in community development policy during recent decades will be explored, with particular attention to the close relationship which has existed between these efforts and changes in the direction of federal housing policy. In Chapter 2, it was argued that housing programs have often been viewed within the frame of reference of community development policy, since housing constitutes such an important use of the physical space available to any community. Because of this close association, the policy subsystem which handles housing programs overlaps considerably with that which handles community development policy. The same subcommittees in Congress, the same federal agency (HUD), and, often, the same local agencies, handle both housing subsidy programs and community development programs.

Nevertheless, as the discussion in Chapter 2 suggested, there have always been powerful conservative groups interested in community development who have not shared with housing advocates a strong interest in utilizing community development programs to improve the housing conditions of the poor and who, in fact, have often been willing to sacrifice low income housing quality in the name of other goals. Therefore, the alliance between housing advocates and community development advocates has always been an uneasy one, and liberals whose main concern was housing have had to push aggressively for the inclusion of housing goals within various community development strategies.

In addition, as Chapter 2 also stressed, community development policy has had as one of its focal concerns the issue of intergovernmental power relationships, as well as a concern with the power relationships

173

between the public and private sector. Though social welfare policies such as housing subsidies have also been affected by the intergovernmental dimension, these issues have been raised more powerfully and directly through the struggle over urban renewal and other general community development strategies. The way in which these intergovernmental issues have been resolved has profoundly shaped community development programs, and this, in turn, has greatly affected their impact on housing.

In this chapter, the federal government's first major urban redevelopment effort, the urban renewal program, will be traced from its roots in the New Deal era, to its demise in 1974. The struggle which occurred over the housing impact of this program will be given particular attention. In addition, the effects of urban renewal and other urban programs on federal/local relationships and local politics will be examined. In Chapter 8, the ways in which the local and national concerns raised by the impact of urban renewal and other federal categorical programs led to a shift in the nation's community development strategy will be explored. The Community Development Block Grant program which embodied this new approach will be discussed in some detail. Finally, it will be shown that this shift in community development had a major impact on federal housing efforts by helping to stimulate a shift from clearance to housing rehabilitation as the major focus of neighborhood renewal efforts.

Urban Renewal as a Community Development Strategy

The Roots of Urban Renewal

Federal invovement in the physical development of local communities was presaged by the emergency public works projects enacted early in the New Deal. These efforts had as their primary purpose the creation of jobs for the legions of unemployed, but they served an additional public purpose by creating capital improvements which nearly bankrupt local governments could no longer afford. Significantly, the federal construction of low income housing was initially a part of the Public Works Administration program. The Roosevelt Administration saw the clearing of slum dwellings and their replacement with new, low cost housing as one of the useful public purposes which could be served by workers on the federal payroll.

However, it was also significant that local property owners successfully challenged in court the clearance aspect of this early federal housing effort, on the grounds that the goal of "removing blight" was not a legitimate public purpose of the federal government and thus could not justify the use of eminent domain to acquire property (*U.S. vs. Certain Lands in the City of Louisville, Ky.*). At the same time, the door was left open for the use of eminent domain by the local government for the same purpose, with proper state authorizing legislation. This lead to a much more decentralized design for the public housing program, which helped to establish a more general pattern for federal programs—local planning and execution of projects utilizing federal dollars (Mandelker, et al., 1981).

The New Deal also spawned other ideas and trends which would later come to be influential in the community development process. Historians have often stressed the *ad hoc* nature of the entire New Deal effort, seeing it as a series of pragmatic responses to concrete problems more than as a coherent plan for national recovery. (Mollenkopf, 1983) Nevertheless, Roosevelt and many of his advisors were attracted by the prospect of national economic and social planning, and they aspired to a more orderly, comprehensive approach to the problems of the Depression than the political sitaution ultimately permitted them to achieve. In the area of community planning they began cautious experiments such as the Greenbelt program, and, in 1933, a National Planning Board was created. This group undertook a comprehensive study of urban problems which resulted in a 1937 report entitled, *Our Cities: Their Role in the National Economy*. As a political document, this report carried little weight, for its recommendations were virtually ignored by both the president and Congress. Nevertheless, the report gave respectability to the idea that government should respond to the unique problems of urban areas. It also stimulated a wide range of academic research which was to become the basis for future policy initiatives (Gelfand, 1975).

Meanwhile, support for federal urban redevelopment was growing in a seemingly unlikely quarter—the National Association of Real Estate Boards (NAREB). According to Gelfand, the drastic slowdown in urban growth brought about by the Depression aroused concern among many real estate and business investors with a heavy financial stake in central city property. They feared a spiral of decay which would substantially reduce the value of their assets, and they accurately foresaw that prosperity would bring a renewal of the suburbanization which had accompanied increased automobile ownership in the 1920s. These investors conceived of blight as something broader than the existence of residential slums. They defined it as patterns of land use which blocked successful (i.e., profitable) redevelopment of central city land to 'higher' uses, whether commercial, industrial, or residential. They came to believe that local government might, with federal financial backing, play a useful role in removing blight. First, it could use its power of eminent domain to overcome a major obstacle to redevelopment – the assembly of smaller parcels of land into larger ones. Second, using the justification of future tax revenue increases and a new, improved face for the central city, governments might also be persuaded to write down the relatively high central city land acquisition and demolition costs which were also an obstacle to redevelopment.

Therefore, NAREB and its affiliated think tank, the Urban Land Institute, began in the late 1930s to generate proposals for federal involvement in urban redevelopment. NAREB's first proposal called for a program in which neighborhood associations of property owners would decide which properties to redevelop. This was later replaced with the idea of a community-wide redevelopment commission with broad condemnation powers. Eventually, their proposal was refined into legislation, which was introduced in Congress in 1943. Though it never got out of committee, this proposal was an important precursor to the redevelopment provisions of the Housing Act of 1949.

The advocacy of urban redevelopment by such a conservative group generated mixed reactions among the academics and government planners who had been urging the renewal of cities. Gelfand notes that "some took . . . [it] . . . as a positive sign of a new civic awareness among realtors," and he goes on to quote Frederic Delano, who "considered it 'a matter of importance to find the real estate men taking an active interest in trying to solve the problems to which they have been somewhat indifferent and which, it seems to me, they have largely created.'" (Gelfand, 1975, p. 117). In contrast, the more housing-oriented planners found it ironic that NAREB should be proposing federal subsidies to private developers while at the same time it was bitterly attacking the new public housing program as socialistic and un-American.

Nevertheless, as the 1940s progressed, liberal housing advocates began to see some advantages to hitching their wagon to the notion of urban redevelopment. The public housing program had taken a beating from NAREB and its conservative allies in Congress. Perhaps housing advocates could strengthen their position by agreeing to accept subsidies for private development in exchange for some units of public housing to rehouse those displaced by redevelopment. Thus, there began an uneasy alliance between those who saw economic redevelopment as the main goal of such a program and those spokespersons for the poor who wanted to make housing the central focus of redevelopment.

In the end, the two purposes were firmly linked together in the bill, introduced in 1945 by Senators Wagner, Ellender, and Taft, which became the Housing Act of 1949. Much to the chagrin of NAREB leaders, the bill empahsized housing as its main goal. It required that redevelopment take place primarily in residential areas, that decent housing for those displaced be located, and it authorized 810,000 units of public housing to replace and supplement the housing destroyed. This housing emphasis was a short-term political liability in that, as noted in Chapter 4, the public housing provisions sparked a bitter debate which held up passage for four years. Yet, in the long run, the urban redevelopment proposal benefitted from its attachment to housing goals. First, it made the bill more appealing to liberal supporters of social welfare programs than urban redevelopment alone would have been, especially in light of the housing shortages which had developed after World War II. Second, the controversy surrounding public housing deflected critical attention which might otherwise have been focused on the redevelopment provisions. On the other side of the coin, private real estate and business interests found the bitter pill of public housing somewhat easier to swallow when sweetened with the prospect of federal subsidies for economic development. Of the diverse coalition which supported the Housing Act of 1949, Catherine Bauer commented, "Seldom has such a variegated crew of would-be angels tried to sit on the same pin at the same time." (Quoted in Gelfand, 1975, p. 153).

Problems with Urban Renewal

The implementation of urban redevelopment under Title I of the Housing Act of 1949 raised a number of complex housing issues. However, before exploring these issues, a brief overview of the design and impact of the program is in order. As originally set forth, Title I provided federal funding for property acquisition, demolition of structures, and site preparation in redevelopment areas; however, it also required a ⅔-⅓ cost sharing by the federal and the local government. The local government's share of the cost was usually provided in the form of "noncash grants-in-aid"; i.e., various public works carried out by the local government in support of the redevelopment project. Proceeds from the sale of land were used to repay as much of the federal costs as possible; but the cost of acquiring and demolishing existing structures was usually much greater than the price at which the land was sold, so that the net cost represented a substantial federal subsidy to encourage private redevelopment.

As with any new and complex program, implementation was slow to get started. By 1953, only $105 million out of the original $500 million in grants had actually been committed. However, there were a number of economic and political pressures brewing in the early 1950s which contributed to the program's expansion. Suburbia was exploding with new housing and new commercial activity, which reduced the central cities' share of the total metropolitan retail trade from 68 percent in 1948 to 58 percent in 1954. (Gelfand, 1975, p. 158). This was very profitable to many business interests, but to many others, it seemed a major threat to their huge investments in the central city and to their civic pride. These central city-oriented business leaders made common cause with a new group of progressive big city mayors who saw the redevelopment of their cities as a source of long-term political support. Pittsburgh under David Lawrence and New Haven under Richard Lee provided models to other cities in this regard. Initially, much of this work was done with private and local government funds, but the urban redevelopment program proved an increasingly attractive supplement to local efforts. Therefore, applications increased in the last half of the 1950s, in spite of complex federal requirements (Mollenkopf, 1983).

Meanwhile, legislative changes were being made which would ultimately make the program more attractive to localities. The Housing Act of 1954 changed the name of the program from *urban redevelopment* to *urban renewal*, and, to encourage more comprehensive planning, required that each city submit a Workable Program showing how it planned to attack the problem of urban decay. Though this requirement would seem to have imposed more red tape on localities, the Housing and Home Finance Administration (HHFA) left the real planning initiative to local governments, restricting itself to a technical and financial review of applications. More importantly, the new law shifted the program's emphasis away from housing by allowing a larger percentage of projects to be nonresidential in character.

By 1959, when Eisenhower tried to cut back the program as a budget reduction measure, it enjoyed strong enough support that the Democratic Congress was able to block his effort. When the Kennedy Administration took office in 1961, they showed the same favorable attitude toward urban renewal as toward other urban-oriented programs, and funding was increased substantially. More and more cities applied during the early 1960s, so that, by the end of the decade, there were few cities of any size in the United States which did not have at least one urban renewal project planned or underway.

Yet, as the projects multiplied, so, too, did the controversy and criticism surrounding the program. Some of this criticism was voiced by pure laissez-faire conservatives, like Martin Anderson (1964.) He argued that federal funds should not be used to selectively subsidize private developers to carry out projects which would not be feasible or profitable within the "natural" workings of the market system. This criticism reemerged in later years as it became increasingly clear that urban renewal could not stop or reverse the suburbanization of the U.S. metropolis. In 1974, Irving Welfeld, writing for the American Enterprise Institute, questioned the cost effectiveness of what he saw as a government financed attempt to "buck the tide" of polycentric urban residential settlement which had overtaken American society (Welfeld, 1974).

However, many actors in the urban political process felt there was something vital to be preserved for the community as a whole by maintaining a viable central business district and a viable central city community. The new central business districts which emerged in the 1950s and 1960s were administrative, governmental, and cultural centers rather than the dominant commercial hubs they had once been. Yet, many city-oriented economic leaders and government professionals shared the view that a positive image and function for downtown were worth being publicly subsidized.

Liberals whose primary concern was amelioration of the plight of the poor also recognized a close association between the fate of the central cities and the fate of the poor. In general, urban aid and aid to the poor continued to be closely linked, and any move to withdraw funds from community development altogether would have been resisted as contrary to the interests of the large concentrations of low income people living in these areas. Although civil rights advocates began to talk about opening up the suburbs and although the Fair Housing Act of 1968 gave them a new tool to do this, the central city was realistically seen as the main point at which housing and other services would continue to be delivered to the poor.

Nevertheless, the urban renewal program itself became the target of increasing criticism from liberals, as well as doctrinaire conservatives. While accepting the need to aid the central cities, a growing number of liberal critics became concerned with the housing and neighborhood impact of the program. Since this is the facet of urban renewal which is of most importance to the present work, these liberal concerns will be discussed in some detail. For purposes of analysis, these problems may be grouped into three basic categories: (1) Problems of project duration; (2) Problems of relocation; and, (3) Problems of neighborhood impact.

TIME — THE ENEMY OF URBAN RENEWAL, On a late spring day in 1970, a group of about 100 demonstrators (of which this author was one) marched from downtown Louisville, Kentucky, south to an urban renewal site adjacent to the University of Louisville. To protest the fact that this land, which had once contained low income housing, had lain vacant for several years, we planted a Poor People's Garden among the remaining rubble, using the argument that if the land couldn't house the poor, at least it could feed them. This protest symbolized the hostility which the long delay between clearance and rebuilding engendered in many citizens. The site we cultivated was only a part of the dozens of acres of cleared land adjacent to Louisville's central business district which lay vacant for periods of five to ten years before any new construction was begun.

Five years later, as an administrator for the Richmond Redevelopment and Housing Authority (Richmond, Virginia), I obtained an insider's view of the causes of such delays. Richmond's renewal efforts were much more oriented to replacing demolished housing with low to moderate income housing than were Louisville's, yet frustrating delays still detracted from the program's image and impact.

One of Richmond's typical projects, Fulton, had been designated in the city's Community Renewal Program in 1966. After three years of planning and community organizing, property acquisition finally began in 1969. One site within the project had been designated for Section 236 housing, to provide at least some low and moderate income replacement units. Acquisition and condemnation of property, relocation of its occupants, and demolition of structures on that site took at least two more years. Then, the site was graded and filled to raise it out of the James River's 100 year flood plain, which proved to be a more expensive and time consuming process than anticipated.

Meanwhile, the Richmond Authority ran afoul of HUD's site selection criteria which, as noted in Chapter 5, sought to avoid an excessive concentration of new subsidized units in low income areas. In a classic federal catch 22, the agency was halted by one set of regulations while trying to comply with another set — namely, urban renewal regulations (to be discussed below) requiring that redevelopment of cleared residential areas include a substantial proportion of low to moderate income housing. The Authority was eventually able to show that private developers had constructed enough comparable units of subsidized housing in outlying areas to satisfy HUD's requirements, but not before an additional delay had occurred. Still another year's delay resulted from the inability of HUD, the developer, and the Virginia Housing Development Authority (which was providing low interest financing) to agree on various cost and design issues. Finally, ground was broken late in 1976, with occupancy beginning some 18 months later, over ten years after the project had been initiated.

A national survey of program impact by Heywood Sanders shows that the delays encountered in Louisville and Richmond were very typical. Each city and each project had its own set of reasons for delay, some of which could be attributed to local agency errors. But the sheer complexity of the process was the fundamental reason for the delays in project completion. Problems of planning and political organization; legal problems with the acquisition of property; problems of coordination between the renewal agency, other local government agencies, private developers, HUD, or other federal programs — none of these were amenable to quick resolution. However, as Sanders suggests, time was a major enemy of public acceptance of the program, and delays intensified the other criticisms leveled at it. The years of further decay and destruction in project areas which elapsed before any renewal actually began created a negative image which it was hard for the eventual new development to erase.

RELOCATION. Of all the issues raised in connection with urban renewal, the issue of the displacement and relocation of low income residents was the most powerful catalyst for opposition. The scene in which an elderly person is evicted from his/her home of 30 years while the bulldozer operator revs his engine outside has become a staple of television and movies, and the villian of the piece is usually labelled *urban renewal* regardless of the private or public nature of the redevelopment which caused the eviction. Yet, on a less emotional level, data began to accumulate during the first 15 years of the urban renewal program's operation which showed a severe problem of housing destruction and displacement. With the public housing component reduced and the emphasis on commercial redevelopment increased in the late 1950s, the program quickly destroyed many more units of low income housing than it was able to replace. To be sure, many of the units destroyed were far below prevailing standards of decent habitation, but they did provide shelter for persons with few other housing choices. And, to representatives of the poor and minorities who were becoming increasingly politically active in the 1960s, this massive physical assault on their neighborhoods was the ultimate indignity. Coupled with extensive displacement due to highway construction and to private redevelopment, urban renewal displacement seemed one more way the poor were being shoved aside to meet the needs of upper income groups.

Chester Hartman summarized a decade of studies of the impact of displacement on the poor in a 1971 article in the *Virginia Law Review*. These studies found the impact to be largely negative, in both economic and psychological terms. In most cases, persons displaced had to occupy more expensive units in only marginally better structures as a result of their move. Homeowners, though compensated for their dwellings at market value, were often forced to become tenants, because the prices paid for their substandard homes were too low to permit the purchase of even a modest replacement unit (Hartman, 1971). Equally harmful, in many cases, were the psychological effects of being uprooted from a home and a neighborhood which the family had occupied for many years. Marc Fried titled his classic study of the effects of relocation from a Boston neighborhood, "Grieving for a Lost Home," because he found that the psychological stress suffered by many of those displaced resembled that associated with the death of a close friend or relative (Fried, 1966).

Moreover, many displaced persons sought shelter in neighborhoods adjacent to their previous area of residence. In many cases, this was an attempt to maintain old community ties, while in others it signalled a perceived or actual lack of choice of alternative areas of the city in which they could live. Economic constraints limited their choices, and for the disproportionate share of those relocated who were black, racial discrimination was also a limiting factor. Of course, the rapid influx of low income tenants into areas near urban renewal sites, areas which themselves were often physically and economically marginal, often tipped the balance in favor of rapid deterioration, thus creating a new slum to replace the one which federal funds were demolishing.

The response of federal and local officials to the problems of relocation was limited and slow in coming. The local business-government coalitions pushing for urban renewal, to the extent that they were concerned about the poor at all, tended to accept the traditional view of the slums as primarily a physical problem. They felt that if the physical blight could be removed, the problems of the poor inhabitants would somehow disappear, as they were dispersed into other areas. In addition, local officials were reluctant to add the cost of adequate relocation benefits to the direct costs of the program, and they found little community acceptance of large scale subsidized replacement housing to aid those displaced. The business and real estate interests backing urban renewal were interested in converting cleared land into more profitable uses and not in using cleared sites for low income housing. Other neighborhoods, of course, displayed their usual reluctance to have low income housing thrust into their midst.

The federal government was, at least formally, given the role of watchdog over the displacement and rehousing of existing residents of urban renewal areas. The 1949 Act required that, in order to qualify for funding, localities had to guarantee that an adequate supply of "decent, safe, and sanitary" replacement housing be available ". . . at rents or prices within the financial means of the families displaced . . . " (Quoted from the statute by Hartman, 1971). However, federal urban renewal officials had little incentive to further slow down an already lengthy and complex process by requiring genuine, effective relocation planning. They, like local officials, wanted to demonstrate results by getting more cities to participate and by completing projects faster. Therefore, relocation planning became little more than a paper exercise (Hartman, 1971; see also, Greer, 1965).

Perhaps of greater importance than the apathy of federal urban renewal administrators was the lack of federal resources directed at rehousing the poor, for not even conscientious relocation planning could work in the absence of suitable replacement units. This lack of resources had two dimensions. First, throughout most of the first 20 years of urban renewal, new units of subsidized housing were being produced in numbers far too small to replace those demolished. Second, direct relocation payments to displaced households were either nonexistent or inadequate to fully compensate them for their losses. Both of these dimensions of the problem require further examination.

The overall ebb and flow of subsidized housing programs from 1950 to 1973, described in earlier chapters, had an obvious impact on the availability of replacement housing. In the case of the very poor, public housing was virtually the only type of housing which could meet the 1949 Act's criterion of "decent, safe and sanitary housing within their ability to pay." Thus, the abandonment of the Act's commitment to 810,000 units of public housing meant the loss of relocation resources as well. Only as public housing construction increased in the 1960s and as new subsidized housing programs came on line in 1968 were enough units being produced to have a positive impact on relocation.

Moreover, since land and resources for low income housing were already in short supply before urban renewal got underway, it was recognized early by many urban planners that a general commitment to new low income housing was not enough. Housing plans and commitments tied specifically to urban renewal efforts were also necessary. However, the federal and local response to this need was very sluggish, due to the fundamental drift of the program away from its original housing thrust. At various times, provisions were added to the 1949 Act, such as special FHA financing of housing in urban renewal areas (Section 220) and rehabilitation loans and grants (Sections 312 and 115), which were designed to create incentives to construct or rehabilitate replacement housing. However, these additions stimulated little residential reuse.

It was only in the late 1960s, when the Johnson Administration began to respond to pressure for a change in the priorities of the urban renewal program that its rehousing element changed substantially. In 1966, the 1949 Act was amended to require that, in predominantly residential projects, a "substantial" number of low to moderate income replacement units be constructed (Hartman, 1971, p. 751). Then, in 1967, HUD Secretary Robert Weaver announced that "the conservation and expansion of the housing supply for low and moderate income families" would be a central goal of the urban renewal program (Quoted in Sanders, 1980, p. 108). In further pursuit of this goal, the 1968 and 1969 Housing Acts strengthened the vague language of the 1966 amendment, making it clear that "renewal projects . . . must replace any occupied low or moderate income . . . units demolished . . . with at least an equivalent number of units . . . to be constructed or rehabilitated somewhere within the jurisdiction of the local public agency." (Hartman, 1971, p. 751).

Hartman notes that this language still allowed local agencies some leeway in avoiding replacement housing which was strictly for low income persons. Nevertheless, data presented by Sanders show a marked shift toward residential reuse in programs which were begun in the late 1960s. The average amount of project land designated for residential reuse rose from less than 25 percent before 1968 to nearly 50 percent after that date. Meanwhile, the average amount of land devoted to residential rehabilitation rose from less than 15 percent to between 25 and 30 percent (Sanders, 1980, p. 111). Furthermore, well over half the residential reuse was designated as housing for low to moderate income people. Sanders suggests that the characterization of urban renewal as a destroyer of low income housing which has prevailed in much of the academic literature was much more accurate during the early years of the program than in the years from 1968 until its demise in the mid-1970s.

The other facet of the replacement housing issue was the question of direct compensation to those being relocated. During the early years of the program, compensation for tenants was limited to a small reimbursement for moving expenses. The agency was required to provide aid in finding replacement housing, but studies showed that only a small proportion of those affected took advantage of these services. In 1964, Congress added a Relocation Adjustment Payment of up to $500 to cover the difference between old and new rent, which was expanded to $1000 in 1965. But the problem of the family's ability to remain in a higher priced unit after one or two years was not dealt with (Hartman, 1971, pp. 749–750). Payments to homeowners were limited to the prices offered for their home plus moving expenses. Moreover, until the late 1960s, when

HUD insisted on a single offer based on the appraised price, local agencies were permitted to offer less than their own appraised value and to bargain hard for this low figure. An appeal to condemnation court was, of course, possible, but few owners had the resources or skill to pursue this remedy.

It was not until 1970 that Congress saw fit to increase relocation payments to levels which might truly begin to compensate for the losses incurred and even to improve substantially the household's living conditions. This legislation, the Uniform Relocation Assistance and Real Property Acquisition Policies Act, covered those displaced from highways and other federal projects, as well as urban renewal. For tenants, this act increased benefits to include moving expenses plus a rental assistance payment based on the difference between the tenant's rent before and after relocation for a period of 48 months up to a maximum of $4000. Thus, a tenant paying $50 per month rent before and $100 per month after would receive $2400 plus moving expenses. Tenants with some savings could also qualify for downpayment assistance, in which their savings would be matched up to $2000 for a downpayment on a new home. Homeowners received a maximum of $15,000 over and above the purchase price of their old property, plus moving expenses.

For a piece of legislation involving the expenditure of large sums of money for the benefit of lower income persons, this measure passed Congress with very little debate or publicity. Outcries against displacement had arisen from many groups representing the poor, and reform to quiet this potentially troublesome opposition to urban renewal seemed prudent. Also, persons displaced through no fault of their own could more easily be placed in the category of the deserving poor than low income persons in general.

Very little research on the impact of the Uniform Relocation Act on the fortunes of those displaced has been done. However, along with Christopher Silver, I examined urban renewal relocation in Richmond, Virginia, most of which was done after the passage of the Uniform Relocation Act. We found that displaced persons fared considerably better with its financial support than was typically the case prior to the act. First, most displacees moved into neighborhoods which were in substantially better physical condition than those they left, and most were living among persons of higher income than themselves. Second, because of the homeowner payments and the downpayment assistance, there was actually a net increase in the percentage of owners in our sample from 28.4 to 39.1 percent. Third, those displaced were scattered over relatively wide areas of the city, rather than concentrated in areas immediately adjacent to clearance areas (Hays and Silver, 1980).

Nevertheless, there were continuing problems with relocation. First, the $15,000 payment to homeowners was greatly reduced in value by the housing price inflation of the 1970s. This was a special problem because most of the displaced owners were elderly and living on small fixed incomes and, thus, were limited to houses for which they could pay cash. The average price received for their homes was $6700, giving them a total of $21,700 to purchase a new one (Hays and Silver, 1980). In the early 1970s this could still buy a modest but decent home. Later, this was not the case.

Second, the issue of racial discrimination was not necessarily resolved by the economic support provided by the Uniform Relocation Act. Our Richmond study found that approximately 40 percent of displaced blacks moved into predominantly white census tracts, a not insignificant pattern of dispersal given the high level of segregation which is still typical of U.S. housing markets. However, some of this apparent dispersal was to areas of considerable white flight, thus making it likely that these areas would become resegregated in the future. Sanders (1980) notes that the lable of *Negro removal* which was given to urban renewal was somewhat exaggerated in that, on a national scale, the majority displaced were whites. However, other studies indicate that because of the dual housing market in most U.S. cities, blacks had much greater difficulty finding decent replacement housing than whites.

Finally, the substantial cost of relocation may have ultimately contributed to the program's demise, since it raised substantially the total cost of each project. For example, unpublished data from the Richmond Redevelopment and Housing Authority show that tenants received an average payment of $2500 and that virtually every homeowner received the full $15,000 payment. As a result, relocation was the largest single item in the Richmond Authority's clearance budget, much larger than the cost of buying the property. Such payments represented the project's true costs, in that the burdens of displacement were no longer merely externalities borne by the current residents. Nevertheless, they contributed to the impression that urban renewal was excessively costly and thus buttressed Nixon's arguments for change.

NEIGHBORHOOD IMPACT. The struggles surrounding relocation tended to focus on the individual problems of displaced households in finding a new place to live. Yet these individual struggles often took place in the context of a neighborhood which was being destroyed by the renewal process. Not only were specific families being uprooted, but a whole fabric of economic, social, and political relationships was being permanently disrupted. Families reacted differently to separation from their neighborhood. Some grieved in the manner described by Marc Fried. Others were glad to escape to better areas. But regardless of individual reactions, the urban renewal program was increasingly confronted with neighborhoods as organized entities fighting for their collective existence.

According to one recent study, the idea of a neighborhood as a consciously planned or organized unit has been central to urban life since the beginning of U.S. cities (Silver, 1982). Neighbors have recognized that they are economically and socially interdependent and that they receive a common package of government services, the quality of which is dependent on their socioeconomic status and political clout. This has led to neighborhood political organizations aimed at improving existing conditions, keeping 'undesirables' out, and pressuring City Hall for a better share of services.

Though the importance of neighborhoods in general has long been recognized, the types of neighborhoods labelled *slums* have frequently been characterized as pathological in nature. From nineteenth century moralistic tracts denouncing the slums as human cesspools to seemingly more sophisticated twentieth century discussions of the culture of poverty, the physical concentration of the poor has been seen as reinforcing and enhancing their alienation from the rest of society. Dilapidated housing; poor sanitation; the temptations of crime and drugs; inferior schools; and a street culture which discourages normal (i.e., middle class) achievement—all of these neighborhood factors have been seen as barriers to the individual's escape from poverty. This analysis has at times been used to support the conclusion that if the physical concentrations of the poor are broken up, some of their pathologies may also be reduced.

However, two alternative views emerged in the 1950s and 1960s which helped generate opposition to urban renewal. One view emphasized that whatever pathology exists in low income neighborhoods arises primarily from the economic and social deprivations of poverty and the inability of individuals to change their situation. Therefore, even though neighborhood influences may be the proximate causes of an individual's failure to advance, the underlying causes relate to the economic structure of the society. Unless more dignity and material well-being is brought to those in low status occupations and unless more opportunities for upward mobility are created, people will continue to adapt in terms of some version of the culture of poverty, no matter how self-defeating it might appear to an outsider. This view supports the conclusion that displacement of the poor out of one area will simply lead to their absorption into another slum environment or to the creation of a similar environment in an adjacent area (Stone, Whelan, and Murin, 1979).

The second view emphasizes the positive aspects of the culture of poor and working class urban neighborhoods. Scholars such as Herbert Gans (1962), Jane Jacobs (1961), and Gerald Suttles (1968) stressed the intricate and often supportive social relationships which exist beneath the drab and sometimes violent exterior of these areas. Many of the poor live out their entire lives in a single neighborhood, and, though it symbolizes to them their poverty and their limitations, it is also familiar territory in which habits and relationships useful to survival are developed. To remove this neighborhood structure suddenly and forcibly is, in this view, to add even more stress to their existence. It means cutting people loose from whatever moorings they have been able to establish for themselves in an unfriendly world.

These reevaluations of the nature and causes of low income living patterns coincided with an increasing amount of political organization by low income neighborhoods. Much of this organization was spontaneous, stimulated, particularly in black areas, by the civil rights movement and modelled after the tactics used by Saul Alinsky in Chicago's working class areas. However, the organization of these neighborhoods was also greatly encouraged by the federal government's own new solution to the problems of low income areas – the War on Poverty. Far from trying to eliminate these neighborhoods and convert the land to 'higher' uses, Community Action Agencies were designed to protect them from neglect, abuse, and encroachment by City Hall or the private sector.

The Community Action Program was, in its own way, as narrow in its approach to poverty as was physical renewal. As several critics have noted, it attributed poverty to the powerlessness of the poor and tried to cure it by political organization, while devoting few resources to correcting the underlying maldistribution of skills and income. Yet, in many cities, the Community Action Agencies did help to create new political leverage for low income neighborhoods, and this leverage was used to tackle concrete problems confronting them. This was particularly true for black neighborhoods, whose leaders had been the most thoroughly excluded from local political structures (Donovan, 1967; Moynihan, 1969; Piven and Cloward, 1971).

To the residents of low income areas, the prospect of massive displacement due to urban renewal was a problem requiring action. Thus, urban renewal agencies began to encounter organized, articulate opposition where once they could have expected passivity or only mild protest. The economic and political interests behind urban renewal still held most of the high cards and could often win the game anyway, but the political costs of redevelopment were raised considerably. In addition, the federal government was, in effect, put on both sides of the fence. On the one hand, it was encouraging grand schemes for economic redevelopment which involved major changes in the face of the city, particularly in areas outsiders considered blighted. On the other hand, through the War on Poverty and other participatory programs such as Model Cities, it was encouraging the empowerment of those groups most likely to suffer the direct costs of such schemes.

In response to these pressures, HUD began to require local renewal agencies to do some community organization of their own. After 1968, local agencies had to set up a Project Area Committee (PAC) during the early stages of each project, made up of elected representatives from the target area. These committees were consulted on plans for the area and often suggested both major and minor changes in direction. Though the authority to approve the Redevelopment Plan lay ultimately with the local governing body and with HUD, agencies found it very advantageous to secure solid PAC approval before approaching higher authorities. A supportive PAC could, for example, mobilize area residents to fill City Council chambers on the night the plan was to be approved. A hostile PAC could, in contrast, make trouble for the agency throughout the process.

Counterpressures from low income neighborhood organizations also contributed to the passage of the various measures aimed at softening and redirecting the program's impact. Offering rehabilitation as an alternative to clearance could help mollify opposition, especially when accompanied by low interest loans and grants to area property owners. Promising to replace a portion of the demolished housing with new units for low and moderate income persons was also a way to reduce opposition. Finally, after the passage of the Uniform Relocation Act, the prospect of its rather substantial financial benefits stimulated many less committed residents to 'take the money and run' rather than to support efforts to save the area. If, as Heywood Sanders suggests, urban renewal was a somewhat different program in the early 1970s than in the early 1960s, the influence of aroused urban neighborhoods can be credited with some of these changes.

Urban Renewal and the Urban Policy Environment

It has been suggested here that a gradual evolution of the urban renewal program took place, changing it from a program which simply brushed aside low income individuals and neighborhoods (in favor of uses more suitable to local political and economic elites) to a device at least partly targeted at improving the physical environment of the poor, either through conservation of their exisitng housing or through rehousing them in new units. This change in the direction of physical renewal did not, however, resolve the even more fundamental issue of the relationship between physical improvment of neighborhoods and the total improvement in the lives of the persons affected. Even if an area could be physically renewed with a minimum of displacement, there still remained the question of how the area's residents had really benefitted from such renewal. Unless their fundamental lack of resources and opportunities were improved, or, at the very least, they received services which improved their social as well as physical environment, had the quality of their lives been genuinely improved? Conversely, would the physical improvements themselves last if other social problems contributing to physical decay were not dealt with?

The answer among those knowledgeable and active in urban policy was, inreasingly, "No!" The longer that poverty remained in the public eye, the more apparent became its multifaceted nature. The causes and solutions to the problems of the poor raised issues of physical health, mental health, employment, education, crime, transportation, recreation, and many others besides housing and community development. Each of these issues touched, in turn, on the basic quality of life of all urban residents, not just the poor. Those concerned with a particular problem constantly found themselves blocked by a nearly seamless web of related problems which seemed to prevent a totally satisfactory solution to that problem alone.

For this reason, the overall increase in government concern about the poor and about urban areas which characterized the late 1960s stimulated new programs in all the areas just mentioned. After years of debate as to whether or not the federal government should get invovled, the prevailing liberal consensus seemed to dictate federal action on as many of the problems as possible. This multifaceted approach also enhanced support for the total effort in the short run, in that many different groups in society were eager to get a piece of the action in solving urban ills.

Yet, in the long run, the effort to attack so many problems at once inevitably led to confusion and conflict. Each program spawned a complex set of relationships between executive, legislative, administrative, and citizen centers of power at all levels of government. As programs multiplied they challenged the prerogatives of various political leaders, administrators, and interest groups. No single program could be expanded or redirected without affecting and being affected by the total size and complexity of the federal effort. Moreover, while it was possible as an intellectual exercise to devise ways to consolidate or coordinate related programs, it was much more difficult as a political exercise. When push came to shove, few actors were willing to give up power in order to make the total system more rational.

Thus, by the late 1960s the number and complexity of federal programs had become a political issue in its own right. Liberals became concerned about the effect of chaos and duplication on the ultimate efficacy of programs, while conservatives seized on this problem as one more bit of evidence that government efforts on behalf of the poor could never succeed. The continued passage of a variety of programs also triggered conservative concerns about the growth in the total amount of resources being devoted to such purposes.

Therefore, in order to understand why community development policy underwent a major transformation in the early 1970s it is not only necessary to understand earlier community development efforts and the problems they spawned. It is also necesary to examine the issue of programmatic complexity and its political expression in the form of demands for program consolidation. It was in the context of this broader issue that the Community Development Block Grant (CDBG) program emerged and became the centerpiece of federal community development strategy. Thus, the discussion of the CDBG program in Chapter 8 will begin with a look at this issue.

Community Development Block Grants

The Creation of Community Development Block Grants

As a framework for a discussion of the problems which led to the movement toward grant consolidation and decentralization in the early 1970s, it is useful to review the pattern of multiple involvement of all types and levels of public bodies in formulation, administration, and review which was typical of the many categorical programs which developed in the 1960s. In the usual pattern of development, a problem was perceived and a program formulated at the federal level, often at the initiative of the president and his advisors. Nationally organized interest groups, whether representing private citizens or public agencies, often had input into presidential decisions or helped shape the compromises and alterations of presidential plans emerging from Congress. The administrative responsibility was conferred on whatever federal agency seemed most appropriate to the members of the national coalition backing the program. The agency then developed regulations to implement the program, again with input from interest groups and political decisionmakers. Two slightly different coalitions dealing with related areas could generate two programs with fairly similar objectives, which, in retrospect, would appear duplicative. Yet, each set of decisionmakers might make a legitimate argument for its responsibility for the problem and might fear that their concerns would be ignored if their program were eliminated or consolidated.

The political commitments behind specific programs and administrative procedures became solidified further as authority passed down through state and local channels. Programs involving an area of traditional state responsibility, such as welfare administration, might rely on state agencies and their local offices to administer the federal funds. Or, as was more frequently the case, authority might be delegated to mayors, city administrative agencies, local independent boards or commissions, or even nonprofit corporations separate from the local governement structure.

This process in itself contained the seeds of conflict in that federal objectives, procedures, and timetables were usually different from those of the local or state administrative units. Conflicts over objectives reflected differences in political values between levels of government (such as the federal government's greater commitment to enforcing equal opportunity statutes), but there were also numerous conflicts over the complexity of federal procedures and the slowness of federal reviews and approvals. For the political reasons mentioned in Chapter 2, it was easier for the federal government to *initiate* such programs; however, once the program was in place, it was the local agency delivering the service which was under the most pressure to produce results for its clientele. The federal government was now in the monitoring and reviewing role, and, though federal agencies were often reluctant to totally block local action, they did attempt to gain leverage by imposing complex technical requirements and by holding projects to their own timetable.

In spite of these conflicts, specialized local implementing agencies were able to learn the requisite procedures and otherwise work out a *modus vivendi* with their federal counterparts. Also, as the federal money began to flow, these local units developed a strong stake in the continuation and expansion of the program(s) in their charge. Thus was created the pattern of vertical, functional integration of categorical areas of governmental activity to which former North Carolina governor Terry Sanford gave the name "picket fence federalism." Each categorical program represented not only a coalition at the federal level, but an alliance between agencies and interest groups at all levels of government with a common interest in the survival of the program.

These alliances tended to be highly resistant to coordination by political executives, no matter which level of government tried to initiate it. When Kennedy's advisors began to formulate an attack on poverty and, later, when Johnson took a new look at neighborhood development in low income areas, the desirability of coordinating the efforts of various federal agencies was readily apparent to those involved. Yet, the mere creation of an umbrella agency, such as the Office of Economic Opportunity (OEO) or the Model Cities Administration, was not enough to insure the success of such coordination. The resistance of the political and administrative alliance around each program was so strong that only constant, strong, presidential intervention could force agencies to cooperate, and, given the broad concerns and responsibilities of the presidency, such constant pressure was unlikely to occur. Thus, according to Peterson and Greenstone (1977), the OEO embarked on a program of political organization of the poor in order to develop its own constituency, *after* its initial efforts to establish a coordination role on the federal level foundered on agency resistance. Similarly, according to Frieden and Kaplan (1977), the Model Cities program, which was supposed to coordinate and concentrate services in certain distressed neighborhoods, was weakened by lack of cooperation at the federal level, even before it began to administer the program locally.

If presidential plans and initiatives had difficulty in changing the existing administrative patterns, it is not hard to see why governors and mayors soon became frustrated at their lack of control. Both were engaged in building political support behind their own priorities, and they found that the acceptance of much needed federal funds often brought with it conflicting priorities. Ironically, the whole system of grants-in-aid to state and local governments was designed to allow these governments to shape their own programs. Yet, because program control was often conferred on separate agencies, rather than on state or local executives, the latter had a sense of losing, rather than gaining, control over programs in their jurisdiction.

The extension of funds to neighborhood-based organizations created further potential for conflict. These organizations often had less success in taking on established agencies and programs than did the political executives just mentioned. Procedural changes were difficult enough to obtain, but, more importantly, the extension of federal funds to OEO or Model Cities was not accompanied, in most cases, by sufficient additions to the funding of categorical programs to enable them to respond on a large scale to the problems of a given neighborhood. Meanwhile, federally funded neighborhood groups were putting political heat on local executives and councils, who could not effectively control the direction of the programs they were being asked to change. Where local government did respond, it was inclined to follow traditional patterns of spreading benefits out among a number of neighborhoods in order to maximize political influence. This pattern did not sit well with the federally organized poor, who felt that resources should be concentrated in their areas. The local "pork barrel" also potentially violated federal criteria for eligibility and distribution in specific programs. Thus, local officals felt even more encircled by demands they could not or did not want to meet.

Finally, competition between localities for federal largesse created further conflict. Some local governments, particularly in the larger cities, had been in the business of soliciting federal funds for years. They had developed the staff, the expertise, and the political contacts to successfully push for federal dollars. As the range of federal activities expanded, communities previously too cautious or too conservative to get involved began to feel pressure to bring in federal money. Since they entered the game later, these communities perceived themselves as at a disadvantage in obtaining grants. They began to complain that federal dollars were being handed out on the basis of grantsmanship rather than real needs.

It was in the context of these multiple conflicts that the concept of revenue sharing took root and flowered. Liberal economist Walter Heller, the first to set forth this concept in rigorous form, argued that the expansive and flexible nature of the federal tax base, in contrast to the relatively inflexible tax mechanisms available to state and local governments, necessitated a continuing federal role in financially aiding these governments. However, he also saw a need to give states and localities greater flexibility in setting objectives and in administering federal dollars. He felt that the continued use of categorical grants for certain basic federal purposes was necessary but he also felt that, if given extra dollars beyond this, local governments could be encouraged to demonstrate creativity in meeting local needs (Reagan, 1972).

This idea received increasing attention throughout the 1960s. Johnson appointed a commission to study it, but because he was basically cool to the idea, he did not even publish the commission's report, let alone try to implement its recommendation that revenue sharing be tried. Nevertheless, the bipartisan Advisory Commission on Intergovernmental Relations strongly endorsed the idea in 1967, and numerous bills embodying various versions of revenue sharing were introduced in Congress. By 1969, when Richard Nixon took office, the idea had been endorsed by the National Conference of Governors, the National Conference of Mayors, the National Conference of State Legislative Leaders, and the National Association of Counties (Reagan, 1972, p. 90).

As the above discussion suggests, revenue sharing had the potential to appeal to both liberals and conservatives, especially at the local level. However, it was generally a concept which fit more comfortably in the conservative agenda than the liberal agenda. Paul Dommel, in what is the clearest and most succinct of many treatments of the history of revenue sharing, points out that the great majority of the revenue sharing bills introduced in Congress in the late 1960s were introduced by political conservatives, and it was not until an administration that, despite its pragmatism, was basically conservative came into power in 1969 that the idea moved to the top of the policy agenda (Dommel, 1974, p. 55). In examining the way Nixon's supportive rhetoric attached revenue sharing to conservatives' focal concerns, it becomes apparent why this is the case.

There were three interrelated themes in Nixon's approach to the issue. First, echoing the long-term conservative concern with the total amount of resources going to aid disadvantaged groups, he decried as excessive the expansion of federal activity represented by categorical grants. In his August 1969 message proposing the "New Federalism" program of which revenue sharing was a part, he asserted that, ". . . a majority of Americans no longer support the continued extension of federal services. The momentum for federal expansion has passed its peak; a process of deceleration has set in."

Second, he linked revenue sharing to the attack on the competence and responsiveness of the federal bureaucracy, which was another conservative theme of his administration. Later in the 1969 speech just cited, he said that, during the five years prior to his election, "the problems of the cities and the countryside stubbornly resisted the solutions of Washington." (Reagan, 1972, p. 97), thereby suggesting that the federal bureaucracy was simply not capabale of understanding what the people really needed. During his 1972 campaign, he intensified his attack on the federal bureaucracy. In an October 1972 speech he asked, "Do we want to turn more power over to the bureaucrats in Washington in the hope that they will do what is best for all the people? Or do we want to return more power to the people and to their state and local governments, so that the people can decide what is best for themselves?" (Nixon's remarks quoted in Lilley, Clark and Iglehart, 1973, pp. 76–79; see also Nixon, 1971)

In making such statements, Nixon seemed to identify the federal government entirely with the bureaucracy, as if agencies running programs were *sui generis* rather than created by a popularly elected president and Congress. Such statements reflected Nixon's intense desire to curtail bureaucratic power, thereby reversing the liberal momentum which he and his advisors felt had been built into its structure by the two previous administrations. A study of the attitudes of federal civil servants in 1970 by Aberbach and Rockman quotes a "manual" prepared by the Nixon White House for its political appointees to various agencies: "Because of the rape of the career service by the Kennedy and Johnson Administrations this Administration has been left a legacy of finding disloyalty and obstruction at high levels while those incumbents rest comfortably on career civil service status." (Aberbach and Rockman, 1976, p. 456). The study goes on to show that Nixon's image of career civil servants as much more liberal than himself was essentially accurate, especially for those in social service departments such as HUD and HEW.

Third, he linked revenue sharing to a shift in power within lower levels of government, especially at the local level. Revenue sharing would not only reduce the influence of federal agencies over localities; it would also reduce the influence of local agencies with direct ties to federal agencies and enhance the influence of local elected officials. Early in Nixon's first term, Daniel Patrick Moynihan voiced the administraton's criticism of what he called "para-governments"; i.e., nonprofit organizations set up outside the local political structure to receive federal funds directly. In his view, the top elected officials at each level of government should be the ones to set local priorities and disburse federal funds (Lilley, Clark, and Iglehart, 1973).

It was within this general ideological framework that Nixon began, in the latter half of his first term, to develop his specific proposals for revenue sharing. However, these proposals also showed the pragmatic orientation of his administration, in that they were designed to attract the broadest possible range of support. To do this, he proposed two basic types of revenue sharing; general revenue sharing, in which a virtually unrestricted grant would be dispersed to state and local governments; and special revenue sharing, or block grants, in which groups of related categorical programs would be replaced by grants covering broad functional areas, within which state and local governments could allocate funds to the programs they felt could best serve the overall function. The six functional areas selected for block grants by Nixon were health, education, police, manpower, medical care, transportation, and community development (Clark, Iglehart, and Lilley, 1972, p. 1927). The general revenue sharing proposal was expected to appeal to liberals in that it was extra money on top of the categorical programs, as in Heller's original proposal. The block grants went to the heart of Nixon's attempt to curb federal influence in that they actually replaced existing programs.

Not surprisingly, the general revenue sharing proposal had a much easier time in Congress than the grant consolidation measures, even though Wilbur Mills, the powerful chair of the House Ways and Means Committee, led the opposition to it. In his view, revenue sharing led to a loss of accountability, on both the federal and the local level. On the one hand, the federal government was simply handing over billions of dollars to the states and localities without any controls over the way it was to be spent. On the other hand, state and local governments were spending funds which they had not taxed their own citizens to obtain, thereby giving them less incentive to spend it wisely. Mills delayed the legislation for a significant period of time, but, under intense pressure from the White House and from others in Congress, he eventually agreed to report it. The State and Local Fiscal Assistance Act became law early in 1972, with Nixon adding a heavy dose of symbolism by signing it in front of Independence Hall in Philadelphia (Reagan, 1972).

When the special revenue sharing proposals began to be considered by Congress, the opposition was much stronger, and this time the debate focused more directly on who would benefit and who would lose. Many proponents of aid to the disadvantaged felt that the poor and minorities would be the big losers if spending priorities were allowed to be set at the local level. Walter Hundley, head of the Seattle Model Cities program and an outspoken critic of block grants, put the opponents' argument very forcefully:

> I am convinced that the only real salvation for the disadvantaged, and for poor blacks in particular, is the direct intervention of the federal government. Local political pressures militate against giving to blacks any priority for public monies, as the federal special impact programs do now. That's why local government is not ready for the burdens which Nixon wants to give it (Clark, Iglehard, and Lilley, 1972, p. 1923).

Wilbur Cohen, former HEW Secretary under Lyndon Johnson, broadened the argument from a concern specifically with the poor and minorities to a concern about the federal government's ability to clearly and precisely set national priorities. He pointed out that targeting money for a program to deal with a specific problem, rather than lumping a variety of related programs into block grants, involves a clear federal commitment to solving that problem. It builds a constituency of persons who are concerned with that problem that would not exist for a broader area, and the federal commitment backed by dollars induces communities to become concerned that would otherwise have ignored the problem. In addition, he argued that the very specificity of categorical programs enabled faster action on social problems. "If Ehrlichman's criteria is, solve the problem slower, and maybe a little more cheaply, with more local people," Cohen said, "that's one statement of the problem. But I wouldn't state the problem that way. . . . in the kind of society we have . . . we've got a lot of social problems, and we've got to deal with them through strong, federal action." (Clark, Iglehart, and Lilley, 1972, p. 1921).

These arguments enjoyed wide support in the Democratic Congress and, bolstered by the direct interests of many organized groups in existing programs they helped to block much of what Nixon had proposed. In the areas of transportation, health, and education, where the beneficiaries of existing programs were most numerous and well organized, the block grant proposals died quickly. In law enforcement, the existing Law Enforcement Assistance Agency (LEAA) program was widely seen as providing sufficient state and local latitude. Only in manpower and community development did any legislative movement at all take place.

The reasons why community development revenue sharing made progress while other areas did not are complex, but they revolve around the nature of the constituencies surrounding these programs. Local govenment officials had, by this time, become a potent lobby in Washington, represented by a variety of organizations. Whereas other categorical grants had been funnelled through groups specializing in those issues, local chief executives had traditionally had a greater say in policies of physical development. Many had succeeded in the grantsmanship game, but many others had failed, and virtually all were attracted to the general idea of greater discretion in the handling of federal funds. Though they had fought hard since the New Deal to gain federal attention to community development needs, they were naturally attracted to the possibility of getting the money with fewer controls.

Nixon was also appealing indirectly to another constituency in proposing community development revenue sharing. This consisted of middle class residents of central cities, suburban communities, and smaller cities and towns who were little concerned or affected by the problems of the poor. The Democrats had felt it essential to appeal to the disadvantaged as well as the middle class to build a winning coalition. Nixon, on the other hand, felt he had little to lose and much to gain politically by redirecting federal dollars toward those whose definition of urban problems revolved around public works, services, and amenities for their own neighborhoods rather than aid to the poor. (See Mollenkopf, 1983, for a more complete discussion of this point) During the debate on revenue sharing, the level of public awareness of this policy change and its implications was not high, but Nixon could anticipate favorable responses when federal funds began to flow to this group.

The broad outlines of the legislative struggle over the Housing and Community Development Act of 1974, which included the CDBG program, have already been sketched in Chapter 5. However, having emphasized the housing aspects of the bill earlier, it is now necessary to review in more detail the struggle over the community development aspects of this legislation.

Although Nixon had outlined his New Federalism program in 1969, it was not until 1971, that he launched a major push for his revenue sharing package. A proposal for community development revenue sharing was made in April 1971. It included the consolidation of the urban renewal, model cities, and neighborhood facilities programs, replacement of the categorical grant application process by a statutory formula for allocating funds to each community, a reduction in federal administrative requirements, and the assignment of decision-making responsibilities to general purpose local governments instead of specialized, quasi-autonomous agencies (HUD, 1977, p. 38).

This proposal made no progress in the House or the Senate during 1971 or 1972. Instead, the housing subcommittees of both chambers each drafted their own legislation, retaining much more of the federal oversight which had characterized the categorical programs. The Senate approved the bill written by its subcommittee, but the House version was blocked by the Rules Committee and did not reach the floor before adjournment.

The battle was resumed in 1973, with a new Congress and a newly reelected president. After having shown his determination by declaring the Moratorium on housing programs in January, Nixon introduced another proposal in March—the Better Communities Act. This new measure contained modifications designed to answer some of the objections raised in Congress. It included three more programs in the block grant—open spaces, water and sewer grants, and public facilities loans—but it contained a "hold harmless" provision to protect the funding levels of communities already receiving large amounts of aid. Nevertheless, this bill was again stalled for most of 1973.

One reason for the delay, according to Nathan, was the Moratorium itself. As noted in Chapter 5, Nixon had instituted it, in part, to pressure Congress into action on housing and community development issues. In the long run, this strategy proved effective. However, in the short run, many pro-housing legislators did not want to approve a major initiative in the community development area without some positive housing action on Nixon's part. Therefore, they waited until the fall of 1973, when Nixon put his housing proposal on the table, before they were willing to move on the block grant proposal. Thus, the close relationship between housing and community development measures which had characterized the debates of the 1940s reasserted itself in the 1970s. Supported by slightly different coalitions, they needed to be combined into the same legislation in order to command sufficient support for congressional and presidential approval (HUD, 1977, p. 36).

The other reason why community development legislation was delayed was the need to work out multiple disagreements concerning the provisions of the new CDBG program itself. Seeing that some kind of block grant was inevitable, those who had supported categorical programs shifted their strategy to working for as limited and controlled a block grant program as they could obtain. They were eventually able to exact compromises on most of the major points Nixon had originally outlined in his 1971 proposal.

The most bitter struggle occured over the allocation of funds among localities by formula rather than through competitive applications. This proposal was central to the redistributive impact of the measure, since almost any standard formula based on quantifiable characteristics of cities would take money away from communities which had been most active and successful at grantsmanship and give it to those which had been less involved. Critics of the "formula entitlement," as it was called, raised three basic objections.

First, the underlying concept of a formula distribution system was attacked as unfair. The Senate's housing subcommittee concluded that, due to the complexity and variety of urban problems, *no* formula could accurately determine whether one city had a greater need for community development funds than another (Magida, 1974, p. 1372). Backed by most of the housing and urban development interest groups, the Senate did not include such a formula in its version of the measure, and only reluctantly agreed to the use of a formula in conference committee. The formula which was approved utilized population, number of overcrowded housing units, and the amount of poverty, with the last factor weighted twice.

Second, criticism was directed at the type of data used to rate communities according to the formula. The accuracy of its principal data source, the U.S. Census, had already been questioned in connection with general revenue sharing, and the prospect of millions more dollars riding on population and poverty counts added new heat to the controversy. The main criticism was that the Census systematically undercounted blacks and other urban minorities, a point supported by the Census Bureau's own admission that it had undercounted blacks by 7.7 percent in 1970, in contrast to a 1.9 percent undercount for whites (Magida, 1974, p. 1373). Critics also pointed out that inaccuracies would occur due to the ten year time lag between censuses. In response, Representative Thomas Ashley, (Dem., Ohio), a long time housing advocate, supported the data used and said of the formula's critics, "The formula will be practical and feasible. Those complaining about the lack of subjectivity are those who have had grants far in excess of equity and more than they can use." (Quoted in Magida, 1974, p. 1373). Evidently, a majority of Congress agreed, for these objections did not block passage of the formula entitlement.

Third, protests were raised about the immediate impact of conversion to the formula on cities currenlty enjoying much higher levels of funding under categorical programs. Such communities, which tended to be larger, older urban areas, were, of course, unhappy about the whole formula idea, but they were especially dismayed by the prospect of a *sudden* drop in funding. This, they argued, would result in administrative chaos and numerous unfinished projects. Therefore, once having resigned themselves to the formula, they concentrated on strengthening the hold harmless provision that would gradually reduce funding to formula levels.

The Nixon Administration was very reluctant to provide such a cushion because of its impact on program costs, but it found a great deal of support for these communities' predicament in Congress. As a result, the final bill included a very gradual, six year phase in of the formula entitlements. During the first three years of the CDBG program, cities currently utilizing categorical grants would be allowed a hold harmless grant, calculated on the basis of their prior level of activity. During the following three years, this would be phased down by thirds, until the formula entitlement level was reached in the sixth program year.

This debate over the use of formula entitlements highlights an ironic twist taken by the struggle over local versus federal discretion in community development. One of Nixon's main criticisms of the categorical grant system was its inflexibility. He objected to the fact that both the purpose for which federal dollars could be used and the way in which funds could be applied to each purpose were specified by federal decisionmakers. However, the block grant system, while giving cities flexibility in *how* to spend the money they received, imposed a new rigidity by utilizing a predetermined, mechanistic formula to determine *how much* a community would receive. This system gave less money to those communities which had shown the most interest in community development, while it rewarded those which had shown little interest in the past. Advocates of the old system pointed out that under it, a community which contained a political coalition demanding solutions to its problems and/or activist leaders wanting to deal positively with them could respond with aggressive pursuit of federal funds in the areas it thought most vital. This was a clear indication of a *felt* need for those funds, which might be a more accurate reflection of true needs than any automatic formula.

Another major struggle surrounding the passage of CDBG concerned the degree of administrative control which would be retained by HUD. The original Nixon proposal had called for no review of locally devised community development programs — the funds would simply be passed along with no strings, as in general revenue sharing. However, this degree of delegation to local governments was unacceptable to the housing subcommittees of both the House and the Senate and to other Democratic congressional leaders as well. They wanted to maintain at least a general level of federal oversight, to insure that the money was spent for legitimate purposes. The administration held out longer on this issue than on any other and was accused of "more Watergate arrogance" for its refusal to compromise. However, as 1974 progressed, the administration showed more flexibility. The bill which finally passed required that localities submit annual applications for CDBG funds, but the HUD review process was to be much less extensive than under categorical programs. HUD was given 75 days to review each application after which it would automatically be considered approved unless objections had been raised; and HUD was only to disapprove applications on the basis that clearly impermissible or inappropriate activities had been included or that "the needs and objectives described in the plan are 'plainly inconsistent' with available facts and data." (HUD, 1977, p. 55).

Nevertheless, HUD was not left without a basis for critical review and even rejection of local applications. The 1974 Act incorporated the following broad, national objectives toward which CDBG expenditures were to be directed:

1. The elimination of slums and blight and the prevention of blighting influences and the deterioration of property and neighborhood and community facilities. . . .

2. The elimination of conditions which are detrimental to health, safety, and public welfare, through code enforcement, demolition, interim rehabilitation assistance, and related activities;

3. The conservation and expansion of the Nation's housing stock in order to provide a decent home and suitable living environment for all persons. . .

4. The expansion and improvement of the quantity and quality of community services . . . which are essential for sound community development. . . .

5. A more rational utilization of land and other natural resources and the better arrangement of residential, commercial, industrial, recreational, and other needed activity centers;

6. The reduction of the isolation of income groups within communities and geographical areas and the promotion of an increase in the diversity and vitality of neighborhoods. . . .

7. The restoration and preservation of properties of special value for historic, architectural, or aesthetic reasons. (Act summarized in HUD, 1977)

Moreover, the Act specified that the needs of low to moderate income people were to be given the highest priority in community development activities. These goals were vague enough to allow localities plenty of latitude; however, by echoing themes established in earlier housing and community development legislation continuity was maintained, and HUD was given some basis for a critical review of local programs.

Another significant administrative requirement was added by Representative Thomas Ashley, in an effort to preserve a strong linkage between community development and housing. This was the Housing Assistance Plan (HAP) mentioned in Chapter 6. This plan required that all participating jurisdictions: (1) survey the conditions of their existing housing stock; (2) determine the extent and character of present housing needs and estimate the housing needs of those persons 'expected to reside' in the jurisdiction; and, (3) establish a realistic annual goal of the amount and kind of housing assistance to be provided (HUD, 1977, p. 56). In defending this provision, Ashley argued that, "If there is anything we have learned in the last few years, it is that we cannot have sound community development without a close-tie in with housing assistance and that we cannot have effective housing programs without local governments providing . . . a healthy community environment for housing." (Quoted in HUD, 1977, pp. 55–56).

The Passage of CDBG—An Overview

The passage of the Housing and Community Development Act in August, 1974, clearly set a new direction in community development policy. The federal government would not be totally uninvolved in urban areas, as it has been before the Depression, yet, at the same time, the influence of political and administrative judgments at the national level would be reduced in favor of greater local control. The Department of Housing and Urban Development would retain a broad oversight function, as a safeguard against gross misuse of federal funds, but the detailed planning and decision making would shift to local government. Local officials had complained that the typical urban renewal application was two and one-half feet thick and took two years to process. Now they would undergo a much shorter and more streamlined review.

Yet, in another sense, the CDBG program did not represent as much a totally new direction as a restoration of relationships which had existed in earlier years of federal involvement. In spite of all the paperwork, urban renewal had, in the 1950s and early 1960s, basically underwritten projects conceived by local political and economic elites. Such normally antigovernment groups as NAREB had pushed for federal help in saving their investments in central business districts from the onslaught of suburbanization. If the literature on urban renewal is to be believed, this is essentially what urban renewal provided in its early years—a way to legally displace uses and people considered 'undesirable' in favor of improvements to the local tax base and private investment opportunities. Some of the other physical development programs added in the 1960s, such as grants for sewers and water, open space, and neighborhood facilities, also served a very broad improvement purpose with which both economic elites and middle income voters could identify.

However, as the 1960s progressed, the direction of federal involvement changed. At first it was a new program, the War on Poverty, which signalled that federal dollars would support political involvement by disadvantaged groups not previously carrying weight in local politics. This new approach, while distinct from traditional community development efforts, eventually helped to stimulate change in the community development process itself. The social services approach of Model Cities, plus changes in urban renewal which moved it toward benefitting, rather than merely displacing, the urban poor, were the products of these pressures. Simultaneously, many other categorical programs benefitting the poor burgeoned rapidly.

All of these activities were stimulated by presidential leadership that adhered to the liberal ideology more intensely than any other since the New Deal. Kennedy, Johnson, and their advisors believed that active problem solving in urban areas by the federal government was essential to system survival, for all of the social cost reasons outlined in earlier chapters. Since many political leaders and interest groups at all levels of government shared their concerns with an array of specific problems, they enjoyed considerable support for the enactment of their numerous categorical programs.

However, within the framework of the liberal thrust provided by presidential leadership, the process of program enactment was essentially incremental. In the classic pattern of U.S. governmental decision making, no one planned out in advance the cost or administrative structure required to solve all the problems of urban areas or even to solve one particular set of problems thoroughly. Kennedy and Johnson deliberately pursued this incremental strategy, because they understood that it was easier to build slightly different coalitions around specific issues than to sell a comprehensive attack on a whole range of problems. Those hostile to government intervention in general could often be persuaded to support programs dealing with a problem of sufficient personal concern.

This piecemeal accumulation of programs was politically successful in the short run, but in the long run, it left the Great Society vulnerable, once the cumulative impact of all these programs began to be felt. State and local officials who had initially welcomed federal funding began to feel frustrated and limited by the sheer multiplicity of federal goals and administrative requirements. More importantly, they began to find the direction of federal involvement increasingly troublesome. Federal agencies were pushing them toward provision of services to, and political recognition of, groups whose needs had not been reflected in the local policy process before. The paragovernments about which Moynihan complained so bitterly were making life much more complicated for local officials by increasing the number of organized groups they had to please. In short, although federal money was still seen as a useful tool for accomplishing some of their purposes, it was also increasingly seen as an obstacle to control of their political environment.

The conversion to Community Development Block Grants may, thus, be seen as a correction of the balance of power in favor of those groups who had traditionally set the direction of community development. To be sure, blacks and other disadvantaged groups would never again be as underrepresented as they had been before the 1960s. Yet, with CDBG it was anticipated that local elected officials, and the popular and elite coalitions surrounding them, would once again be firmly in control of the community development process.

The situation was further complicated by the issue of fund distribution between communities. Nixon was much more politically beholden to white, middle class suburban areas than to ethnically diverse, often working class central cities. He was also more politically beholden to the South and West than to the Northeast and North Central regions of the United States. Nixon wanted an urban aid formula which would give these areas a share of federal largesse without appearing to abandon the traditional recipients of grants. The struggle over the hold harmless provision made it apparent that many who supported the block grant concept did not support this intercity redistribution, and the issue would arise again during the implementation of the program. Nevertheless, a new, middle class constituency was written into urban aid by CDBG.

In light of these considerations, the rhetoric with which Nixon and others justified these changes cannot be taken at face value. Nixon talked a great deal about the "distortion of local priorities" which resulted from categorical grants. However, while the federal bureaucracy can often be a blunt and inflexible instrument, there is nothing *inherently* illegitimate about the national government setting priorities for all its citizens and then trying to insure that these priorities are carried out. One can, in fact, make a strong argument that is unfair to allow local political and administrative forces to fundamentally alter benefits which should be available nationally to all persons in certain categories. This distortion is only a serious problem if, like Nixon, one disagrees ideologically with the priorities set by the federal government and feels that the priorites set by local governments are likely to be better.

Nixon's rhetoric also emphasized the confusion and complexity of federal programs, as if this were some ultimate moral evil that had to be corrected at all costs. Certainly, efficiency and order are important values, but one may legitimately ask what other values should be sacrificed in order to achieve them. When the political mood of the country favors the solution of a certain set of problems, it is to be expected that a wide variety of actors will get involved, and that programs dealing with a wide variety of problems will be put forward. The resulting programs may duplicate and conflict with one another, but collectively they represent a momentum toward solving the problem which can be constructive. In a world where perfect efficiency and coordination are virtually unattainable, perhaps it is better to have government agencies tripping over each other in their eagerness to solve some important national problem than to allow the problem to be ignored.

Was the Nixon team primarily concerned with the duplication and waste in categorical programs or with the overall policy directions they represented? Based on an overview of the revenue sharing debate, the latter concern seems much more prominent. Many ways could have been devised to eliminate waste and inefficiency short of wholesale combination into block grants. Here, as in the case of housing subsidy programs, Nixon seems to have seized on the very real shortcomings of existing programs as a political weapon to bring about changes in the underlying direction of federal involvement.

The Implementation of Community Development Block Grants

In the following pages, four aspects of the implementation of the CDBG program will be examined. First, the overall impact of the program on the level of federal spending for community development will be looked at. Second, its impact on the distribution of funds between cities will be examined. Third, its impact on the distribution of funds among projects and claimants within local communities will be discussed, along with the political struggles these basic issues engendered in the late 1970s. Finally, with these more general discussions as a background, the direct impact of the CDBG program on housing in urban areas will be assessed. Particular attention will be given to the shift toward housing rehabilitation as the central strategy in urban housing improvement the CDBG program helped to engender.

The Impact of CDBG on Federal Community Development Spending

When the Housing and Community Development Act of 1974 was passed, fears were expressed by some community development advocates that the change in the structure of the program would serve as a smokescreen for a reduction in federal involvement. Certainly, Nixon had encouraged such fears by suggesting that a block grant structure would render less powerful the competitive push of national constituencies for funds directed at their special problems. However, an analysis of the impact of the program on federal spending levels shows a rather more complex picture in this regard.

Figure 12 shows the total dollar outlays for community development

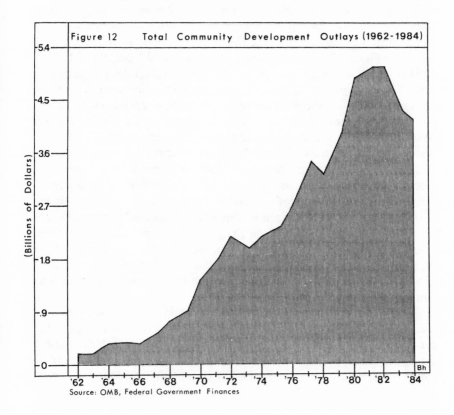

Figure 12   Total Community Development Outlays (1962-1984)

Source: OMB, Federal Government Finances

activities by the federal government in each fiscal year from 1962 to 1984, as reported by the OMB. It should be kept in mind that there is often a lag between appropriations (budget authority) and actual program outlays due to the length of time needed to execute such programs. This figure reveals a steady increase in outlays during the 1960s, followed by a rapid increase (over 100 percent) in outlays from 1969 to 1972. This increase reflects the spending initiatives of the late Johnson years and Nixon's initial reluctance to cut back in this area. The dip in expenditures during 1973 and 1974 reflects the impact of the Moratorium, and it is followed by an increase after the 1974 Act went into effect. CDBG spending leveled off in 1978, after an initial burst of activity, but outlays grew rapidly after that to a 1981 peak of over $5 billion. The sharp drop after that reflects the large Reagan cutbacks in all types of federal grants-in-aid.

This rising trend in the absolute amount of community development spending during the 1970s must, of course, be looked at in relation to inflation and in relation to total federal expenditures. Figure 13 includes both these factors by showing community development outlays as a percentage of total federal outlays during the same 22 year period.

One striking characteristic of community development expenditures shown by Figure 13 is that they have never exceeded 1 percent of federal outlays in the entire 22 year period for which the OMB has compiled data. This fact gives conservative rhetoric about the massive commitment of federal funds to urban development a slightly hollow ring. A second important fact this graph reveals is that the steady rise in absolute dollar amounts shown in Figure 12 actually represents a steady, if fluctuating, level of outlays when looked at as a proportion of total expenditures. The rapid dollar rises of the 1969–1972 period did represent a substantial proportional increase in federal community development spending, but after a peak of just over 0.9 percent in 1972, the remainder of the decade was characterized by fluctuation between 0.7 and 0.85 percent. The Moratorium caused on sharp dip, while a rapid rise in other federal expenditures not matched by community development caused the 1978 dip. Of course, Reagan's cuts after 1981 represented a large proportional as well as absolute decline in community development expenditures.

Although these data on overall federal outlays give us some idea of the level of resources committed to community development, they also conceal two other major sources of retrenchment within the block grant program. First, it should be recalled that the urban renewal program, which accounted for a major portion of community development expen-

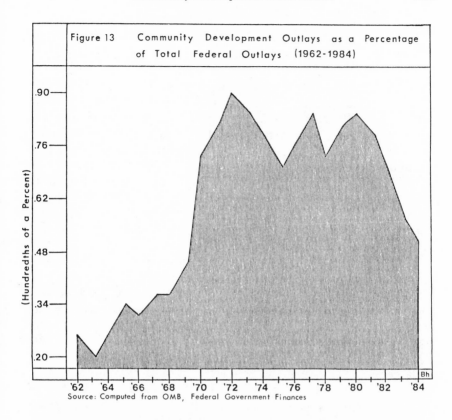

Figure 13   Community   Development   Outlays   as   a   Percentage
of Total   Federal   Outlays   (1962-1984)

Source: Computed from OMB, Federal Government Finances

ditures beforer 1974, had required a one-third matching expenditure by
localities. Under the new program, this one-third share was not required,
and communities began to spend federal funds on the very kind of
physical improvements they had previously funded themselves in order
to earn federal dollars. The precise impact of this change would require a
complex analysis beyond the scope of this book. Nevertheless, given the
size of the local commitment formerly required, it is very likely that a
noticeable shrinkage in the impact of community development expenditures occurred as a result of this change.

Secondly, retrenchment occurred as a result of the splitting of the
community development pie among a larger number of communities.
The increased levels of funding after 1974 were not directed at the same
universe of problems addressed previously. They were, rather, accomodating many new claimants while avoiding sudden cutbacks in
communities formerly using these funds. This distributional impact of
CDBG will be explored in the next section.

CDBG—Distribution Among Communities

The effects of the new CDBG program on the distribution of funds among communities were, in general, those that could have been predicted from the basic design of the program. Under the categorical programs, funds had tended to flow to the central city more than to suburban areas. Under CDBG, suburbs received more, in spite of the double weighting of the poverty factor. Under the categorical programs, the older central cities of the Northeast, North Central, and Midwest had received a disproportionate share of funds. Under CDBG there was a shift toward the South and West. Under the categorical grants, metropolitan areas (SMSAs) had received almost all the funds. Under CDBG, they continued to receive the lion's share, but 20 percent of the dollars were set aside in a discretionary fund for smaller, nonmetropolitan communities.

However, analysis of these trends is made more complicated by the fact that additional political struggles took place during the period of implementation resulting in significant midcourse changes in direction. Therefore, it is necessary to look at the original direction the program would have taken, in contrast to the direction it actually took and in contrast to the direction taken by the categorical grants it replaced.

For the first two years of the program's implementation, its impact on large central cities that had been active in categorical programs was muted by the hold harmless provision. The total amount of federal community development funds was increased by Congress, and these larger cities shared the increment with metropolitan and nonmetropolitan areas not previously active, but since their individual funding levels were not reduced, this was only mildly troublesome. However, as the full implementation of the system of formula entitlements loomed closer, its rather substantial redistributional impact became more apparent. The first two columns of Table 8 contrast what various jurisdictions received under the categorical system (as reflected in their hold harmless share) with what they would have received had the CDBG allocation system originally passed in 1974 gone into effect.

These data reveal the precipitous decline which would have occurred in the share of funding received by central cities in SMSAs had the original formula taken full effect in the sixth year of the program, fiscal 1980. Funds would have been redistributed from these traditional beneficiaries of categorical grants to virtually every other type of jurisdiction. In spite of the protection which was supposed to be afforded to large urban areas by the double weighting of the poverty factor in

TABLE 8

CDBG DOLLAR SHARES BY TYPE OF RECIPIENT

Type of Recipient	Hold Harmless Allocation (Based on Categorical Programs)	Original Formula Allocation 1974 Act	Dual Formula Allocation 1977 Act
SMSA Total	87.5%	80.0%	81.3%
Entitlement Jurisdictions	74.0	48.0	62.5
Central Cities	69.6	42.4	55.5
Satellite Cities	4.4	5.6	7.0
Urban Counties	–	11.0	12.0
Non-Entitlement Jurisdictions	–	21.0	6.8
Non-SMSA Jurisdictions	12.5	20.0	18.7

Source: HUD, *City Need and Community Development Funding,* 1979.

the formula, many of these areas would have seen massive amounts of funds flowing from their projects into the relatively prosperous suburban communities surrounding them.

It also became apparent that a regional redistribution of funds would occur as a result of full implementation of the 1974 formula. Figure 14 shows projections made by the Brookings Institution's first year CDBG evaluation as to the regional impact of the change. It shows the percentage of funds received by each of the nine U.S. Census subregions under the categorical programs, in contrast to the percentage they would have received under full implementation of the 1974 formula. It also shows per capita expenditures as a proportion of the national average both before and after the change.

As may be seen from this map, the New England, Middle Atlantic and North Central regions would have lost from one-fourth to one-half of their funds and would have dropped from relatively high per capita expenditures to levels well below the national average. In contrast much of the South and West would have gained in their share of funds and in per capita expenditures.

The Brookings study went on to show that the cumulative result of

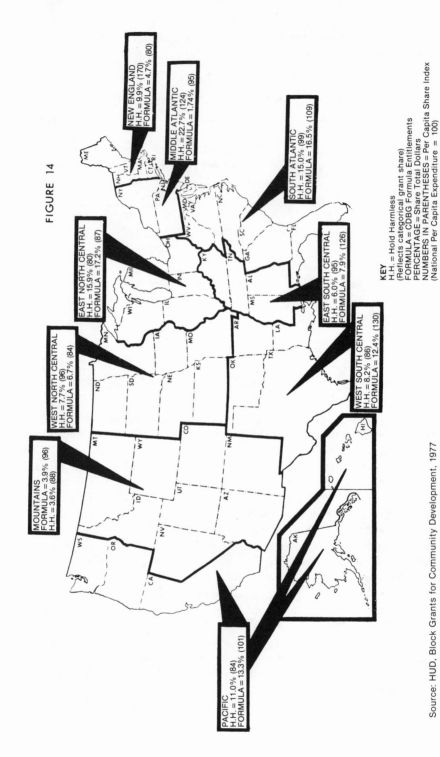

FIGURE 14

NEW ENGLAND
H.H. = 9.9% (170)
FORMULA = 4.7% (80)

MIDDLE ATLANTIC
H.H. = 22.7% (124)
FORMULA = 1.74% (95)

SOUTH ATLANTIC
H.H. = 15.0% (99)
FORMULA = 16.5% (109)

EAST NORTH CENTRAL
H.H. = 15.9% (80)
FORMULA = 17.2% (87)

EAST SOUTH CENTRAL
H.H. = 6.0% (95)
FORMULA = 7.9% (126)

WEST NORTH CENTRAL
H.H. = 7.7% (96)
FORMULA = 6.7% (84)

WEST SOUTH CENTRAL
H.H. = 8.2% (86)
FORMULA = 12.4% (130)

MOUNTAINS
FORMULA = 3.9% (96)
H.H. = 3.6% (88)

PACIFIC
H.H. = 11.0% (84)
FORMULA = 13.3% (101)

KEY
H.H. = Hold Harmless
(Reflects categorical grant share)
FORMULA = CDBG Formula Entitlements
PERCENTAGE = Share Total Dollars
NUMBERS IN PARENTHESES = Per Capita Share Index
(National Per Capita Expenditure = 100)

Source: HUD, Block Grants for Community Development, 1977

both redistributions would have been a drastic loss of funds by some of the most distressed cities in the United States. They constructed an index of the degree of economic disparity between central cities and their suburbs, and they found that the cities which measured highest on this index were some of the biggest losers of funds. Based on their findings, the Brookings evaluation team recommended a new formula to reduce the flow of funds away from the most socially and economically distressed areas. The two indicators they found to be most closely correlated with distress were the age of a city's housing stock and the extent of population decline. They suggested, therefore, that these factors be included in a new distribution formula, in lieu of the overcrowded housing factor previously used. However, to prevent the change from too drastically reducing the newer cities' share, they suggested that, instead of substituting the new formula for the old, a dual formula system be adopted, in which each city would get the larger of the two amounts computed with both formulas. Under increasing pressure from the representatives of larger urban areas, the Ford Administration recommended the adoption of this dual formula method in its lame duck budget message of January 1977.

Jimmy Carter had reason to be even more enthusiastic about the dual formula idea than Ford, since the traditional Democratic urban coalition had contributed greatly to his election. Therefore, the Carter Administration retained the idea in the legislative proposal which was to become the Housing and Community Development Act of 1977, and it expanded its impact by substituting a measure of growth lag for population loss. This meant that cities experiencing growth rates lower than the national average would receive increased funding, as well as those cities actually losing population.

In spite of the fact that the dual formula did not directly cut the funding of any entitlement city, the measure precipitated an intense debate in the House, which divided its members along regional lines. Representatives from the South and West denounced the age of housing factor as arbitrary discrimination against the more recently settled parts of the country. As Representative Jerry Patterson (Dem., California) succinctly put it, "The real issue here is: Do we want to address poverty or do we want to address old houses?" (Quoted in HUD, 1978, p. 24). Northeastern and Midwestern representatives argued, on the other hand, that the poverty factor alone would not prevent the rapidly growing Sunbelt cities from receiving funds that were needed much more desperately by the declining cities of the Frostbelt. In the end, the dual formula survived an attempt to delete it from the law by a vote of 261 to 149. Congresspersons from the East voted 110 to 1 in favor of the dual formula and members from the Midwest supported it by a 105 to 7 margin. Those from the South and West voted to delete the dual formula 132 to 18 (HUD, 1978, p. 25).

The impact of the new formula is clearly shown in the third column of Table 8. Under it, entitlement cities retained a 62.5 percent share of CDBG funds, substantially less than their share under the categorical grants but a marked improvement over their share under the original 1974 formula. Most of this gain was allocated to central cities, at the expense of the smaller, suburban communities. The regional distribution was also affected, in that the Northeast and North Central regions regained some of the share of funds they had claimed under the categorical grants.

In addition to the formula change, the Carter Administration successfully initiated in 1977 a new program designed to further correct the shift of funds away from the older, more distressed cities. This was the Urban Development Action Grant (UDAG) program. This program enabled economically declining central cities to support large redevelopment projects of a commercial, industrial, or residential nature which were beyond the scope of CDBG but which would offer improvements in employment and tax base. Although the projects envisioned for UDAG were similar in purpose to many of the urban renewal projects of an earlier era, the new program reflected the caution of the 1970s in that it required the *prior* commitment of investment funds by private firms in an amount 5 or 6 times that of the federal investment. The program reflected a renewed interest in leveraging private central city investment through direct cash subsidies, low interest loans, or public financing of land assembly or public improvements needed to make a project economically viable. This program added $500 million per year to community development coffers during the late 1970s and early 1980s.

The political struggle over the CDBG formula in the late 1970s showed the ability of representaives of the older, larger urban areas in general and of the central cities in particular to mount effective political pressure and to recoup at least part of their losses from the 1974 Act. The way this issue emerged and was dealt with illustrates once again the complexity of community development issues in political and ideological terms. In one sense, aid to declining urban areas was the type of government inervention liberals tended to favor and conservatives questioned. The cumulative effect of market decisions was to favor some cities over others and, within cities, some areas over others. The conservative ideological position leans toward enhancement of or, at the least, noninterference with these trends. This outlook was reflected in the 1974 Act in that it broadened the set of legitimate targets for governmental community development aid to include the problems of better off communities as well as the declining central cities.

Yet, this redistributive pattern also triggered opposition which cut across ideological lines. Economic and political elites in many cities were negatively affected by the formula, and their loyalty to their own communities did not permit acquiescence to too drastic a reallocation of funds. Each community's power structure remained committed to its ultimate economic viability, even though national economic criteria might classify the area as declining. Thus, the formula struggle pitted region against region and central city against suburb, rather than liberal against conservative. To the extent that the poor were concentrated in declining areas, they would potentially benefit from the dual formula; but, their actual level of benefits would depend more on another struggle — the struggle over the use of funds within urban areas.

CDBG — Distribution Within Communities

The guidelines established by Congress and by HUD for CDBG gave local officials something less than *carte blanche* in guiding the flow of federal dollars, yet their control over the planning and execution of specific projects increased substantially. As a result, each city had to create its own mechanism for planning programs and allocating funds. According to the 1978 Brookings evalution (HUD, 1978a), most of these new mechanisms reflected the desire of local chief executives for more direct involvement than before. During the first two years, many cities spent CDBG funds to finish out existing urban renewal and model cities commitments. This tended to perpetuate the influence of existing agencies and to maintain the direction they had set. However, most chief executives tried to place the administration of CDBG much closer to their own office. Some urban renewal agencies were abolished and some had their staffs absorbed by new community development offices headed by a deputy to the mayor or city manager. Others remained intact but now had to deal directly with city, rather than federal, officials.

In addition to the more extensive involvement of local chief executives, the Brookings study notes the importance of citizen involvement. HUD required as a minimum that public hearings be held to inform local citizens of the availability of the money, but most communities went beyond this and created citizen advisory boards, representing both community leaders and people in targeted neighborhoods. The term *advisory* is important, since most executives maintained ultimate control over the program, yet these groups did provide a means by which the needs of various neighborhoods could be heard and weighed.

Citizens' groups tended to gain influence as the program moved into its later years of implementation. During the first year, plans were drawn up quickly by mayoral or agency staffs to meet tight HUD deadlines. Moreover, local citizens knew very little about the program or the flexibility it provided to local officials. As the application procedure became more routinized and as more community groups became aware of the relatively unrestricted funds it provided, the number of demands for a share of the pot increased. At this point, the new participatory mechanisms became one means of resolving conflicting citizen pressures. In addition, members of local legislative bodies became more active in reviewing individual projects as the programs progressed. They, too, saw the block grant as a source of funding for projects of importance to their districts.

Both increased chief executive involvement and increased citizen involvement encouraged the spreading effect in the use of funds which many had predicted at the program's inception. Mayors, city managers, and councils were generally anxious to please as many local constituencies as possible with this new source of funds. Categorical program guidelines might have enabled or compelled them to concentrate millions of dollars in a single urban renewal or model cities area. Now, with some of these constraints removed, their attention turned to projects benefitting the entire community or to smaller scale projects which enabled them to spread funds among many neighborhoods.

This spreading effect led to two major conflicts between HUD and local officials — the conflict over socioeconomic targeting and the conflict over geographic targeting. With regard to socioeconomic targeting, the 1974 Act specified that "maximum feasible priority" be given to low and moderate income persons in utilizing block grant funds. Since "maximum feasible priority" was as vague a term as "maximum feasible participation" had been in the War on Poverty, this was a rather flexible guideline. Yet, in spite of a few well-publicized cases of suburban golf courses or tennis courts being built with CDBG funds, there was no wholesale abandonment of community development activities in lower income areas. What concerned HUD officials, and a number of liberal interest groups, was that a slow drift of funds from low income projects to city wide projects or to projects benefitting prosperous areas would occur. HUD saw its role as one of preserving the original legislative intent by insisting on continued concentration of effort in low to moderate income areas, while local officials felt that the flexibility accorded them by the 1974 Act was being negated by HUD's regulatory efforts.

Although HUD officials tended to take this position from the inception of the program, their resolve to push communities in this direction was strengthened by the appointment of Patricia Roberts Harris as HUD Secretary by Jimmy Carter in 1977. In testimony before the House Subcommittee on Housing and Community Development just after the appointment she said, "We will expect communities to direct development and housing programs toward low and moderate income citizens. I do not consider this to be just *an* objective of the block grant program—it is the highest priority of the program and we in the federal government must see to it that the thrust of the program serves that objective." (Quoted in Dommel, 1980, p. 466). HUD proceeded to give concrete expression to this point of view by proposing regulations which would have required that 75 percent of all CDBG funds be used to directly benefit low and moderate income persons, while 25 percent could go to other projects.

This proposal met stiff opposition from Representative Thomas Ashley and other community development specialists who felt that aid to the poor was only one of several important goals of the 1974 Act. After some intense verbal sparring during late 1977 and early 1978, HUD issued final regulations on the subject which acceded to congressional pressure and allowed localities more flexibility than the rigid 75 percent to 25 percent ratio. However, the department continued to push localities to spend as much of their grant on low and moderate income areas as possible, and the Brookings evaluation team concluded that they were partially successful. In the cities sampled by Brookings, spending directed at low to moderate income persons increased from 54 percent to 62 percent of total expenditures over the first four years of CDBG (Dommel, 1980, p. 469).

HUD also stressed a second form of targeting—geographical—which ran counter to the local spreading of funds. Federal officials tended to believe that sound community development strategy involved the concentration of funds and activities in well-defined areas, rather than the spending of funds on a communitywide basis. They felt such concentration would make the effects of various programs mutually reinforcing, and that permanent improvement in neighborhood conditions, rather than a series of piecemeal solutions to immediate problems, would be more likely to result. In pursuit of this goal, which of course was similar to that of Model Cities and the War on Poverty, they pushed localities to concentrate programs in specific census tracts and even disapproved some applications on the grounds that activities such as housing rehabilitation were too widely dispersed. This concern overlapped with their concern with socioeconomic targeting, since it was in lower income areas that, in their view, intensive activity should take place.

The HUD push for geographic targeting culminated in a series of new regulations in 1977 and 1978 which gave formal designation to areas of concentrated activities—Neighborhood Strategy Areas (NSA). Communities were required to show that these areas were mainly residential and that enough resources were being committed to meet major community development needs. Communities were pressured to designate areas as NSA and to shift resources into them for city-wide projects (HUD, 1981a).

The reaction of local officials was somewhat skeptical. The Brookings team quotes one local official's comment that, "If HUD wants to play NSA, we'll play NSA." (HUD, 1981a, p. 91). However, the Brookings evaluators found that, in their sample of participating communities, there had been a noticeable shift toward neighborhood targeting. In the fourth and fifth program years, benefits were more concentrated in fewer census tracts, and the boundaries of target areas tended to contain fewer people than in earlier years. Interestingly enough, it was the cities with the worst social and economic problems that had the least geographic targeting, while economically advantaged communities targeted more. This suggests that even scattered projects were directed at serious needs rather than dissipated on nonessential services (HUD, 1981a).

Table 9 summarizes the activities proposed in CDBG applications received by HUD for fiscal years 1979–1981. These are plans, not actual expenditures, but they indicate the direction in which the program had moved.

Public works, redevelopment activities, and related public services stand out in these data as major activities. However, the most striking feature of this table is the large concentration of funds in the area of housing rehabilitation, which represented about one-third of CDBG expenditures in FY 1979 and grew to 40 percent in FY 1981. These data suggest that the importance of housing as a community development goal had increased greatly as a result of the shift to CDBG, continuing the trend noticeable in the urban renewal program during the early 1970s. The reasons for this lie in broad changes in concepts of proper housing strategy which took place in the 1970s. They also lie in the political dynamics of CDBG program implementation just described. Both these aspects of the growth of housing rehabilitation as a community develop-

TABLE 9

PLANNED USES OF CDBG FUNDS: 1979–1981

Type of Activity	1979	*Fiscal Year* 1980	1981
Redevelopment	17.9	15.9	14.6
Housing			
Code Enforcement	2.7	2.4	2.6
Rehabilitation of Public Residential Structures	6.8	4.4	5.9
Public Housing Modernization	1.5	1.4	1.4
Rehabilitation of Private Structures	23.1	28.8	31.3
Subtotal	34.1	37.0	40.2
Parks and Recreation	4.9	4.1	3.4
Public Works	20.4	20.4	19.6
Public Facilities			
Senior centers	0.8	0.7	0.5
Handicapped centers	0.4	0.4	0.4
Neighborhood centers	3.3	3.5	2.4
Subtotal	4.5	4.6	3.3
Economic Development	4.5	5.9	6.2
Public Services	9.7	9.0	9.2
Other	4.0	3.1	3.5
TOTAL	100.0	100.0	100.0

Source: HUD, *Community Development Block Grant Report*, 1982a.

ment strategy will be explored in the context of the overall impact of CDBG on housing policy.

Community Development Block Grants and Housing Policy

The close political linkage between housing and community development which had existed since the 1940s and which reemerged in the passage of the 1974 Act has already been discussed. In this section, the implementation linkages between the two will be explored. A general link may be found in the use of CDBG funds to provide physical improvements in neighborhoods which would enhance the residents' total environment. Since the neighborhood is part of the housing package a family purchases, improvements in the area can enhance the quality and value of their housing. For both budgetary and political reasons, communities tended to do much less clearance under CDBG than under the urban renewal program. Thus, physical development could be directed at supporting the viability of existing neighborhoods.

In addition to this general link, there existed two more specific ways in which the CDBG program shaped the direction of housing policy. One was the incorporation of the Housing Assistance Plan (HAP) into the CDBG application. The other, alluded to above, was the extensive development of housing rehabilitation programs as a major object of CDBG expenditures. Each of these relationships deserves further exploration.

The Housing Assistance Plan

As was discussed earlier, the 1974 Act required each locality to submit a Housing Assistance Plan as part of its CDBG application, which was to be followed by HUD in allocating units of federally assisted housing to that community. The immediate impact of this requirement was to strongly encourage communities to be conscious of housing needs when planning their CDBG strategies and to compel them to collect more detailed information on their housing stock. The data they gathered varied in quality. Some communities hired consultants to carry out sophisticated surveys of housing needs. Others merely manipulated 1970 census data to produce numbers they hoped HUD would find plausible. Yet, Raymond Struyk suggests that regardless of variations in the accuracy of the data collected, the HAP had a positive impact on the level of awareness of local political leaders concerning housing needs, since it had to be debated and approved along with the rest of the CDBG application (Struyk, 1979).

At the same time, the HAP process demonstrated the complexity and difficulty of federal-local relationships in such a situation. Although the HAP was designed to make the planning of housing needs a local activity, HUD was required to monitor and assess the reasonableness of local plans. In order to carry out this role, HUD Area Offices obtained their own, independent data the housing stock of the communities in their jurisdiction. This led local officials to complain that area offices often attached little credibility to local data and, instead, insisted on substituting their own figures. An internal HUD memorandum reporting on a meeting with local officials stated that: "Most respondents said that they take what the Area Office gives them. First you submit a set of numbers and 'then you play games'; you put down the bottom numbers and the Area Office divides them up." (Quoted in Struyk, 1979, p. 14).

Two other factors which detracted from the full utilization of the HAP as a planning tool should also be mentioned. First, the state housing agencies had their own allocations of units which were not included in the HAP and which could greatly affect the program mix in some locations. Second, the numbers of units actually available under congressional appropriations were usually only a small percentage of any community's total need. Therefore, there was a tendency not to take the total need figures seriously, since the actual units built would never come near that level.

Nevertheless, Struyk concluded that the HAP's apparent enhancement of local housing planning was a good reason for continuing to require it. He suggested improvements in the process, including a more strict adherence by HUD to the congressional intent of decentralization and the control of all local housing allocations by the HAP (Struyk, 1979, p. 20-22).

CDBG and Housing Rehabilitation

Throughout most of the history of U.S. housing policy, the idea of utilizing rehabilitation of existing structures as a strategy for improving the housing stock existed mostly as an afterthought. While lip service was paid to the notion that rescuing existing structures might be an economically desirable alternative to new construction, this activity was given very low priority. The financing of rehabilitation was possible under FHA's mortgage insurance program, but the number of units rehabilitated was dwarfed by the agency's massive commitment to new construction. The Housing Act of 1954 included rehabilitation as an eligible activity under the urban renewal program, but the dominant strategy was still clearance and rebuilding.

This deemphasis on rehabilitation was in keeping with the spirit of community development in the post-World War II era. The emphasis then was on the *new*—new factories, new commercial developments, and new housing in the suburbs reached by new cars on newly built freeways. Progress was measured by the degree to which open countryside could be filled with crisp, clean new dwellings equipped with the modern conveniences now within the financial range of middle class families. Central cities, therefore, tried to compete with this suburban development with sleek new office towers and other new uses of blighted areas. The idea of converting an old warehouse into shops or restaurants, which is typical of the plans which captivated urban dwellers in the 1970s, would have seemed eccentric to all but a few in the 1950s.

In the case of housing rehabilitation, the negative impact of the general cultural emphasis on the new was reinforced by some very concrete economic and administrative problems. As a planned, public activity, housing rehabilitation has been, on the whole, slower and much more difficult than new construction. There are several reasons for this.

First, mass production has proven very difficult to utilize in rehabilitation. Whereas a new development can be erected with a limited number of floor plans, and large scale purchase of materials, existing houses and neighborhoods often contain numerous variations in design and condition. Therefore, each rehabilitation job must be tailored to the needs of a specific structure and family, a process which requires considerable administrative, as well as construction time, and which discourages economies of scale. Moreover, the economic structure of the housing rehabilitation industry reflects its technical characteristics, in that firms specializing in rehabilitation tend to be small operations. Agencies experimenting with large scale rehabilitation have, therefore, found it difficult to recruit private firms willing to carry out their plans (see the National Commission on Urban Problems, 1969 and Hartman, 1975 for discussions of these problems).

Second, housing rehabilitation requires a very different set of relationships between government agencies and citizens than does suburban new construction or clearance of older areas. During the first 15 years of the urban renewal program, agencies bent on clearance and armed with the power of eminent domain could relatively easily overcome neighborhood resistance, especially when the target area's citizens were poor, inarticulate, and unorganized. The process required little cooperation from the areas affected. In contrast, rehabilitation requires such cooperation from the very beginning of the process, at both the neighborhood and the individual level.

At the neighborhood level, agencies must work with existing property owners to reverse the "prisoner's dilemma" situation described by Davis and Whinston (1966) in their classic article on the economics of urban decline. According to their model, property owners in older areas are reluctant to invest in repairs for fear that other property owners will not match their investment. Since property values in a given area are interdependent, the owner will be worse off if he/she invests while others do not than if no one invests or if others invest while he or she does not. A rehabilitation program targeted at a specific neighborhood must, therefore, engage in extensive and time-consuming neighborhood organization (or work to strengthen existing organizations) in order to create a psychological atmosphere in which individual property owners are convinced that their investment will pay off. Various forms of coercion (such as the ability to condemn property that does not comply with certain standards) may be used to back up persuasion, but if they are not used extremely sparingly, they will enhance, rather than weaken, resistance.

Cooperation must also be secured from individual property owners during the rehabilitation process. In order to encourage participation in the program, the property owner must be allowed some choice as to the type of work to be done on his/her property. This requires negotiations between the owner and the agency, and it may also require the inclusion of certain visible amenities the property owner can enjoy, as well as basic (but less visible) structural repairs, such as new plumbing and heat. This may lengthen the process and increase the cost of each dwelling.

It is not, of course, absolutely necessary to utilize existing property owners as the vehicles for rehabilitation. Several federal programs have purchased and rehabilitated small numbers of dwellings. However, it has, in general, been more difficult to justify politically the coerced purchase of a dwelling and the displacement of its occupants if it needs modest repairs and is in a moderately deteriorating area than if it is dilapidated and located in an area which has been labeled blighted (i.e., in need of clearance). The notion of leaving a neighborhod physically intact has seemed to fit, in the minds of most policymakers, with the utilization of existing owners, although displacement through various forms of rehabilitation has also occurred.

In addition to the technical problems of construction and the sociopolitical problems of securing neighborhood cooperation, rehabilitation has also encountered a third set of problems—those associated with finances. Rehabilitation of existing structures in older, declining areas is at best a risky venture, as evidenced by the higher foreclosure rates among Section 236 and Section 221(d)(3) rehabilitation units than among newly constructed units. Unless the area in which the structure is located is substantially upgraded, owners often have difficulty attracting tenants at rents which will support even subsidized borrowing for rehabilitation.

Finally, rehabilitation programs have encountered opposition in some communities on ideological grounds. Though clearance has been resisted by doctrinaire conservatives, the notions of removing blight and of beneficial reuse of land have appealed to a broad political spectrum as legitimate public purposes which justify interference with private property rights. In contrast, rehabilitation of structures which remain in private hands has met resistance on dual grounds: (1) that forced inspection and rehabilitation violates the property rights of landlords and homeowners; or, (2) that direct subsidies to private owners which enhance the value of an asset they hold represent an unfair benefit to a few owners at the expense of others. The first attitude has shown up in the rulings of local judges, who are extremely reluctant to convict or punish landlords for code violations. According to Chester Hartman, "Few judges take housing violations as seriously as they take other types of cases, nor do they have sufficient background in housing or knowledge of the particular defendant and his patterns of operation to make a sound judgement." (Hartman, 1975, p. 66). The second attitude has shown up in frequent protests by property owners in other sections of a city when a specific geographic area is designated for rehabilitation aid. This has made local officials reluctant to assist any but the lowest income owners.

None of these fundamental problems was eliminated by events of the 1970s, yet rehabilitation grew rapidly during this decade to become the most popular community development strategy. This rapid increase may be accounted for by other cultural, economic and political factors which overrode these traditional obstacles to the utilization of this strategy.

On the cultural level, the American belief that "new is better" was, if not eliminated, at least chastened by the events of the 1970s. First, the environmental movement began to bring to public consciousness the heavy costs of growth in general and new urban development in particular, in terms of air and water pollution and in terms of the loss of open space and farm land. Second, the energy shortages of the 1970s led to the growing conviction, among at least some segments of the population, that resources were finite and that the continued consumption of more fuel, more raw materials, and more land for new products might eventually lead to disaster. Both of these movements stressed the desirability of reuse and recycling of existing resources, and the reuse of existing neighborhoods and structures fell naturally within this area of interest. Also, these movements called attention to older technologies and lifestyles which were less wasteful of the envinroment and of natural resources. Mass transit, intensive urban land uses such as row houses, the passive solar heating features incorporated into older houses—all of these elements which had seemed destined for the trash heap in the early postwar decades were now more attractive and useful.

These changes also helped bring into sharper focus the social and aesthetic critique of suburbia which had always been an intellectual current in the U.S. (Daniel Elazar's 1966 article, "Are We a Nation of Cities?" gives attention to this current.) Malvina Reynolds' song about "little boxes made of ticky-tacky," whose inhabitants allegedly acted in blind conformity, had earlier expressed intellectuals' association of suburbia with middle class philistinism. (Reynolds, 1964) Now these "little boxes" could be seen as wasteful and environmentally damaging, as well as aesthetically and socially distasteful. To these aesthetic arguments, which admittedly appealed only to a few, there were added some practical economic disincentives to suburban life as well. Many suburbs were, by the 1970s, becoming increasingly congested and were suffering from some of the same problems of crime and social alienation as the central cities. Moreover, the energy costs of long commuting distances were beginning to hit the pocket books, as well as the social consciences of middle and upper middle class persons.

In this atmosphere, the 'back to the city' movement took hold and flourished among a certain segment of the middle and upper middle class. In an oft described pattern, a few middle class families would renovate older structures in neighborhoods filled with rooming houses and lower income apartments. These 'pioneers' (It is interesting to note that terms from the early frontier such as 'pioneer' and 'homesteading' brought another set of symbols to play in this process) would discover that these older houses, many of which had been built by the well-to-do of the nineteenth centry, had design and aesthetic elements not available at any reasonable price in the suburbs—large rooms, parquet floors, stained glass, carved woodwork, etc. By restoring these elements (and modifying them to modern tastes) these early renovators attracted others, with the result that the filtering process which had seemingly doomed the area was suddenly reversed. Property values rose, rental property became owner occupied, low income persons were forced to move elsewhere, and the area became, in the new terminology of the decade, *gentrified.*

Since the writers and intellectuals who shape the direction of the media and academic research were among the social stratum most involved in this process, (i.e., the urban upper middle class), the phenomenon of gentrification quickly captured much public and academic attention. Features on upper middle class couples fixing up old townhouses became a staple of Sunday newspaper supplements and national magazines. Urban policy researchers began to explore the dynamics and implications of reverse filtering. Judging from the intensity of this interest, it was easy to conclude that a major national trend was in the making.

In addition, there were some hard data which indicated a change in patterns of urban housing investment and ownership. Franklin J. James reports that the middle 1970s saw a modest increase in the proportion of central city dwellers owning their own homes and a proportionally faster increase in the value of central city housing than in suburban housing. He also reported a significant increase in the level of investment in the upgrading of existing housing, as measured by the U.S. Census's Survey of Residential Alterations and Repairs (James, 1980, pp. 131–135).

Doubts were soon raised, however, about the scope and direction of the back to the city movement by more intensive and critical demographic research. One fact that quickly became clear was that, as noted in Chapter 3, this new flow of people back to the city was really a trickle. Even the most sanguine estimates showed a relatively few families and a relatively few neighborhoods involved. Moreover, this trickle was largely counteracted by the continued exodus of other middle class families (especially white) to the suburbs. (Sternlieb, et al., 1980; Palen and London, 1984)

In addition, much of the evidence indicated that it was more a 'stay in the city' than a back to the city movement. Young single or recently married persons, a group traditionally attracted to the central city, were the main ones who chose to invest in older areas, rather than move to the suburbs, as their economic status improved. While this in itself was not an insignificant trend, it did not represent a choice of the central city over the suburbs by the middle class persons of child-rearing age who had traditionally lived in outlying areas. Also, analyses by Philip Clay and others showed that considerable reinvestment was being made by families of more modest means who already lived in the central cities (Clay, 1980). Such "incumbent upgrading" was not as likely to make the newspaper's Sunday Supplement and so did not attract as much attention as gentrification.

At the same time, it was clear that the impact of the back to the city movement was greater than could be measured by the numbers of people involved. First, the revitalization which did take place was generally spread out over highly visible and strategically located neighborhoods close to downtown. A few hundred families occupying as many units in a previously decaying section could have a major visual and psychological impact, and could turn the area into a showcase for the entire central city. Second, the fact that it was so striking a reversal of a decades-old exodus of the white middle and upper middle classes gave it a psychological significance beyond the actual numbers involved. Planners, policymakers, and other interested urban dwellers began to anticipate (and hope) that these few families might be the "thin edge of the wedge".

Finally, and most importantly for the present analysis, the back to the city movement gave added respectability and impetus to the use of housing rehabilitation as a community development strategy. Its growth coincided with an increasing desire among planners and policymakers to find a less costly and disruptive mechanism for urban revitalization than total clearance, a desire reflected in the growing use of rehabilitation in urban renewal programs prior to the 1970s (Sanders, 1980). Analyses such as Grigsby's classic study of filtering (1965) had focused attention on the long-term process of physical and social decay which turned neighborhoods into slums. These suggested that it would be less costly to intervene in the process *before* it had advanced to the point where total clearance was necessary. While neighborhoods undergoing gentrification were generally those with special architectural (and in some cases historical) appeal, the fact that private individuals could, virtually unaided, intervene in this process and turn a neighborhood around suggested that planned, public intervention might be successful in a broader range of declining urban neighborhoods.

Even though housing rehabilitation played a minimal role in federal housing programs during the 1950s and 1960s, there were a number of programs which contributed administrative models and a wealth of implementation experience to the new rehabilitation push of the 1970s. The most important of these were the Section 312 and Section 115 programs. The Housing Act of 1954 had enabled localities to utilize urban renewal funds for housing rehabilitation, but for all the reasons mentioned, it was difficult to get either public or private agencies excited about central city residential renovation. Therefore, pressure developed at the federal level for programs which would give more concrete incentives to carry out rehabilitation, particularly as the destruction of housing by urban renewal became more widespread. The Section 312 program was part of the Housing Act of 1964, while the Section 115 program was enacted a year later, but they were so closely linked in implementation as to be, in effect, one program (Hartman, 1975, p. 73). In addition to their use in urban renewal areas, localities could also use them in areas designated for concentrated code enforcement. This came to be known as the FACE (Federally Assisted Code Enforcement) program.

The Section 312 program program provided loans of up to $15,000 to property owners at 3 percent interest for 20 years. At first, this rate constituted only a small subsidy in relation to market rates, and the main benefits of the loans were: (1) that they were available in areas where private banks would not extend credit; and, (2) that they were an alternative to demolition for property owners in the path of urban renewal.

However, as private market interest rates gradually increased, the interest subsidy itself became greater and greater, until, by the late 1970s, a 3 percent loan seemed almost like free money in comparison to double-digit private rates. As an added incentive for participation, these loans could be used to refinance existing mortgages, if that were necessary to make the rehabilitation financially feasible for the property owner. Hartman notes that this sometimes made the monthly payment after rehabilitation *less* than it was before (Hartman, 1975, p. 73).

The Section 115 program made grants of up to $3500 available to property owners whose incomes were too low to support a loan of any sort, and grants of up to $3000 were available as supplements to Section 312 loans, in cases where the recipient could afford a reduced loan. The three types of aid — grants, loans, and loan/grant combinations — could thus span a fairly wide range of incomes, mostly at the lower end of the scale. The impact of these programs, measured in terms of total units upgraded, was limited during the first decade of their existence. According to HUD's 1979 Statistical Yearbook, a total of 66,045 units had been rehabilitated under Section 312 by 1974. Nevertheless, certain basic administrative patterns were set which carried over into the CDBG era.

One pattern established by Section 312 was a strong preference for loans to homeowners over loans to investor owners. This design was related both to positive perceptions of homeowners and to negative perceptions of investor owners. On the positive side, homeowners were seen as a stable, responsible element in the community, a perception similar to that which helped stimulate Section 235. To encourage owners to reinvest in their homes was to aid residents who would continue to care about the overall condition of the area in order to preserve their investment. This perception was borne out by the administrative experience of many agencies, which generally found the homeowners in each rehabilitation area the most eager to organize and to participate in the program.

On the negative side, investor owners tended to be viewed, especially on the local level, as slumlords who were undeserving of federal aid. They were often, though not always, higher income individuals residing outside the target area, and the prospect of giving them subsidized loans was not appealing, in spite of the fact that low income tenants were intended as the ultimate beneficiaries. Added to these perceptions were serious practical problems with their inclusion. Contrary to the popular stereotype of profiteering, many operated their properties on a very slim margin (Stegman, 1979). This meant that any additional financing costs were hard to sustain while maintaining a minimal return on their investment. This made investor owners reluctant to participate, to the point that some would demolish their units rather than bring them up to code, even when low interest loans were available. It also meant that their participation often led to increased rents for the improved units. Hartman, Kessler, and LeGates (1974) found that FACE programs in San Francisco and elsewhere led to considerable displacement of low income tenants, either due to demolition or to rent increases.

The targeting of these programs at homeowners influenced, in turn, the segment of the low income population served by housing rehabilitation. Deteriorating areas of rental housing in which many of the poor lived were passed over. U.S. Census data show that, in 1978, 51 percent of those with incomes under $10,000 owned their own homes. (Hays, 1982a) Though a large percentage in comparison with other industrial societies, it was still much less than the rest of the population; and homeownership was disproportionately concentrated among one type of poor person—the elderly. Many of these persons had high enough incomes during their working lives to purchase a modest home, but their fixed retirement incomes did not permit them to maintain it. In contrast, other poor families tended not to have the resources even to begin the purchase of a home, especially as home prices escalated during the 1970s.

Another characteristic of housing rehabilitation which emerged from the Section 312/115 program was the emphasis on neighborhoods with modest levels of decay, i.e., with structures in what HUD called "deteriorating" rather than "dilapidated" condition. Many dilapidated dwellings were structurally unsound or obsolete to a degree that would make any rehabilitation investment of dubious value. But, beyond this, the program's heavy reliance on a financial contribution from property owners limited the amount which could be spent on each structure. Thus, the program would only work in less seriously deteriorated areas where rehabilitation costs were affordable by residents. Such a strategy was justified as avoiding excessive per structure costs and as preventive medicine for neighborhoods that had not yet become slums. Nevertheless, it further narrowed the segment of low income persons served.

When the CDBG program was enacted, Section 115 was folded into the block grant, but Section 312 continued to be funded separately, due to its great political popularity. Therefore, rehabilitation programs using CDBG funds tended to closely parallel or to consciously supplement this older program. Grant programs were established to replace Section 115, and loan programs with slightly higher or lower interest rates than Section 312 were set up, in order to reach a broader segment of property owners within affected neighborhoods. Though the amount of Section 312 funds available from HUD fluctuated greatly during the 1970s, my 1980 survey of rehabilitation programs in a national sample of 154 communities revealed that it was still the single largest source of funds for these localities. (Hays, 1982b)

One significant way in which CDBG programs did differ from earlier efforts was in their greater emphasis on the *leveraging* of private loan funds through the use of limited CDBG subsidies. In most such arrangements, a local bank would make the loan at the market interest rate, while CDBG funds would be used either as a grant to lower the principal or as an interest subsidy. The public agency might further protect and subsidize the private lender by depositing public funds at low interest rates, as security against defaults. This arrangement was advantageous to the public sector because the total number of units served was greater than if CDBG funds were loaned out directly. It was also advantageous to private lenders who had come under increasing pressure during 1970s to make more credit available in lower income, central city, and minority areas. Neighborhood groups were increasingly critical of redlining, and Congress attempted to limit this practice by requiring financial institutions to publicly report loans made by geographic area. Cooperation in a CDBG program was one way in which they could increase their lending in central city areas, with some protection from risk (see Agelasto and Listokin, 1975, for a careful examination of this issue).

In spite of such changes, the basic direction and impact, as well as the structure, of the CDBG loan programs remained very similar to that of Section 312 and Section 115. Most communities kept their upper income limits low, so as to keep the program targeted at lower income groups. However, they also continued to exclude, or give lower priority to, investor owners, and they targeted neighborhoods with only modest levels of decay. Thus, these programs still served only a narrow segment of the low income population.

CDBG Politics and Housing Rehabilitation

Having shown how long-term cultural, economic, and political trends encouraged a new emphasis on housing rehabilitation in the 1970s, it is now necessary to highlight the relationship between this particular community development strategy and the political dynamics of CDBG implementation. There are a number of reasons why housing rehabilitation appealed so strongly to CDBG decisionmakers in so many localities. One was, of course, steadily increasing federal pressure to utilize such a strategy. The 1974 Act allowed rehabilitation only as a supplement to other activities, but this limitation was dropped in the 1977

Act, and such activity was strongly encouraged by HUD. However, there were also strong elements within local political arenas which pushed CDBG policy in this direction.

First, cities traditionally active in urban renewal were generally receiving less money than before and, therefore, could not afford the massive investment in acquisition, relocation, and demolition required by further clearance projects. In Richmond, Virginia, for example, the Housing Authority spent over $30 million in federal and local funds over a ten year period in a single urban renewal project. In contrast, the city's entire hold harmless allocation was approximately $10 million for each of the first three years of CDBG, and it dropped to $4.5 million in 1980, when the formula allocation took full effect. Housing rehabilitation was attractive to that city because it promised to make a substantial impact in many more neighborhoods with the more limited funds available.

Second, housing rehabilitation fit the need of localities to spread out the dollars among a larger number of claimants. Whereas clearance lent itself to concentrated efforts in the worst neighborhoods, rehabilitation lent itself to more modest efforts in several, less deteriorated neighborhoods. The fact that numerous, well organized neighborhood groups existed in many localities also enhanced the normal desire of local political leaders to please as many citizens as possible with a given expenditure of funds. Many cities made housing rehabilitation loans available on a city wide basis, but HUD's pressure for geographic targeting discouraged this. Therefore, the more common pattern was to select a few declining areas and to combine rehabilitation loans and grants with modest public improvements so as to provide at least the image of a long term commitment to the upgrading of those neighborhoods. In this way, the demands of groups whose needs had been neglected in the past could be satisfied.

Interestingly enough, there is little evidence of direct support for gentrification by CDBG loan and grant programs. While the income ceilings on these programs generally included moderate, as well as low income recipients, these ceilings were too low to permit aid to upper middle class renovators. One federal program, urban homesteading, was established separately from CDBG by the 1974 Act. Under it, repossessed FHA houses were sold to new owners at a nominal cost in exchange for a substantial investment in rehabilitation on their part. (Hughes and Bleakly, 1975) The high cost of rehabilitating these structures limited this program mainly to middle and upper middle income families, but, while CDBG funds were used to defray urban homesteading costs in some areas, this was not a major form of rehabilitation activity. CDBG programs, to the extent that they did aid those returning to or remaining in the city, gave assistance mainly to those more modest areas in which incumbent upgrading was taking place.

In light of the excitement generated by the back to the city movement this low level of CDBG involvement might seem surprising. One might expect that communities would be eager to use funds to attract and retain higher status residents. Yet, the constituency for such support was not yet large in most communities, and the residents of most successful gentrification areas seemed to be making it on their own, without government aid or guidance. Also, local governments could have become targets for the critics of displacement by the new gentry. Such criticism became more prominent during the late 1970s, although a relatively small number of low income families were actually displaced in this fashion. (Palen and London, 1984) In sum, existing residents of modest means could put more effective pressure on city government than could the small numbers of returning gentry.

A third reason why housing rehabilitation fit into the political environment of CDBG was that it was less disruptive of existing neighborhoods and settlement patterns. Though concerns continued to be raised about displacement, this strategy was, for obvious reasons, less likely than earlier strategies to cause massive dislocation. Unlike clearance, rehabilitation did not portend a direct transfer of the use of a geographical area from one group to another. This was appealing to communities which had not previously had extensive community development activities and where housing problems were not severe enough to create pressure for clearance. It was also appealing to previously active cities which were encountering increased neighborhood resistance to massive change. The negotiation and cooperation involved in rehabilitation fit better within a political environment containing many organized constituencies than did earlier slum removal strategies.

Finally, one can discern a compatibility between housing rehabilitation and the generally lowered expectations about federal involvement in urban problems which charactertized the 1970s. In the 1950s and 1960s, liberal reformers and many conservative business interests as well hoped that federal dollars could be used to transform their decaying central cities into new, more hospitable environments. Urban renewal succeeded in transforming parts of the central city in the desired directions but with dollar costs which seemed high in relation to the objectives achieved, and with the added human costs of the destruction of low income neighborhoods. In contrast, housing rehabilitation promised steady, rather than dramatic, improvements, and it concentrated on delivering physical improvements as a service to property owners already in place. As such, it was a gentler form of government intervention but also one containing lower expectations for radical change in the urban environment.

Housing and Community Development Under CDBG — An Overview

In this chapter and Chapter 7, a rather ambivalent relationship between housing policy and community development policy has been revealed. In a number of important respects the two have been closely interdependent. In terms of its actual impact, housing is undeniably an important aspect of the community development process. It is hard to imagine any other single factor which has a greater effect on the appearance and liveability of a community than the condition of its housing stock. In political terms, those legislators and interest groups mainly concerned with housing have found it necessary to band together with those whose main concern was other types of community development in order to push through crucial pieces of legislation such as the Housing Act of 1949 and the Housing and Community Development Act of 1974.

Yet, in other respects, the thrust toward community development and the thrust toward housing improvement have worked at cross purposes. Economic and political elites pushing for major physical changes in their communities have been concerned mainly with economic development and civic pride. Housing, especialy for those on the lower end of the economic scale, has been at best an afterthought and at worst an end to be sacrificed to the goal of overall civic betterment. Urban renewal, the centerpiece of community development policy for many years, was first proposed by NAREB, a group unalterably opposed to any public sector role in providing low income housing; and, true to the thrust of NAREB's initial proposals, urban renewal destroyed more housing than it erected during its first 15 years. Only under intense pressure from those negatively affected did urban renewal begin to evolve into a program which could contribute to, rather than detract from, the housing quality of lower income persons, and shortly after the tools were in place to make it a pro-housing effort, the program was abolished.

In light of this complex relationship, how can the housing impact of CDBG be judged? On the positive side, the upgrading of housing in low to moderate income areas via rehabilitation did move to center stage in the CDBG process. Communities found it a popular and useful way to spend their grants, one that pleased both HUD and local constituencies. If one compares the typical CDBG program with the early urban renewal projects, in which thousands of low to moderate income units were destroyed and their inhabitants left to fend for themselves, one may conclude that CDBG was a much more pro-housing community development strategy. If, on the other hand, one compares CDBG to the strategy that seemed to be evolving out of the categorical programs in the late 1960s, the comparison becomes more troubling. There are at least two aspects of CDBG which are points of concern.

First, CDBG housing efforts seem to have bypassed the most desperate slums, and the low income persons inhabiting them. Some public housing has been refurbished and some land has been cleared for new low income housing construction; but, for the most part, CDBG programs are aimed at areas where decay is less advanced. Severely dilapidated and/or abandoned slum properties generally require clearance—they cannot be economically restored to meet modern definitions of standard housing. Clearance is an expensive process, and it disrupts the lives of some low income people in ways that dollars or new housing cannot totally compensate. But if a commitment is made to undertake clearance activities with improved housing as the ultimate goal, it can pay off in the long run for the low income population as a whole. Dangerous or unhealthy units can be replaced by publicly subsidized housing which, while not without problems of its own, generally provides living quarters much superior to those it replaces. Many communities had seriously begun to use their urban renewal funds in this way during the last years of the program, and CDBG did little to replace this commitment to the positive aspects of slum clearance.

Second, CDBG rehabilitation is essentially a slow, gradual approach. Because of the complexity of the process and the limited funds available, it has not produced massive numbers of upgraded units. Data from my national survey revealed an average output of four to five rehabilitated units per month in the cities which responded, and rates of output increased only slightly with the size of the community (Hays, 1982a). As an alternative measure of output, national yearly CDBG rehabilitation expenditures were divided by $10,000, the average per unit rehabilitation amount reported in the survey. Again, the result was just under 100,000 units per year, far less than subsidized new construction was producing during the same period (Hays, 1982b). These findings received further confirmation in a recent GAO report on CDBG housing rehabilitation programs (U.S., GAO, 1983). This is not to deny that rehabilitation is an important, even essential, part of an urban housing strategy. It is to say, however, that sole or primary reliance on rehabilitation is unlikely to produce large numbers of upgraded units within a reasonable time period. Only new construction will generate *volume*. In addition, unless it is backed up by deep housing cost subsidies, rehabilitation is unlikely to benefit the very lowest income segment of the population.

Third, under CDBG, housing rehabilitation has to compete for funds with a variety of other legitimate community development needs. In addition to the public works and public facilities for which localities may use federal dollars, there has been an increasing concern with economic development. Without a stable economic base which provides employment at adequate wages, no community can expect the housing improvements it makes to last. Thus, many communities, especially those in economic decline, have diverted funds from other community development purposes in a desperate effort to revive their economic base. Though economic development activities are still a smaller percentage of CDBG expenditures than housing rehabilitation, it would be very difficult for most communities to fund both activities adequately out of the same pool. Thus, some special commitment to each is needed in order for federal funds to have a greater impact.

As noted in this and the previous chapter, positions on community development policy do not sort themselves out as clearly along the liberal/conservative dimension as do positions on housing subsidies to the poor. Most of the major community development programs have drawn support from both liberals and all but the most doctrinaire conservatives. Nevertheless, such efforts have enjoyed the most enthusiastic support among liberal administrations while undergoing some reductions and curtailments during more conservative administrations. Also, liberals have pushed community development policy in the direction of providing more direct benefits to low and moderate income persons.

These positions are consistent with the definitions of these ideologies given in Chapter 2. *Both* liberals and conservatives tend to support government interventions in the market which enhance the position of market winners. Certainly, a community development strategy aimed at upgrading central business districts is an intervention designed primarily to benefit key groups of market winners. Liberals, however, support additional interventions to modify market outcomes in ways they feel will stabilize the entire system, particularly interventions on behalf of groups severely disadvantaged by market outcomes. Thus, they have pushed community development in the direction of upgrading the housing and neighborhood environments of those lower on the economic scale.

The CDBG program was developed and pushed through by a moderately conservative administration. In a variety of ways described in this chapter, it represented a long-term disengagement of the federal government from urban problems, particularly from the problems of those distressed cities which had competed most vigorously for categorical community development funds. The more modest kinds of housing and neighborhood upgrading typical of CDBG programs reflect this underlying spirit of disengagement. At the same time, liberals were strong enough during most of the period when CDBG was being formulated and implemented to exact restrictions on its direction as the price for the program's existence. The establishment of national goals for the program, the subsequent emphasis on the low to moderate income goal during the implementation process, and the softening (via the dual formula) of the redistribution away from large, decaying cities were the most important restrictions imposed. The influence of these restrictions is apparent in the types of programs funded by CDBG. Housing rehabilitation programs, though slow and limited, are still *housing* programs and are still, for the most part, directed at low to moderate income residents. Public improvements, too, have been directed in such a way as to support the upgrading of declining areas.

In sum, CDBG has been in harmony with the lowered voices and lowered expectations which Richard Nixon envisioned for the 1970s, yet it is far from the total retrenchment liberals feared and some conservatives wanted. It remains to be discussed, in the final chapter of this book, how the Reagan Administration has tried to turn this modest disengagement into a rapid federal withdrawal from community development and other urban problems.

CHAPTER 9

The Future of Housing
and Community Development Policy:
Reagan and Beyond

A Change of Direction: The Reagan Administration

Ronald Reagan's landslide victory over Jimmy Carter in 1980 was, in many respects, the culmination of the trends of the previous decade. First, economic problems which had plagued the nation throughout the 1970s took a turn for the worse in the last two years of the decade. Another oil price shock in 1978 moved energy prices to unprecedented levels, triggering a general acceleration of inflation (see Figure 3). In an attempt to control this new round of inflation, the Federal Reserve kept relatively tight control over the money supply. This, plus the inflationary expectations of investors, drove interest rates to new highs, which, in turn, contributed to an economic downturn in 1979. The intensification of both facets of the stagflation problem helped create the widespread perception that government management of the economy was no longer effective. More concretely, hundreds of thousands of workers were unemployed in the traditional Democratic strongholds of the Northeast and North Central regions.

The quality of the Carter Administration's leadership also became an issue in the 1980 election. As suggested in Chapter 6, Carter was himself unenthusiastic about continuing the movement toward increased governmental activities initiated by his Democratic predecessors. The prevailing economic pessimism among political elites, plus their perception of a revolt of taxpayers against an enlarged government role, made it hard for Carter to generate support for even his modest new proposals among moderate members of his own party as well as among the opposition. Add to this the legislative ineptitude of the Carter team, and one has a recipe for political disaster.

Thus, the behavior of voters in the 1980 election was, as in 1968, more a repudiation of the past administration's performance than a clear mandate for Reagan's philosophy (Pomper, 1981). In sharp contrast to

239

Carter's uncertain leadership image, Reagan exuded confidence that his proposals would "turn the country around." His question, "Are you better off than you were four years ago?" seemed to hit home with voters discontented with recent events. However, regardless of whether or not the voters knew exactly what they were getting in 1980, the election brought into power the most ideologically conservative administration since the 1920s. This set the stage for a major shift in the expenditure patterns and programmatic philosophies of the federal government. Housing policy could hardly have avoided the effects of this shift.

Reagan's well-known program for turning the country around included rapid increases in defense spending designed to enhance the nation's global influence; deep reductions in the social welfare and grant-in-aid programs which had been initiated in the 1960s; tax cuts to stimulate the economy; and the combination of a balanced budget with tight money to help restrain inflation. In practice, these goals proved to be incompatible for a number of complex reasons.

First, the largest category of domestic spending consisted of entitlement programs; programs such as social security, Medicare, Medicaid, food stamps, and unemployment insurance in which the government had a legal obligation to provide benefits to all eligible persons. The bulk of entitlement funds went to the elderly and the short-term unemployed, groups with sufficient political clout to discourage drastic cuts in their benefits. In addition, because these were entitlements, the only way to control their costs was through politically unpopular eligibility restrictions, rather than incremental adjustments in appropriations (Congressional Quarterly, Inc., 1982). In 1981, entitlement programs constituted 48 percent of the budget, while defense spending constituted 24 percent. Therefore, a combination of gradual increases in entitlements and rapid increases in defense spending more than counterbalanced budgetary savings resulting from cuts in other program areas (Palmer and Sawhill, 1982, p. 80).

Second, the Reagan projections that these goals could be simultaneously achieved were based on the expectation that the economy would recover rapidly due to the stimulus of his tax cuts. This recovery did not, of course, quickly materialize, due, in large part, to the continued use of restrictive monetary policies to keep inflation in check. In fact, the nation slid into the deepest recession of the postwar era in 1982. Added to the fact that federal spending had been reallocated but not reduced and to the cuts in tax rates, the recession left the federal government with deficits much larger than those Reagan had campaigned against so vigorously in 1980.

As of this writing, the jury is still out on the long-term impact of Reaganomics on the macroeconomic well-being of the United States. On the positive side, the recession drastically reduced the rate of inflation, and a loosening of monetary restrictions in late 1982 helped stimulate a modest economic recovery which has continued through late 1984. On the negative side, unemployment remained very high, and the large federal deficits showed few signs of going away, unless defense spending were cut or new taxes added, neither of which was acceptable to the Reagan Administration. However, what is most important for the present discussion is what happened *on the way to* the rather uncertain economic policy outcome just described. Based on the strength of his electoral victory and based on the appeal of his plan for economic recovery, Reagan was able to push through Congress a package of substantial cuts in virtually all areas of domestic federal spending except the entitlement programs. These cuts amounted to approximately $40 billion in FY 1982. In the process of achieving such cuts, the Reagan Administration displayed considerable skill in utilizing its political resources to influence Congress.

The administration's principle tool was the set of procedures set up in the 1974 budget reform act. This act had been passed in an attempt by Congress to give itself more leverage vis-a-vis the president in budgetary decisions. The act established the House and Senate Budget Committees, which were to review the president's budget as a whole and to draft a budget resolution reflecting overall congressional priorities, which would provide guidelines for the appropriations process. Ironically, the Reagan team used this process to enhance presidential influence over budget outcomes. Building on his Republican majority in the Senate and on considerable support from conservative Democrats in the House, he worked closely with congressional leaders in 1981 to produce a First Budget Resolution which conformed closely to his desired cuts. He then made it stick by pushing through a reconciliation bill which forced program authorizations by individual committees to conform strictly to the limits set in the First Budget Resolution. In doing so, he was able to override the traditional centers of support for domestic programs; i.e., substantive committees tied to agencies and program clientele. With equal skill, Reagan also pushed through his drastic tax cuts, including the most restrictive measure of all with regard to revenues – the indexing of tax rates to prevent their automatic rise with inflation.

By Reagan's second year, congressional suypport for his initiatives had waned, and the defenders of various domestic programs were better prepared for the onslaught. As a result, additional deep cuts in nonentitlement domestic spending which Reagan requested encountered much stiffer opposition. Nevertheless, the overall decline in such expenditures was maintained because earlier decisions proved difficult to reverse. Congress had supported defense increases, and many members feared that any backtracking in this area would make them vulnerable to charges of undermining national security. To rescind tax cuts already given or to cut back entitlements were also political risks many were unwilling to take. Therefore, restoration of funding for other domestic programs would inevitably result in increased deficits, leaving Reagan the opportunity to blame Congress for the sea of red ink. As the second Reagan term begins, the attempt is again being made to use the deficit as leverage for more drastic domestic program cuts.

One other major impact which the Reagan Administration had on the course of domestic programming came through its control of the federal bureaucracy. Those appointed to key cabinet and subcabinet positions generally came from the most conservative end of the political spectrum, and they usually came into domestic program agencies with a mandate to curtail their activities as much as possible. In symbolic recognition of one of HUD's main constituencies, Reagan appointed a black, Samuel Pierce, as Secretary of HUD; however, in doing so, he chose one of the least aggressive advocates of housing for the poor that he could have found in the black community (Stanfield, 1983c). In addition, budget cuts and reorganizations led to Reductions in Force (RIFs) which tended to demoralize the remaining administrators. Where administrative discretion allowed, agencies were pushed toward reductions in regulations of local governments and private businesses and toward tightening of eligibility for social welfare programs.

The Reagan Administration was not immune to the frequently observed tendency of presidential appointees to go native and protect their agencies from White House cuts. Even Pierce went to bat for the CDBG program in the face of OMB Director, David Stockman's budgetary axe. However, the extreme disparity between the conservative ideology of many appointees and the basically liberal purposes of the agencies they headed minimized this tendency.

The continued evolution of housing policy in the first Reagan term was, as shall be shown, influenced by the ongoing policy dilemmas described in earlier chapters. However, the influence of the overall policy environment just described was also very powerful. This environment reflected the efforts of a group of political leaders with ideological assumptions deeply at odds with the existing course of policy to redirect that course. The ideas of balancing the budget and reducing federal spending were important from their conservative point of view, but they soon gave way to two higher priorities; cutting taxes and redirecting federal spending toward defense and away from social welfare programs. They found it politically impossible to reduce the largest welfare state programs, those affecting millions of working and middle class citizens. Therefore, they focused their attacks on more recent programs which were directed more exclusively at the narrower and weaker constituency of the disadvantaged. This having been done, they seemed willing to accept the large deficits resulting from their other priorities. Housing subsidy programs were among the primary target group for cuts. Housing efforts carried out under Community Development Block Grants were also affected, though, as shall be shown, they proved somewhat less vulnerable.

Housing and Community Development Policy Under the Reagan Administration

Housing Trends in the Early 1980s

Before discussing Reagan's housing initiatives, it is appropriate to look briefly at those changes in economic conditions affecting housing during the early 1980s with potential impacts upon policy. Such data have been painfully slow in coming for the first four years of the decade, and detailed information is generally not available for years later than 1983. However, some patterns may be tentatively discerned. They generally show a continuation of trends observed in the late 1970s, with some important variations.

Perhaps the most important change has been a marked increase in the proportion of U.S. families falling below the poverty line. Table 2 in Chapter 3 showed a decline in the percentage of families in poverty from 11.0 percent in 1970 to 10.1 percent in 1979. Comparable data for 1982 show that the poverty rate forthe United States as a whole rose to 13.1 percent in a three year period. In addition, a detailed breakdown shows even more rapid increases in the central city poverty rate (14.3 percent to 19.0 percent) and the black poverty rate (29.9 percent to 34.9 percent), rates which were much higher than average to begin with (U.S. Bureau of the Census, 1984, pp. 33-39). The Reagan Administration did, of course, challenge data such as these on the grounds that noncash benefits (e.g., food stamps and subsidized housing) were not included in the computation of poverty rates. Moreover, 1982 data reflect the depths of the recession of that year, from which the nation has since partially recovered. Nevertheless, the large cuts in housing and other benefit programs which

Reagan made clearly occurred against the backdrop of a halt, if not a major reversal, in the slow decline in poverty which characterized the 1970s.

Meanwhile, the cost of housing of all types continued to rise, albeit at a slower rate in keeping with the overall slowing of inflation which occurred in the early 1980s. The 1983 Annual Housing Survey reported a 25 percent rise in the median value of owner occupied dwellings between 1980 and 1983 and a 30 percent rise in rents. At the same time, the median income for tenants increased only about 20 percent, with the result that 61.4 percent of central city tenants and 54.9 percent of suburban tenants were paying over 25 percent of their income in rent, in contrast to the 1980 figures of 55.2 percent and 51.4 percent reported in Table 4. (U.S. Bureau of Census and Department of Housing and Urban Development, 1984) The Consumer Price Index for housing costs shows a similar trend for these years and indicates that this trend continued into late 1984 (U.S. Bureau of Labor Statistics, *CPI Detailed Reports* for appropriate months).

All of these data suggest potentially serious difficulties for lower income persons in finding decent housing, but one other trend also had a negative impact. This was the drastic decline in housing construction starts during the 1980-83 period. Throughout the 1970s, as was shown in Table 3, yearly starts of 1-4 unit dwellings fluctuated from over 1,500,000 to 950,000, while starts of dwellings with 5 or more units ranged from 900,000 to 200,000. In contrast, 1-4 unit starts ranged from 800,000 in 1981 to 1,200,000 in 1983, while starts of 5 + unit dwellings ranged from 300,000 to 500,000 (U.S. Federal Home Loan Bank Board Journal, April, 1984). Such continued low levels of production did not bode well for the filtering process by which most low income persons would acquire housing in the 1980s and suggested a need for the continuation of subsidized rental construction. Nevertheless, as shall be shown, Reagan's strategy involved drastic reductions in new construction subsidies and a reliance on exisiting moderately priced rental housing mostly produced by filtering.

Housing Subsidy Programs

The major features of housing subsidy proposals and actions under the Reagan Administration may be divided into two categories. First, there were the extensive budget cuts for these programs alluded to above. Second, there were the structural changes in housing subsidy programs which were recommended. These two aspects are best treated as analytically distinct, even though they have been closely intertwined in the ongoing political struggle.

In his budget coup of 1981, Reagan succeeded in cutting the amount of new budget authority for Section 8 and public housing in the FY 1982 budget to approximately $17.5 billion, just over half the $30 billion which had been appropriated in Carter's FY 1981 budget. (The reader will recall that actual expenditures [outlays] from this budget authority are spread out over many years in the form of contracted subsidy payments.) In addition, he pushed through a recission of approximately $4 billion in budget authority left over from previous years. However, these cuts were small in comparison to those requested in 1982 for the FY 1983 budget. In his budget proposal for that year, Reagan asked for what was, in effect, a negative appropriation; that is, no additional budget authority for new units, plus a net recission of $2.5 billion in budget authority from previous years (National Low Income Housing Coalition, 1983b, p. 10).

Reflecting its new willingness to give at least a qualified "no" to the Reagan Administration, Congress balked at such deep cuts. In the House, the defenders of subsidized housing had a strong new advocate, Representative Henry Gonzalez (Dem., Texas), as chair of the Housing and Community Development Subcommittee of the Banking, and Urban Affairs Committee. He insisted that such cuts were unacceptable and gained enough support from his colleagues to battle the administration to a stalemate on new authorization legislation for housing programs. The result of the lack of authorizing legislation was an initial HUD appropriations bill containing no new budget authority and no recissions. However, in a later compromise, $8.6 billion in new budget authority for FY 1983 was added through a continuing resolution.

In 1983, Reagan again tried to cut new budget authority to the bone, asking for $500 million for FY 1984. Congress again proved determined to keep some new housing efforts going, and just over $12 billion was appropriated. By 1984, the administration was seeking to soften its image of hostility to social welfare programs and its FY 1985 budget request of $6.3 billion was much closer to what Congress had appropriated in the previous two years. In contrast to the prolonged battles of earlier years, the HUD appropriations bill was one of the first approved in 1984, and it contained an appropriation of $7.9 billion for new housing subsidies.

Looked at from one perspective, the appropriations of FY 1983–1985 may be seen as a testimony to the powers of resistance of the housing subgovernment and to the residual popularity of housing subsidy programs in Congress. However, from another angle, this battle may be seen a a confirmation of the ability of ideological changes in presidential leadership to shape the terms of the debate. Housing advocates did not go down to total defeat, yet they were clearly fighting a rear guard action on behalf of their programs. The amounts approved still represented a reduction in budget authority from pre-Reagan levels of over two-thirds. It would take several years for the full impact of this reduction to be felt, due to the extended time frame of housing programs. This is why the yearly outlays shown in Figure 11 and the subsidized housing starts shown in Figure 10 declined only gradually in the early 1980s. But this was clearly a drastic change in the order of magnitude of the federal effort, one which would lead to a deeper drop in production than that which occurred in the mid-1970s.

Meanwhile, the Reagan Administration also proposed administrative changes in the Section 8 program designed to more directly and immediately affect yearly outlays. First, they proposed, and received, congressional approval of a gradual increase in the percentage of income which families in Section 8 units had to pay for rent from 25 to 30 percent. Second, they proposed that the cash value of food stamps received by Section 8 tenants be counted as income for purposes of computing the rent to be paid. As of this writing, Congress has refused to approve this cost cutting measure which, according to the National Low Income Housing Coalition, would fall most heavily on the lowest income tenants. Finally, they succeeded in lowering the levels to which Fair Market Rents would have risen in the normal course of things; first by delaying the publication of new FMRs for two years and, second, by instituting a new formula which calculated them on the basis of the 40th percentile of area rents, rather than the median, which had previously been used. Protest from local housing agencies was muted by a hold harmless provision which prevented any area's current FMR from actually being reduced.

During the same period that the Reagan Administration was pushing hard for reductions in the level of federal housing subsidy effort, it was also conducting a review of the structure of federal housing programs. Early in the administration, key officials indicated that a new form of housing allowance, "housing vouchers," would be a central concept. However, in order to review, elaborate, and justify program options, the President's Commission on Housing was appointed in 1981. According to Rochelle Stanfield, membership on this commission was limited to those who basically shared Reagan's conservative political outlook, rather than being representative of a broad spectrum of opinion as were previous commissions. This was because the administration wanted concrete proposals that matched its desired direction, rather than broad statements upon which a diverse commission could agree (Stanfield, 1982b). The Commission's final report, issued in the spring of 1982, accurately represents the central thrust of the Reagan team's thinking about subsidized housing.

In keeping with the affinity of Reagan and his advisors for housing vouchers, the central housing subsidy recommendation of the Commission was a voucher-like program called the *Housing Payments Program*. The following is a summary of the major features of the program recommended by the Commission:

1. It would be administered by the same agencies which were currently administering the Section 8 Existing Housing program, and they would continue to enforce minimum housing standards.

2. Eligibility would be restricted to those below 50 percent of the local median income, not 80 percent as in Section 8, so that the program would, in the Commission's words "be directed to those most in need."

3. A "payment standard" would be substituted for the Fair Market Rent. Like the FMR, this standard would be calculated on the basis of the cost of a typical unit of that size in the community, with the subsidy computed as the difference between 30 percent of income and the standard. However *the rent in the unit actually occupied could be more or less than the payment standard*. As a result, households would be "rewarded" with extra cash income for other purposes if they found a less costly unit. Also, households who chose to spend more than 30 percent of their income on housing could do so and still receive the subsidy.

4. The government should "move toward" direct payment of the subsidy to the tenant, but local agencies could maintain their current practice of paying the landlord, if they so desired. (U.S. President's Commission on Housing, 1982, pp. 23-30).

The principal arguments used by the Commission to justify this new program were very similar to those raised on behalf of a free market, voucher approach throughout the 1970s. First, they reiterated the argument that the chief housing problem experienced by the poor is excessive housing cost, not poor housing conditions. Using Annual Housing Survey data, they calculated that, "Of the 10.5 million very low income renters [less than 50 percent of median income] identified in the 1977 Annual Housing Survey, 6.5 million paid more than 30 percent of their incomes for rent, while 2 million lived in inadequate housing. " (U.S. President's Commission on Housing, 1982, p. 12). On this basis, they concluded that the provision of cash rent supplements was much more urgent than the construction of new, standard, subsidized units.

Second, they relied upon the reduced cost argument which had been around at least since Nixon's report, *Housing in the Seventies*. They provided data showing the substantially lower per/unit costs for Section 8 Existing Housing than for Section 8 New Construction, and they argued that less constrained cash subsidies to tenants would push costs even lower. They cited evidence from the EHAP Demand Experiment that tenants would use only part of an unconstrained cash grant for housing, while spending the rest on other consumer goods. They also took note of the tendency of rents in the Existing Housing program to be pulled upward toward the Fair Market Rent ceiling.

Third, they took pains to refute the notion that cash subsidies would cause the poor to pay more for less by driving up prices within the restricted housing market available to them. Again, they cited the results of EHAP, in this case the Supply Experiment which showed that even a fairly extensive program did not increase rents in the communities affected. With regard to minorities, they recommended continued strict enforcement of fair housing laws, but they noted favorably the HUD findings (discussed in Chapter 6) that: (1) minorities were better represented in the Section 8 Existing Housing program than in Section 8 New Construction; and, (2), a significant number of minority households used their subsidy to shop for housing in physically better, more racially integrated areas.

In spite of its strong advocacy of concentrating federal subsidies on existing units, the Commission's report did express concern that the overall supply of standard, low income units might not be adequate, especially in localities with very tight housing markets. Their proposal for dealing with this problem was a radical decentralization of new construction programs. They recommended that new construction be included as an eligible activity under the Community Development Block Grant program. Extra funds would be added to the grants, using a separate formula based on the extent of local housing needs. However, the Commission recommended that the ultimate decision to spend or not to spend these extra funds on new construction be left to local governments. In support of this proposal, the Commission praised the willingness of localities to utilize CDBG funds for housing purposes, and they praised local creativity in devising leveraging schemes which stretched federal dollars by stimulating private investment.

In many respects, the political atmosphere was propitious for acceptance of the types of programmatic changes recommended by Reagan's Housing Commission. The same conservative coalition in Congress which had supported Reagan's budget cuts was receptive to alternative program designs which promised lower costs and less active governmental intervention in market transactions between tenants and landlords. In addition, a decade of debate and experimentation had brought many liberal advocates of low income housing around to the position that it was both necessary and desirable for programs involving cash subsidies of existing units to shoulder an increasing share of the task of housing the poor. Nevertheless, the structural changes the administration eventually proposed ran into much stronger opposition than did his budget cuts.

One may glean from contemporary accounts of the housing debate in the *Congressional Quarterly* and the *National Journal,* two basic reasons for the stalemate over programmatic change which emerged in the first three years of the Reagan Administration. The first was the disagreement over the composition of the federal housing subsidy effort. Throughout most of the debate, Regan and his advisors were intransigent in their insistence that *no* units whatsoever be allocated to new construction programs. Not only were allocations to Section 8 New Construction cut to zero, but also the Housing Commission's proposal for a housing block grant was modified so that only rehabilitation of existing rental units would be included. According to the *National Journal,* Reagan's HUD Secretary Samuel Pierce, as well as a number of congressional Republicans, urged the inclusion of a modest number of units of new construction as a compromise essential to the passage of a bill containing the new voucher program. Liberal lobbyists such as Cushing Dolbeare, president of the National Low Income Housing Coalition, stated their willingness to endorse housing vouchers, as long as they were supplemented by some newly constructed units, in order to keep the overall supply of low income housing adequate, and many members of Congress supported their position. Within the administration, however, David Stockman's concern with the long-term costs of new construction subsidies prevailed, and Reagan opted for total stalemate with Congress over housing legislation rather than compromise on the issue of new construction. (Stanfield, 1983a)

The second set of issues around which opposition to Reagan's program centered pertained to the relationship between his proposals for programmatic change and his push to drastically reduce total housing subsidy costs. Several actions by the Reagan Administration aroused hostility among housing advocates, because they led to the perception that his new programs were, in reality, little more than a smokescreeen for emasculating the federal effort.

First, Reagan did not propose his voucher plan as part of a package of new funding for additional units. Rather, he proposed to pay for it with funds recaptured from prior budget authority for Section 8 units.

This use of negative funding to initiate housing vouchers was totally unacceptable to housing proponents in Congress. Second, Reagan coupled his housing voucher proposal with various administrative efforts, described above, to cut deeply the total amount of subsidy going to each household. Again, this made an otherwise acceptable concept unacceptable to many housing advocates. They supported the cost savings inherent in the housing voucher approach as legitimate ways to spread benefits to a larger group of the disadvantaged without hurting individual households. However, additional subsidy cuts were seen as punitive, unjustified, and as one more bit of evidence that the Reagan Administration's real concern was in saving money, not serving the poor. In an interview with the *National Journal*, Cushing Dolbeare complained that, "Reagan is giving housing vouchers a bad name." (Stanfield, 1983a, p. 843).

Third, the level of funding provided for the housing block grant eventually proposed by Reagan was very low, in addition to being directed only at rehabilitation. The total amount proposed in the FY 1983 budget was $150 million, and another program which had been a major supplementary source of funds for CDBG rehabilitation, the Section 312 program, was virtually eliminated. Such acts pointed to the use of the block grant proposal to cover a reduction in the overall level of funding. Such a maneuver was widely perceived by liberals to be the basis for Reagan's proposals for block grants in other social service areas. There was also concern among housing advocates that localities would not have the technical capacity to carry out new housing construction, a concern underlined by a GAO report which stressed that the primary housing experience of CDBG programs had been the making of loans to homeowners. (U.S. GAO, 1983). This report also noted that local housing officials themselves found the idea of housing block grants unacceptable unless substantial additional funds were provided. For these reasons, the block grant proposal generated as low a level of enthusiasm as the housing voucher program.

In the end, Reagan did succeed in substantially changing the direction, as well as the scope of housing subsidy programs. Congress refused to approve housing vouchers except on an experimental level, yet the proportion of units going to Section 8 Existing Housing was greatly increased, and Section 8 New Construction was eliminated except for use in conjunction with Section 202 housing for the elderly and handicapped. Yet, the preservation of this small effort, plus continued appropriations for some new public housing units, indicated that Congress was unwilling to abandon the new construction strategy altogether. Also, a new program of housing development grants, modeled after the UDAG program, was authorized, although its ultimate scale and impact is uncertain as of this writing.

Community Development Block Grants

The fate of CDBG under the Reagan Administration was not nearly as grim as was that of housing subsidy programs. One reason was that the overall design of the program fit closely with Reagan's ideological predisposition toward consolidation of categorical programs and a return of federal dollars to state and local control. In fact, CDBG served as a model for the reorganization of federal social welfare activities into state or locally controlled block grants. Reagan's ideology also predisposed him favorably to UDAG, with its use of federal seed money to promote private investment in the central city.

Another reason was the popularity of these programs among local political and economic elites. As indicated in Chapters 7 and 8, community development has generally enjoyed a somewhat broader base of political support than have housing subsidy programs. Though groups representing mayors and other local officials often lobby for both housing and community development funding, the community development programs gain additional support from local and national business interests who have less enthusiasm for social welfare programs. The pool of money channelled into CDBG is largely under local government control and can be used in ways that do not disturb local political arrangements. Also important is the fact that CDBG money, while it has been concentrated in low and moderate income areas, is available for general community improvement and for various kinds of subsidies to market winners. This last point was even more the case with UDAG, which had aided numerous private investors in potentially profitable involvement in downtown revitalization.

To say that community development programs were relatively better off is not to say, however, that they emerged unscathed from the Reagan drive to reduce and reorganize nonentitlement domestic expenditures. According the the *National Journal*, OMB Director Stockman, during the initial push to reduce domestic spending in 1981, recommended the elimination of UDAG and drastic reductions in CDBG. Backed by local government lobbyists, HUD Secretary Pierce fought successfully to preserve the CDBG program. At the same time, ". . . wealthy private interests, such as the hotel chains that take advantage of action grants, . . . talked convincingly to presidential counselor Edwin Meese III and White House chief of staff James A. Baker III . . ." and their intervention helped to insure that UDAG also escaped the budgetary axe

(Stanfield, 1983b, pp. 1645–1646). Nevertheless, as Figures 12 and 13 show, absolute funding levels for community development were slated to fall off sharply from their peak in the late 1970s; and, given the still growing federal budget, to drop even more sharply as a percentage of federal outlays.

There were also a number of structural changes in community development which were attempted, with varying degrees of success, by the Reagan Administration. First, the administration of CDBG funds for small, non-entitlement cities was shifted from HUD to the state governments. As a result, HUD began allocating these funds to a responsible state agency which then reviewed the applications of smaller cities. In a NAHRO workshop I attended some community development officials predicted that this devolution of authority would lead to the same kind of spreading effect that has occurred in some larger communities with regard to local CDBG projects. That is, state political leaders would try to give small amounts to as many communities as possible, rather than concentrating on large projects in a few cities. A recent HUD report cited by Mary K. Nenno confirmed that the average number of recipients in each state had increased by 75 percent, and that the average grant per recipient had declined from $485,000 to $219,000 under state administration. The report also noted an increased emphasis on economic development and public facilities and a decreased use of CDBG funds for housing programs (Nenno, 1983, p. 146).

Second, HUD reopened the debate on targeting of CDBG funds by announcing that it would interpret the administrative mandate of the Housing and Community Development Act of 1974 differently than had the Carter Administration. Rather than insist that the primary beneficiaries of CDBG funds be low and moderate income persons, the Reagan Administration stated that the other two broad goals of the 1974 Act, "the elimination of slums and blight" and "meeting urgent community needs," would be treated as coequal. This had the effect of giving localities more flexibility in the types of activities they could fund with block grants. Such a move was not well received in the housing and community development subcommittees in Congress, and bills were proposed which would change the 1974 Act to put more explicit emphasis on targeting funds to low and moderate income persons. In the HUD reauthorization bill passed by Congress in late 1983, a compromise was reached in which 51 percent of CDBG funds had to be spent on low and moderate income persons.

Third, the Reagan Administration offered, as its only new urban aid proposal, a program implementing the concept of "enterprise zones" about which Reagan had talked extensively in his 1980 campaign. The enterprise zone program would have designated certain areas of cities as "distressed" and then would have granted relief from federal taxes and regulations to private firms engaging in economic development within these areas. State and local governments would also have been urged to follow suit in granting tax relief. This proposal made it through the Senate in 1983 and was added to the bill repealing tax withholding on interest and dividends; however, it was deleted from the bill in conference committee. Whether or not it will ultimately gain congressional approval remains in question as of this writing.

Behind the specific proposals for change in community development programs made by the Reagan Administration lies a larger question of the long term survival of such programs during a second Reagan term. Early in his first term, Reagan proposed his ambitious New Federalism plan. (It really should have been called the *New* New Federalism, to distinguish it from Nixon's initiatives in the early 1970s.) Under this plan, many of the federal government's domestic responsibilities would have been turned over to the states and localities, with a gradual phase-in of financial responsibility over several years. Such an idea has long been dear to the hearts of many conservatives, for the reasons outlined in Chapter 7. As part of implementing this plan, CDBG would have been merged with General Revenue Sharing and turned over to the Treasury Department to administer. The New Federalism proposal stirred widespread opposition among state and local officials, who protested their own fiscal incapacity to handle many of the large federal programs. As a result, the effort was subsequently deemphasized by the Reagan team.

However, Reagan remains philosophically committed to more and more devolution of authority to state and local governments, and the New Federalism may be revived in his second term. In addition, the continuing large deficits are seen as unacceptable by both Democrats and Republicans, and Reagan again announced in late 1984 that CDBG and UDAG were under consideration for total elimination in the FY 1986 budget, as part of a plan to reduce these deficits. Thus, the survival of CDBG and any other federal assistance which is even remotely targeted by federal decisionmakers remains in serious doubt.

The Overall Impact of the Reagan Administration

It is clear that many in the Reagan team envision a complete turnaround in housing and community development policy. Like Nixon (but perhaps more fervently and dogmatically), they believe in the disengagement of federal agencies from direct and active intervention on behalf of the disadvantaged, and they want states and localities to solve community development problems, either with their own resources or by stimulating private sector investment. However, like Nixon, their initiatives have been blunted by the strong support which federal housing and community development programs still enjoy in Congress and among state and local leaders. Reagan has had a Congress much more sympathetic to disengagement and retrenchment than Nixon ever had, yet defenders of these activities have managed to preserve at least the skeletons of their programs. And, as both proponents and opponents tacitly recognize, as long as the skeleton is there, it can be brought back to life and have the flesh restored to its bones during more politically propitious times.

In defending their programs, housing and community development advocates in Congress have a built-in advantage over the president — they are specialists focusing on specific programs while he has multiple concerns and priorities. If current observers are to be believed, Reagan has been less willing to bargain on specific features of programs than have earlier administrations. Cushing Dolbeare said of herself and other housing advocates, "We've learned to ignore Reagan. Appealing to him is a wasted effort. Congress is more willing to deal with us and we're going to deal with them." (Quoted in Stanfield, 1982a, p. 2167). At the same time, the relatively low priority which housing issues have with Reagan means that he has not fully committed his political resources to the changes he wants in this area. Cutting the budget, not structural reform, has been his administration's main priority, and here they have had to give in on minor levels of funding which have kept the programs clinging to life.

However, the contrast between the political atmostphere surrounding housing and community development in the early 1980s with that of 15 years ago is still striking. The momentum behind federal activism in these areas was very strong 15 years ago, and the debate was mainly focused on how much the federal government should help, not whether it should help. Nixon slowed but could not reverse this momentum, yet he and other critics were able to create considerable doubt about the efficacy of the federal role, in effect keeping the issue of "whether" alive. With increasing economic problems, and loss of faith in federal action even among liberals, the stage was set for the more serious attempt at reversal which has occurred in the last three years. Subsidies still flow to low income households, due to the built-in inertia of such programs, but the long-term outlook is not positive, unless a change in mood and philosophy in a liberal direction is forthcoming. Unlike 15 years ago, when the ground was fertile for new ideas and proposals, defenders of federal housing and community development activities must use their remaining centers of influence to salvage bits and pieces of programs. Meanwhile, it remains fashionable to argue either that problems do not exist or that the federal government cannot do anyting about them.

The Future of Housing Policy

In concluding this analysis of housing policy trends, it seems appropriate to discuss briefly the future of U.S. urban housing policy. This discussion will begin with a brief review of the major conclusions about the policy-making process in the United States which have been supported by this study. Then, it will focus on the implications of what has happened in the past for future policy outcomes. Finally, the direction this author feels housing policy should take, in contrast to the direction it probably will take, will be discussed.

It was suggested in Chapter 1 that the relationship between the broad ideological orientations of members of the political/economic elite and the unfolding of policy in a particular area of concern is a complex but important one. One the one hand, shifts in power between coalitions within the political/economic elite which have different ideological orientations can drastically affect outcomes in a wide range of policy arenas. Executive or legislative leadership can provide an environment in which a certain set of programs will thrive and expand or it can threaten their very existence. The history of housing subsidy programs presented in Chapters 4, 5, and 6 clearly shows that the commitment to government efforts to deal with the housing problems of the disadvantaged has ebbed or flowed depending on the conservative or liberal philosophy of different presidential administrations and on the strength of conservatives or liberals within Congress.

At the same time, each policy area has its own unique set of actors and issues — its own internal frames of reference within which problems are viewed. Social welfare goals and community development goals have both been relevant to the kinds of housing policies which have emerged, and each of these sets of goals has drawn support from a slightly different group of actors. In addition, certain central, recurring problems have shaped the housing policy debate throughout the 50 years of federal involvement. In connection with housing subsidies as social welfare measures to benefit the poor, questions of quantity, quality, cost, and equity have been raised. In connection with community development policy, the central question of intergovernmental power relationships has greatly influenced the housing outcomes of these programs. These questions have been raised in different ways at different times, and different answers have been appealing to liberals and/or conservatives. Nevertheless, there is striking continuity in the kinds of questions which emerge as each new policy initiative is debated.

Finally, it has been shown that participants in the housing policy arena can mount their own lines of defense provided by the fragmented U.S. political system to enhance their programs' share of the pie and/or to protect them from interference by outsiders such as the president. This capacity lends some continuity to policy although much less than traditional subgovernment models of policy making would lead us to believe. Those committed to the survival of a certain set of programs may play a crucial role in blunting or altering the impact of executive or legislative initiatives, but they still find themselves basically in a reactive position, vis-à-vis the overall direction of policy.

The central question raised by the consideration of the future of housing policy is, "Can this process produce a set of policy outcomes which is, in some sense, optimal?" In thinking about this question, one immediately confronts a central dilemma of decision making which is especially difficult to resolve in a society which makes it decisions in an at least partially democratic fashion. This dilemma centers on the role of dissensus and consensus in the growth and development of the social and political system.

On one side of the dilemma is the widely shared view, articulated so forcefully by John Stuart Mill, that clashing points of view help to clearly identify alternatives and that the process of compromise produces policy outcomes which meet the needs of all actors to the greatest extent possible. Also supporting the need for clearly expressed opposition in the political process is the argument, very powerfully expressed by democratic revisionists, that such peaceful conflict is the only alternative to violence or autocracy (Kariel, 1970).

On the other side is another model of decision making which is aspired to by many individuals and institutions in contemporary societies, a model which Anderson calls the "rational-comprehensive" model. This model presupposes that rational actors can come to some agreement on the objectives of public policy and sees this as an essential first step in the careful determination of the most efficient means to carry out the objectives. Thus, though debate and conflict are, in this model, necessary at the outset, the establishment of consensus among informed participants is the precursor to progress in solving any given problem (Anderson, 1979). This model has a closer affinity to the scientific and technical decision making which goes on within complex organizations than to the rough and tumble of the democratic political process; however, modern democratic theorists have also stressed the importance of consensus to system stability (Kariel, 1970).

The most rigorous version of the rational-comprehensive model calls for a complete analysis of alternative courses of action *before* one of them is chosen. Extensive information on the costs and benefits of each alternative must be gathered before a rational choice can be made. Critics of this approach have argued, convincingly I think, that this criterion is unrealistic because it demands too much time and resources from decision makers. Real world political actors are under pressure to act quickly and cannot be expected to collect all the data necessary for a totally rational choice before they more ahead. Therefore, they tend to proceed incrementally, making minor adjustments to current practices on the basis of incomplete knowledge of the future.

However, even if a high degree of prior knowledge about probable program outcomes is an unrealistic expectation, perhaps it is reasonable to expect a learning curve to develop from successive attempts to solve a problem. This is a very common way for rational courses of action to emerge in virtually every field of human endeavor, a fact which has been formally recognized in systems analysis through the concent of the feedback loop. It would appear, then, that government actions should at least measure up to this criterion of rationality; namely, that past mistakes lead to corrective actions which, over time, produce a gradual increase in program efficiency and effectiveness.

There are at least two levels on which such learning should occur. First, each program should have its own learning curve. As a program is administered, it is almost inevitable that: (1) vague legislative goals (often deliberately vague for political reasons) will prove difficult to interpret and execute; (2) totally unforseen consequences will emerge; and, (3) ambiguities or loopholes in the program's design will be used to undermine its original purposes by those who have something to gain by doing so. These problems must be dealt with as they occur, through administrative changes or, if necessary, through new legislative action. The second and broader level at which learning should occur is within the policy area as a whole. As different programs are implemented, and their strengths and/or weaknesses revealed, decisionmakers should accumulate knowledge about which types of programs will and will not work. In most policy areas, no single approach will solve all problems. Rather a *mix* of programs will be needed, each targeted at the purposes and clientele it serves best. Though changes and adjustments will always be needed, this mix should become relatively stable over time.

If one looks at federal housing policies in terms of the considerations just mentioned, one may, I believe, discern some important learning which has taken place during the nearly 50 years in which the federal government has been involved in this area. My own brief summary of the most important things which have been learned is as follows:

Subsidized Housing: The approach to housing for the poor which was first used—publicly owned and operated housing—has proved to be the most effective way to house a certain, very low income segment of the population, provided that important lessons from the construction and management errors of the past are incorporated into its design and operation. However, relying on public housing the sole source of low income housing is not practical in a capitalist economy, and too great an expansion in the future would probably generate additional diseconomies of scale. Therefore, programs based in the private sector are also needed.

In such private sector subsidy programs, it has become increasingly clear that a mix of subsidies for new construction, rehabilitation, and existing units is necessary. New construction is needed to maintain an ample supply of low cost housing; however, too great a reliance on new construction raises at least two key issues. One is cost; clearly new construction of privately owned units is very expensive on a per unit basis, especially since investors seem to demand deep tax subsidies, as well as direct rent subsidies, as a condition for risking their money on the disadvantaged. The second is equity; new construction seems to gravitate away from the most desperately poor and those with the fewest housing options (such as large, low income families) and toward serving those poor people considered more desirable and deserving (e.g., the elderly).

Therefore, the use of existing standard units to house the poor is a useful way to spread resources further and to achieve a better mix of families served. However, the design of such programs must take into consideration the limited private market which lower income (particularly minority) families may effectively use and must be vigorous in preventing, through inspections and counseling, the subsidization of low quality units. Also, this approach must be tempered by the realization that the community as a whole has a stake in the quality of housing consumed by individuals, due to the negative externalities created by poor housing. In light of this consideration, Reagan's unrestricted housing voucher approach appears to be a questionable use of housing funds, even though per unit costs are reduced in the short run.

Community Development: The clearance and redevelopment approach embodied in the urban renewal program produced some notable improvements in central cities, especially in central business districts. However, it produced them at a high cost both in human distress and in dollars; and it often proved administratively cumbersome and inflexible with regard to differing local needs.

In contrast, the approach embodied in CDBG has emphasized modest clearance for specific, limited purposes; extensive use of rehabilitation combined with improved public services for existing neighborhoods; and local flexibility in the utilization of funds. This has occurred within the context of a very constructive rediscovery by key segments of American society of the value of renovating existing urban physical resources.

However, for this approach to deliver maximum benefits, it, too, must be used with full realization of its limitations. First, there are times when large sums directed at total improvement of a single section of a community may be justified, and the resources for such large projects should be available to supplement CDBG. The UDAG program meets this need to some degree, but it must be carefully scrutinized to insure that the subsidies provided to private developers are generating substantial benefits for the community as a whole.

Second, the use of rehabilitation as a housing improvement strategy has tended to produce standard units at a slow pace, and it has benefitted primarily that segment of the low income population which own their homes and/or live in only modestly deteriorating neighborhoods. Therefore, the increased reliance on rehabilitation should not lead to the total rejection of replacement of dilapidated housing as a community development strategy. This conclusion ties in with the continued need for new construction of units of low income housing mentioned above.

It should be apparent to the reader that the conclusions just outlined are not fixed, determinant program characteristics but, rather, general concepts and approaches. Even if these conclusions were elaborated beyond the very general statements just given into a comprehensive set of guidelines for housing and community development activity, they would still not constitute a definitive statement of what must be done to successfully utilize public resources in this area. Rather, these guidelines would remain general principles of action, to be applied differently in different situations. This fact points, in turn, to a more general characteristic of learning curves in public policy. Even if policymakers are the most rational and receptive of human beings, the education they receive from past experience cannot totally define or control future decisions or actions. The making of public policy is, like all facets of human existence, in constant flux, and knowledge from the past can never produce ironclad rules which will guarantee future success.

What, for example, is good management in public housing, and what is its role in program success? From the past, one may learn that it is an absolutely essential element in achieving the program's objectives. One may also learn a variety of features of the physical structures which detract from good management, and a variety of techniques both for controlling destructive tenants and for creating positive tenant attitudes toward the project. What one may not learn, however, is *the* program design and implementation strategy which will guarantee that public housing units will be well managed. Ongoing learning will be necessary to achieve anything resembling good management, and some projects in some communities are almost bound to fail.

The ongoing nature of learning in public policy implementation is important to the present discussion because it implies that *commitment* to the activity is an absolutely essential ingredient to the successful utilization of knowledge to maintain and improve programs. This commitment should exist at several levels: a general elite belief in the legitimacy of this type of government activity, supported by favorable, or at least neutral public opinion; a belief in the government's ability to carry out such programs itself or to successfully induce comparable private sector action; a commitment by administrators at all levels to the maximum possible realization of the program's objectives. This commitment must also include a willingness on the part of key political actors to provide sufficient *resources* to achieve these goals — not without regard for the limits imposed by competing needs, but with at least some rationally defensible relationship to the need which exists. Obviously, not all of these levels of commitment will be fully realized at any one time, but some minimum level of each is clearly necessary.

Having established the importance of feedback and learning to successful public programs, and the importance to learning of a solid commitment to the activity in question, we may now return to the question of the role of consensus and dissensus which was raised at the beginning of this section. The housing policy environment described in this book has been characterized by: (1) a lack of consensus as to the basic validity of government intervention on behalf of the poor in general; and, (2) a lack of consensus as to the need for the government to provide adequate housing to those who cannot purchase it on the private market. A substantial segment of the political/economic elite stratum of American society has felt, with varying degrees of consistency and intensity, that such government activity is inimical to the long-term well-being of the capitalist system. They have opposed and/or tried to curtail such activities at every turn. They have occupied key leadership positions at various times throughout the last five decades and have had a major impact on housing policy outcomes, despite the legislative, bureaucratic, and constituency interests supporting a public role in housing and community development.

Based on the above arguments, one would expect that this lack of consensus would have had distinctly negative consequences for the development of housing programs. The history of federal housing policy presented in these pages clearly reveals some of these negative consequences. Among the most important are:

1. A consistently low level of resources (in relation to need) have been committed to housing and community development programs, both at the "micro" level (i.e., excessive per unit cost restrictions and various other false economies) and at the level of aggregate spending. Though Nixon's famous dictum that you can't solve problems by throwing money at them may have some validity, it is also true that many of the problems of various housing programs *could* have been solved with the judicious application of additional resources. Yet, conservatives have generally retained enough power to keep the resources at a lower level than many implementors felt was genuinely necessary.

2. Feedback regarding the difficulties encountered by various programs has been used to argue for their curtailment or abolition rather than as knowledge useful for their improvement. As the public policy literature has made abundantly clear, it is difficult for objective program evaluation to take place in a politically charged environment, and it is even more difficult for such information to be clearly understood by decisionmakers (Nakamura and Smallwood, 1980). Negative information becomes a weapon in the hands of program opponents, and, as a result, proponents become reluctant to generate or disseminate such information or even to give it the serious consideration which it usually deserves.

3. Constant fluctuations in program design, direction, and magnitude result from the ongoing struggle between opponents and proponents of government involvement. New national leadership often feels ideologically committed to abolish the old ways of its predecessors, and it often sees political advantages in setting its own course. The built-in inertia of government (reinforced by the power of subgovernments to protect their turf) reduces these fluctuations to some degree, but, in the end, the lack of continuity often interferes with a smooth learning curve.

Nevertheless, there is a positive side to the dissensus, one which reinforces Mill's contention that the presence and free expression of widely opposing views contributes to the rationality of government decisions. To appreciate this positive side, one must recall E. E. Schatscheider's famous assertion that any organization represents a "mobilization of bias" which tends to discourage the full examination of alternatives (Schattschneider, 1960). When government acts on any problem, organizational commitments are made and program constituencies are mobilized. Legislative decisionmakers are committed to a certain strategy because it matches their image of the problem and pleases key constituencies. Administrators find their careers and egos tied up in certain modes of dealing with problems, and they, too, cultivate clientele support. While the commitment of these actors to an ongoing government role in the area, and even to specific programs or strategies, is, in one sense, essential to rational problem solving, this commitment can also make it difficult to identify or to respond to serious flaws in program structure. Such changes threaten the political and administrative status quo, a set of arrangements and alliances which they have carefully worked out. Moreover, in the case of programs which benefit the disadvantaged, activities are usually carried out *on their behalf* by members of more privileged groups in the society. The history of such programs makes it abundantly clear that actions which benefit these privileged public and private sector providers may not be in the best interests of the program's intended beneficiaries.

As a result, critics who are outside this network of relationships serve a vital function. Conservatives, because they are not strongly committed to the government's taking any action at all, are free to look at the limitations and biases of existing programs from new perspectives. The most important examples of this role discussed in this book are the concepts of housing allowances and revenue sharing. Because of their hostility to large and active public sector organizations, conservatives have been motivated to search for alternative ways of delivering services which involve less complicated administrative structures, such as cash allowances. This, in turn, has helped wean many liberals from an excessive a reliance on complex public bureaucratic structures as the sole means to deliver public services. Similarly, block grants were pushed by conservatives as a means to reduce federal involvement in society, but many of those deeply committed to a federal community development role gradually came to see distinct advantages to more decentralized administration of this process.

The usefulness of these critiques does not, however, negate the importance for successful implementation of commitment to a basic policy direction. Decisionmakers must believe that such activities are necessary and must be willing to search constantly for better means to the end. Only in this way can programs evolve into more efficient and effective problem-solving tools.

The need for such commitment puts the analyst of public policy in a somewhat difficult position. Policy analysts offer themselves as dispassionate observers of the policy process, ready with methodological tools which can assess the potential costs and benefits of future actions and accurately measure the impact of actions already taken. However, the basic value choices upon which the commitment to pursue certain objectives are based are not, in themselves, subject to precise, scientific determination. As Arnold Brecht pointed out many years ago, science can be of great help with the means to achieve goals but is of more limited value in choosing those goals (Brecht, 1959). Throughout this book, I have tried to present both liberal and conservative perspectives on housing policy in an objective and critical fashion. However, I have not attempted to conceal my own value preference for an active government role in meeting housing and community development needs. And, in drawing my final conclusions about the course of federal housing policy, I find I must rely on this basic value preference, which is not necessarily amenable to scientific demonstration.

My basic value premise is that an active role for the state is essential to justice and stability in modern capitalist societies. This role must not be limited to reinforcing market outcomes by rewarding those who are already successful (although investment incentives and public financing of infrastructure can be important and useful activities). It must also include regulation and planning to prevent various undesirable collective consequences of private market transactions, and it must include the provision of essential human services to those who cannot afford to purchase them on the private market. This role may be justified in terms of the long-term growth and stability of the system, in addition to the ethical criterion of the ultimate worth and dignity of individual human beings. Therefore, such a role should be in the rational self-interest of those who are placed in positions of privilege and power by the system.

Given this premise, it becomes essential, in the area of housing policy, that sufficient public resources be committed to the identification of housing and community development needs and the development and/or continuation of programs which met those needs in the most efficient and effective ways possible. Conservatives have argued that such an effort would consume an excessive amount of the nation's resources, i.e., that we can't afford an adequate effort to meet housing needs. There might be a point at which such an effort could become sufficiently costly to detract from other needs, but with combined yearly federal expenditures for housing and community development of less than one-half of 1 percent of the Gross National Product (see Chapters 6 and 8), it would appear that this point is far from being reached.

As to the means for achieving the long sought goal of a decent home and suitable living environment for every American, I would assert, based on the foregoing analysis, that there are no arcane and insoluble mysteries involved in the design and execution of successful public programs. There is no ultimate key to a successful housing policy which our limited rationality has yet to grasp. On the contrary, the tools for achieving varoius pieces of that goal already exist in the program designs which have been developed during the 50 years since the federal government first ventured cautiously into this area. The conclusions suggested throughout this work, and outlined briefly above, are not offered as unique and original insights into the design of a successful housing policy. They will probably seem obvious to most knowledgable observers of this area of public concern.

What, then, is necessary to the development of an effective housing policy? On the one hand, the argument made by a number of conservatives that the public sector is inherently incapable of creating and operating effective programs must be rejected. The historical record does not, in my judgment, reveal *any* housing program which has been a total, categorical failure. Most have succeeded in meeting the needs of hundreds of thousands of persons much better than they would have been met by the private sector, and in most, the successes appear to outweigh the well-publicized failures. To say this is not to deny the seriousness of the failures which have occurred, but, rather, to put these failures in the proper perspective. On the other hand, no program should be undertaken with unrealistic expectations or regarded as a panacea for all housing problems. Conservative critics are correct in asserting that liberals, in their efforts to generate public support for new initiatives, have often oversold the effectiveness of new programs. This tactic makes programs the target of elite and mass resentment and disillusionment when they fail to achieve grandiose objectives within a short period of time.

Ultimately, success depends on learning through experience, which programs work best in meeting which needs, how to administer each program with maximum effectiveness, and what mix of programs works best in dealing with the complex range of housing and community development problems. Neither public housing, nor privately subsidized new construction, nor housing allowances, nor housing rehabilitation will successfully meet all housing needs *by itself*. Similarly, there is no single community development strategy which is the sole key to reversing the decay which has overtaken many urban areas. Sophisticated targeting is required, but sufficient resources must be available so that policy-makers are free to choose, not just one strategy or the other, but *all of the above* when this appears necessary.

Within this process of policy development and execution, extensive debate and dissensus is needed. All programs must be subject to critical review, and there must always be observers who are not locked in to existing ways of doing things. Administrators tend to sink into routine and inertia unless they are periodically called to account for their lack of success in achieving their original objectives. At the same time, it is unlikely that the nation will succeed in meeting the housing needs of its citizens unless there is a strong consensus behind governmental action in this area. Such a consensus cannot be wished into existence. Nevertheless, it is important to recognize that the lack of genuine collective commitment to solving these problems contributes more to their seeming intractability than does any inherent limitation in human rationality or organizational capacity.

In light of these considerations, the direction which the Reagan Administration is pursuing with regard to housing and related human service areas appears as nothing short of tragic. The momentum of prior commitments, and the strong resistance of congressional housing advocates has kept government aid flowing, albeit at reduced levels. However, the reforms Reagan has proposed seem little more than the smokescreens for a basic desire to remove the federal government from such activities altogether. Such a withdrawal of commitment and resources would, in my judgment, prevent the nation from benefitting from the 50 years of learning which have occurred in housing policy. We genuinely do know more than we did 20 or 30 or 50 years ago about providing housing needs. To turn away from the problem—or to pursue the nonsolution of letting the private sector handle it—would be especially tragic in light of this accumulated knowledge. What combination of political events and forces will be necessary to renew our commitment is unclear at this point. Those who believe that we can and should deal with these problems through positive, collective action can only hope that such a combination will occur.

References

Aaron, Henry J. 1972. *Shelter and Subsidies: Who Benefits from Federal Housing Policies?* Washington, D.C.: The Brookings Institute.

— — —. 1978. *Politics and the Professors.* Washington, D.C.: The Brookings Institute.

— — —. 1981. "Policy implications: A Progress Report." in Katharine L. Bradbury and Anthony Downs, eds. *Do Housing Allowances Work?* Washington, D.C., The Brookings Institution: 67–98.

Aberbach, Joel D., and Bert A. Rockman. 1976. "Clashing Beliefs Within the Executive Branch: The Nixon Administration Bureaucracy." *American Political Science Review* 70:456–68.

— — —. 1978. "Bureaucrats and clientele groups: A View from Capitol Hill." *American Journal of Political Science* 22 (November): 819–32.

Agelasto, Michael, and David Listokin. 1977. "Redlining in Perspective: An Evaluation of Approaches to the Urban Mortgage Dilemma", in Donald A. Phares, ed. *A Decent Home and Environment: Housing Urban America.* Cambridge, MA: Ballinger.

Ahlbrandt, Roger S., Jr., and Paul C. Brophy. 1975. *Neighborhood Revitalization.* Lexington, MA: D.C. Heath.

Anderson, James E. 1979. *Public Policy-Making.* 2nd ed. New York: Holt, Rinehart and Winston.

Anderson, Martin. 1964. *The Federal Bulldozer: An Analysis of Urban Renewal 1949–1962.* Cambridge, Mass.: The MIT Press.

Bachrach, Peter, and Morton S. Baratz. 1962. "Two Faces of Power." *The American Political Science Review* 56 (December):947–52.

Bayes, Jane H. 1982. *Ideologies and Interest-Group Politics: The United States as a Special-Interest State in the Global Economy.* Novato, CA: Chandler and Sharp Publications in Political Science.

Beer, Samuel H. 1978. "In Search of a New Public Philosophy." in Anthony King, ed. *The New American Political System.* Washington, D.C.: American Enterprise Institute for Public Policy Research, 5–49.

267

Bekowitz, Marti Anne. 1977. "National Problems and Local Control Tension in Title I of the Housing and Community Development Act of 1974. *Columbia Journal of Law and Social Problems* 13 (no. 3/4):409–463.

Bell, Daniel, 1962. *The End of Ideology: On the Exhaustion of Political Ideas in the Fifties.* New York: Free Press.

Bellush, Jewel, and Murray Hausknecht. 1967. *Urban Renewal: People, Politics, and Planning.* Garden City, New York: Anchor Books.

Berger, Curtis J. 1969. Homeownership for low-income families: The 1968 Housing Act's "cruel hoax". *Connecticut Law Review* 2:30–36.

Best, Michael H., and William Connolly. 1982. *The Politicized Economy.* 2nd ed. Lexington, Mass.: D.C. Hath.

Black, J. T. 1975. "Private Market Renovation in Central Cities." *Urban Land* 34 (November): 3–9.

Blair, John B., and David Nachmias, eds. 1979. "Fiscal Retrenchment and Urban Policy. *Urban Affairs Annual Review* vol. 17. Beverly Hills, CA: Sage Publications.

Boyer, Brian D. 1973. *Cities Destroyed for Cash.* Chicago: Follett Books.

Bradbury, Katherine L., and Anthony Downs. 1981. *Do Housing Allowances Work?* Washington, D. C.: The Brookings Institute.

Bradford, Calvin. 1979. "Financing Home Ownership: The Federal Role in Neighborhood Decline." *Urban Affairs Quarterly* 14 (March):313–336.

Brecht, Arnold. 1959. *Political Theory: The Foundations of Twentieth Century Century Political Thought.* Princeton, NJ: Princeton University Press.

Bryce, Herrington J., ed. 1979. *Revitalizing Cities.* Lexington, Mass.: D.C. Heath.

Buenker, John D. 1973. *Urban Liberalism and Progressive Reform.* New York: Scribner's.

Butler, S. 1980. "Urban Renewal: A Modest Proposal." *Policy Review* 13 (Summer):95–1–7.

Caputo, David A., and Richard L. Cole. 1974. *Urban Politics and Decentralization.* Lexington, Mass.: D. C. Heath.

Caraley, Demetrios. 1976. "Congressional Politics and Urban Aid." *Political Science Quarterly* 91 (Spring):19–45.

Chatterjee, Lata. 1977. "Impact of Leverage on Central City Housing markets." *Growth and Change* 8 (July):8–13.

Chudacoff, Howard P. 1981. *The Evolution of American Urban Society.* 2nd ed. Englewood Cliffs, NJ: Prentice Hall.

Clark, Timothy B., John K. Iglehart, and William Lilley III. 1972. "New Federalism Report." *National Journal* 4 (December 16):1907–1940.

Clay, Phillip L. 1979. The Process of Black Suburbanization. *Urban Affairs Quarterly* 14 (June):405–24.

– – –. 1980. "The Urban Neighborhood in the 1980's: Towards a New Definition of Housing Opportunity." Paper presented to the 1980 Annual Meeting, Urban Affairs Association.

Cobb, Robert W., and Charles D. Elder. 1981. "Communication and Public Policy." in Dan D. Nimmo and Keith R. Sanders, eds. *The Handbook of Political Communication.*" Beverly Hills, CA.: Sage Publications.

Congressional Quarterly, Inc. 1982. *Budgeting For America.* Washington, D.C.

Congressional Quarterly, Inc., Almanac (CQ Almanac). 1965. *Major Housing Legislation Enacted.* 21, 358–87.

— — —. 1966. *Restricted Rent Supplements Funded by Bare Margin.* 22, 245–46.

— — —. 1968. *Housing Bill Provides Home-Buying, Riot, other Aid.* 24, 313–35.

— — —. 1969. *Housing and Urban Development.* 25, 391–403.

— — —. 1970a. *Congress Authorizes $2.9 Billion for Housing Programs.* 26, 727–41.

— — —. 1970b. *Congress Clears Emergency Home Finance Act of 1970.* 26, 277–87.

— — —. 1970c. *Relocation Assistance.* 26, 761–63.

— — —. 1971. *Community Development: Senate, House Hold Hearings.* 27, 841–49.

— — —. 1972. *Rules Committee Kills Housing-Urban Development Act.* 28, 628–35.

— — —. 1973a. *Housing and Urban Development.* 29, 421–23.

— — —. 1973b. *Housing Program Authority Extended to Oct. 1, 1974.* 29, 425–32.

— — —. 1978. *Housing Authorization. 34, 303–11.*

— — —. 1979. *Housing Authorization.* 35, 315–21.

— — —. 1981a. *Reagan Housing Plans Generally Approved.* 37, 111–13.

— — —. 1981b. *HUD, Agencies Funds.* 37, 34–35.

Congressional Quarterly, Inc., Weekly Reports (CQ Weekly Reports). 1972a. *Federal Low-Income Housing Programs Under Scrutiny.* 30 (May 13):1100.

— — —. 1972b. *Growing Issue: Communities vs. Low-Income Housing.* 30 (January 8):51–55.

— — —. 1972c. *Low-Income Housing.* 30 (July 29):1895–96.

— — —. 1973a. *Housing: First Battle in the War Over Spending?* 31 (January 1):40.

— — —. 1973b. *Housing: Nixon Likes Cash Payments, But Not Yet.* 31 (September 22):2518–24.

— — —. 1973c. *Housing Funds: The Nation Seems Unconcerned.* 31 (November 10):2969–72.

— — —. 1973d. *Housing Programs: Administration-Congress Clash.* 31 (January 27):139–41.

— — —. 1974a. *Congress Clears Omnibus Housing Bill.* 32 (August 17):2253–66.

— — —. 1974b. *House Passes Omnibus Housing Bill, 351–25.* 32 (June 29): 1702–06.

— — —. 1974c. *Housing, Urban Development.* 32 (February 2):222.

— — —. 1974d. *Senate Committee Reports Omnibus Housing Bill.* 32 (March 9):621–25.

– – –. 1975a. *Committee Report: 'Contercyclical Aid'.* 33 (August 2):1707–09.

– – –. 1975b. *Congress Clears Emergency Housing Bill.* 33 (June 14):1227–31.

– – –. 1975c. *Congress Clears 'Redlining' Legislation.* 33 (December 20); 2779–81.

– – –. 1975d. *Emergency Housing Aid Reported, Passed.* 33 (April 26):873–75.

– – –. 1973e. *Ford Signs Compromise Housing Legislation.* 33 (July 5): 1435–37.

– – –. 1975f. *Housing Notes.* 33 (September 20):1998.

– – –. 1975g. *House Sustains Ford's Veto of Housing Bill.* 33 (June 28):1353–59.

– – –. 1975h. *Housing/Community Development Action Completed.* 33 (December 27):2857–59.

– – –. 1975i. *HUD Appropriations.* 33 (October 11):2173.

– – –. 1975j. *Neighborhood Decay: Is 'Redlining' a Factor?* 33 (May 17): 1041–43.

– – –. 1975k. *Variable Rate Mortgages.* 33 (June 21):1296.

– – –. 1976a. *Conferees Agree to Revive Public Housing.* 34 (June 19): 1587–90.

– – –. 1976b.*Housing: Continuation of Existing Programs.* 34 (January 24):129.

– – –. 1976c. *Housing: Ford Proposal, Democratic Criticism.* 34 (September 25):

– – –. 1976d. *Panels Want More Variety in Housing Efforts.* 34 (April 10): 829–31.

– – –. 1976e. *Senate Panel Seeks Changes in Housing Policy.* 34 (April 24): 979–80.

– – –. 1976f. *Suburban Public Housing Orders Upheld.* 34 (April 24):958.

– – –. 1978a. *Carter's Urban Package Floundering on Hill.* 36 (July 29): 1960–1963.

– – –. 1978b. *Congress Cool to Renewal of 10-Year Housing Goals.* 36 (July 15):1801–04.

– – –. 1979a. *Carter Proposes Cutbacks in Housing, Urban Programs.* 37 (January 27):145–46.

– – –. 1979b. *Housing Bills Reflect Budgetary Concern.* 37 (June 2):1055–56.

– – –. 1979c. *Senate Approves Cutbacks in Federal Housing Programs.* 37 (July 21):1455–57.

– – –. 1980a. *Congress Approves Cutbacks in U. S. Housing Programs, Boosts Urban Grant Funding.* 38 (January 12):71–75.

– – –. 1980b. *Senate Approves $74.9 Billion HUD Bill.* 38 (September 27): 2847–49.

– – –. 1980c. *Senate Defeats Middle-Income Housing Plan.* 38 (June 28): 1808–09.

– – –. 1983a. *House Approves HUD Bill After Funding is Slashed.* 41 (July 16): 1983.

– – –. 1983b. *Senate's Hopes for Housing Bill Wane.* 41 (September 24):1998.

Converse, Phillip E., et al. 1969. "Continuity and Change in American Politics: Parties and Issues in the 1968 election." *American Political Science Review* 63 (December):1092–1115.

Davis, Otto A., and Andrew B. Whinston. 1966. "The Economics of Urban Renewal." in James Q. Wilson, ed., *Urban Renewal: The Record and the Controversy.* Cambridge, MA: MIT Press: 50–67.

Davis, Otto A., C. M. Eastman, and C. I. Hue. 1974. "The Shrinkage in the Stock of Low Quality Housing in the Central City: An Empirical Study of the U. S. Experience over the Last Ten Years." *Urban Studies* 11 (February):13–26.

DeSalvo, Joseph S. 1976. "Housing Subsidies: Do We Know What We are Doing?" *Policy Analysis* 2 (Winter):39–60.

Dolbeare, Kenneth M., and Patricia Dobeare. 1971. *American Ideologies: The Competing Political Beliefs of the 1970's.* Markham Political Science Series. Chicago: Markham Publishing Co.

Dommel, Paul R. 1974. *The Politics of Revenue Sharing.* Bloomington, Ind.: University of Indiana Press.

– – –. 1980. "Social Targeting in Community Development." *Political Science Quarterly* 95 (Fall): 465–78.

Donovan, John C. 1967. *The Politics of Poverty.* New York: Pegasus

Downs, Anthony. 1973. *Federal Housing Subsidies: How Are They Working?* Lexington, Mass.: D. C. Heath, Lexington Books.

– – –. 1977. "The Impact of Housing Policies on Family Life in the U.S. Since World War II." *Daedalus* 106 (Spring):163–80.

– – –. 1981. *Neighborhoods and Urban Development.* Washington, D. C.: The Brookings Institute.

Dye, Thomas R. 1983.*Who's Running America? The Reagan Years.* Third ed. Englewood Cliffs, NJ: Prentice Hall.

– – –. and L. Harmon Zeigler. 1981. *The Irony of Democracy: An Uncommon Introduction to American Politics.* Fifth ed. Belmont, CA.: Wadsworth, Duxbury Press.

Edelman, Murray, 1964. *The Symbolic Uses of Politics.* Urbana, Ill.: University of Chicago Press.

Edwards, George C. 1980. *Presidential Influence in Congress.* San Francisco: W. H. Freeman and Co.

Elazar, Daniel J., et al, eds. 1969. *Cooperation and Conflict: Readings in American Federalism.* Itasca, Ill.: F.E. Peacock.

– – –. 1966. "Are We a Nation of Cities?" *The Public Interest* (Summer) 42–58.

Elickson, Robert. 1967. "Government Housing Assistance to the Poor." *Yale Law Journal* 76 (January):508–44.

Elmore, Richard F. 1978. Organizational Models of Social Program Implementation. *Public Policy* 26 (Spring):185–228.

Evans, Rowland, and Robert D. Novak. 1971. *Nixon in the White House: The Frustration of Power.* New York: Random House.

Farkas, Suzanne. 1971. *Urban Lobbying: Mayors in the Federal Arena.* New York: New York University Press.

Follain, J. R., Jr. 1979. "How Well do Section 8 FMR's (Fair Market Rent) Match the Cost of Rental Housing?: Data from 39 Large Cities." *American Real Estate and Urban Economics Association Journal* 7 (Winter):466-81.

Fredland, J. E., and C. D. MacRae. 1979. "FHA Multi-Family Financial Failure: A Review of Empirical Studies." *American Real Estate and Urban Economics Association Journal* 7 (Spring):95-122.

Free, Lloyd A., and Hadley Cantril. 1967. *The Political Beliefs of Americans: A Study of Public Opinion.* New Brunswick, NJ: Rutgers University Press.

Freedman, Leonard. 1969. *Public Housing: The Politics of Poverty.* New York: Hold, Rinehart and Winston.

Freeman, J. Leiper. 1965. *The Political Process: Executive Bureau-Legislative Committee Relations.* New York: Random House.

Frej, William, and Harry Specht. 1976. "The Housing and Community Development Act of 1974: Implications for Policy and Planning." *The Social Service Review* 50 (June):275-92.

Fried, Marc. 1966. "Grieving for a Lost Home: Psychological Costs of Relocation," James Q. Wilson, in ed. *Urban Renewal: The Record and the Controversy,* 359-79.

Frieden, Bernard J., and Marshall Kaplan. 1977. *The Politics of Neglect: Urban Aid from Model Cities to Revenue Sharing.* Cambridge, Mass.: The MIT Press.

Frieden, Bernard J., and Arthur P. Solomon. 1977. *The Nation's Housing: 1975 to 1985.* Cambridge, Mass.: Joint Center for Urban Studies of the Mass. Institute of Technology and Harvard University.

Friedman, Lawrence M. 1968. *The Government and Slum Housing: A Century of Frustration.* Chicago: Rand McNally.

Friedman, Milton. 1962. *Capitalism and Freedom.* Chicago: University of Chicago Press.

Fullerton, D. J., and C. D. MacRae. 1978. "FHA, Racial Discrimination, and Urban Mortgages." *American Real Estate and Urban Economics Association Journal* 6 (Winter):451-70.

Galbraith, John Kenneth. 1967. *The New Industrial State.* Boston: Houghton Mifflin.

Gans, Herbert J. 1962. *The Urban Villagers: Group and Class in the Life of Italian-Americans.* New York: The Free Press.

Gelfand, Mark I. 1975. *A Nation of Cities: The Federal Government and Urban America.* New York: Oxford University Press.

Glazer, Nathan. 1967. "Housing Problems and Housing Policies." *The Public Interest* 7 (Spring):21-51.

Goering, John M. 1979. "The National Neighborhood Movement: A Preliminary Analysis and Critique." *American Planning Association Journal* 45 (October): 506–14,

Graul, Barbara. 1976. "Housing and Community Development Act of 1974: Who Shall Live in Public Housing?" *Catholic University Law Review* 25 (No. 2):320–42.

Grebler, Leo, and Frank G. Mittelbach. 1979. *The Inflation of House Prices.* Lexington, Mass.: D. C. Hath, Lexington Books.

Greer, Scott. 1965. *Urban Renewal and American Cities: The Dilemma of Democratic Intervention.* Indianapolis, New York: Bobbs-Merrill.

Grigsby, William G. 1965. *Housing Markets and Public Policy.* Philadelphia: University of Pennsylvania Press.

Grigsby, William, and Louis Rosenburg, 1975. *Urban Housing Policy.* (For Center for Urban Policy Research, Rutgers University.) New York: APS Publications.

Hale, George E. and Marian L. Palley. 1981. *The Politics of Federal Grants.* Washington, D. C.: Congressional Quarterly, Inc.

Harrigan, John J. 1976. *Political Change in the Metropolis.* Boston: Little, Brown and Co.

Harrington, Michael. 1971. *The Other America.* Baltimore, MD: Penguin Books.

Hartman, Chester W. 1971. "Relocation: Illusory Promises and No Relief." *Virginia Law Review* 57 (June):745–817.

― ― ―. 1975. *Housing and Social Policy.* Englewood Cliffs, NJ: Prentice Hall.

Hartman, Chester W., and Dennis Keating. 1974. "The Housing Allowance Delusion." *Social Policy* 4 (January/February):31–37.

Hartman, Chester W., Robert P. Kessler, and Richard T. LeGates. 1974. "Municipal Housing Code Enforcement and Low Income Tenants." *American Institute of Planners Journal* 40 (March): 90–114.

Haveman, Robert H., ed. 1977. *A Decade of Federal Anti-Poverty Programs: Achievements, Failures and Lessons.* Institute for Research of Poverty, Poverty Policy Analysis series. New York: Academic Press.

Havemann, Joel, and Rochelle L. Stanfield. 1977. "Housing as Part of Welfare: An Agency Battles for its Turf." *National Journal* 9 (July 30):1190–92.

Hays, R. Allen. 1982a. "Housing Rehabilitation as an Urban Policy Alternative." *Journal of Urban Affairs* 4 (Spring):39–54.

― ―. 1982b. "Public Sector Housing Rehabilitation: A Survey of Program Impact." *The Urban Interest* 4 (Spring):70–86.

Hays, R. Allen, and Christopher Silver. 1980. "Can you Compensate for a Lost Home? An Assessment of the 1970 Uniform Relocation Act." *Urban Affairs Papers* 2 (Winter):33–49.

Heclo, Hugh. 1977. *A Government of Strangers.* Washington, D. C.: The Brookings Institute.

― ― ―. 1978. "Issue Networks and the Executive Establishment," in Anthony King, ed., *The New American Political System.* Washington, D. C.: American Enterprise Institute for Public Policy Research, 87–125.

Hirshen, Al, and Richard T. LeGates. 1975. "HUD's Bonanza for Suburbia." *Progressive* 39 (April):32-34.

Holleb, D. B. 1978. "A Decent Home and Suitable Living Environment." *Annals of The American Academy of Political and Social Science* 435 (January):102-16.

Huber, Joan and William H. Form. 1973. *Income and Ideology: An Analysis of the American Political Formula.* New York: Free Press.

Hughes, James W., and Kenneth D. Bleakly, Jr. 1975. *Urban Homesteading.* New Brunswick, NJ: The Center For Urban Policy Research, Rutgers University.

Ingram, Helen. 1977. "Policy Implementation through Bargaining: The Case of Federal Grants-in-Aid." *Public Policy* 25 (Fall):499-526.

Jacobs, Jane. 1961. *The Death and Life of Great American Cities.* New York: Vintage Books.

James, Franklin J. 1980. *Back to the City: An Appraisal of Housing Reinvestment and Population Change in Urban America.* Washington, D. C.: Urban Institute.

Kallen, David J., and Dorothy Miller. 1971. "Public Attitudes Towards Welfare." *Social Work* 16 (July):83-90.

Kariel, Henry S., ed. 1970. *Frontiers of Democratic Theory.* New York: Random House.

Keith, Nathaniel S. 1973. *Politics and the Housing Crisis Since 1930.* New York: Universe Books.

Kern, C. R. 1981. "Upper-Income Renaissance in the City: Its Sources and Implications for the City's Future." *Journal of Urban Economics* 9 (Jan): 106-124.

Kettl, D. F. 1979. "Can the Cities be Trusted?: The Community Development Experience." *Political Science Quarterly* 94 (Fall:437-54.

Key, V.O., Jr. 1964. *Politics, Parties, and Pressure Groups.* New York: Thomas Crowell.

Keyes, Langley C., Jr. 1969. *The Rehabilitation Planning Game: A Study in the Diversity of Neighborhoods.* Cambridge, Mass. MIT Press.

― ― ―. 1980. "The Boston Rehabilitation Program," in John Pynoos, et al. eds. *Housing Urban America.* Chicago: Aldine.

Kingdon, John W. 1984. *Agendas, Alternatives and Public Policies.* Boston, Little Brown.

Kolko, Gabriel. 1962. *Wealth and Power in America.* New York: Praeger.

Kristoff, Frank S. 1975. "The Housing and Community Development Act of 1974: Prospects and Prognosis." *Journal of Economics and Business* 27 (Winter):112-121.

Larner, Jeremy, and Irving Howe. 169. *Poverty: Views from the Left.* New York: William Morrow and Company.

Laska, Shirley B. and Daphne Spain, eds. 1980. *Back to the City: Issues in Neighborhood Renovation.* New York: Pergamon Press.

Lasch, Christopher. 1977. *Haven in a Heartless World: The Family Besieged.* New York: Basic Books.

Lazin, Frederick A. 1976. Federal Low-Income Housing Assistance Programs and Racial Segregation: Leased Public Housing. *Public Policy* 24 (Summer):337–60.

— — —. 1980. "Policy, Perception, and Program Failure: The Politics of Public Housing in Chicago and New York City." *Urbanism Past and Present* no. 9 (Winter):1–12.

Levitan, Sar A. 1976. *The Promise of Greatness*: Cambridge, Mass.: Harvard University Press.

Lewis, Michael. 1978. *The Culture of Inequality.* Amherst, Mass: University of Massachusetts Press.

Light, Paul Charles. 1982. *The President's Agenda: Domestic Policy Choice from Kennedy to Carter (With Notes on Ronald Reagan).* Baltimore: The Johns Hopkins University Press.

Lilley, William III. 1972. "(Cities and Suburbs) Chicago Case Shows Courts Hold Key to Mandatory Housing Desegration." *National Journal* 4 (January 22):162–63.

Lilley, William III, and Timothy B. Clark. 1972a. "Urban Report/Block-Grant, Transit, Reorganization Plans Languish in Congress." *National Journal* 4 (September 16):1459–65.

— — —. 1972b. "Urban Report/Federal Programs Spur Abandonment of Housing in Major Cities." *National Journal* 4 (January 1):26–33.

— — —. 1972c. "Urban report/Immense Costs, Scandals, Social Ills Plague Low-Income Housing Programs." *National Journal* 4 (July 1):1075–83.

Lilley, William III, Timothy B. Clark, and John K. Iglehart. 1973. "New Federalism Report: Nixon Attack on Grant Programs Aims to Simplify Structure, Give Greater Local Control." *National Journal* 5 (January 20):76–88.

Lipton, S. Gregory, 1977. "Evidence of Central City Revival." *AIP Journal* 43 (April):136–47.

Listokin, David. 1973. *The Dynamics of Housing Rehabilitation.* New Brunswick, NJ: The Center for Urban Policy Research, Rutgers University.

Lowi, Theodore J. 1979. *The End of Liberalism: Ideology, Policy and The Crisis of Public Authority.* 2nd ed. New York: W. W. Norton and Co.

— — —. 1964. "American Business, Public Policy, Case Studies, and Political Theory." *World Politics XVI* (July):677–715.

Lynn, Lawrence E. Jr., and David Whitman. 1981. *The President as Policymaker: Jimmy Carter and Welfare Reform.* Philadelphia: Temple University Press.

Maas, Arthur. 1951. *Muddy Waters.* Cambridge, Mass.: Harvard University Press.

McClaughry, John. 1975. "The Troubled Dream: The Life and Times of Section 235 of the National Housing Act." *Loyola University Law Journal* 6 (Winter):1–45.

McConnell, Grant. 1966. *Private Power and American Democracy.* New York: Random House, Vintage Books.

McDonough, W. R. 1975. "Buyers, Builders, and Instability in Single-Family Housing Construction." *Journal of Economics and Business* 17 (Winter):150–58.

McFarland, M. Carter, 1978. *Federal Government and Urban Problems: HUD: Successes, Failures, and the Fate of Our Cities.* Boulder, Col.: Westview Press.

McGuire, Chester C. 1981. *International Housing Policies: A Comparative Analysis.* Lexington, Mass.: D. C. Heath, Lexington Books.

Magida, Arthur J. 1974. "Housing Report/Major Programs Revised to Stress Community Control." *National Journal* 6 (September 14):1369–79.

Mandelker, Daniel R. 1973. *Housing Subsidies in the U. S. and England.* Indianapolis, New York: Bobbs-Merrill Co.

Mandelker, Daniel R., et al. 1981. *Housing and Community Development: Cases and Materials.* Contemporary Legal Education Series. New York: Bobbs-Merrill Co.

Mandelker, Daniel R., and Roger Montgomery. 1973. *Housing in America: Problems and Perspectives.* Indianapolis, New York: Bobbs-Merrill Co.

Marcuse, Peter. 1978. "Housing Policy and the Myth of the Benevolent State." *Social Policy* 8 (January/February):21–26.

– – –. 1979. "The Deceptive Consensus on Redlining: Definitions do Matter." *American Planning Association Journal* 45 (October):549–56.

Medley, Richard, ed. 1982. *The Politics of Inflation: Comparative Analysis.* New York: Pergamon Press.

Meehan, Eugene. 1977. "The Rise and Fall of Public Housing: Condemnation Without Trial," in Donald Phares, ed. *A Decent Home and Environment,* Cambridge, Mass.: Ballinger 5–42.

– – –. 1979. *The Quality of Federal Policymaking: Programmed Failure in Public Housing.* Columbia, Mo.: University of Missouri Press.

Mendelson, Robert E., and Michael A. Quinn, eds. 1976. *The Politics of Housing in Older Urban Areas.* Praeger Special Studies in U. S. Economic, Social, and Political Issues. New York: Praeger Publishers.

Meyerson, Martin, and Edward C. Banfield. 1955. *Politics, Planning and the Public Interest.* Glencoe, Ill.: The Free Press.

Mileur, Jerome M., ed. 1974. *The Liberal Tradition in Crisis: American Politics in the Sixties.* Lexington, Mass.: D. C. Heath.

Mills, C. Wright. 1959. *The Power Elite.* New York: Oxford University Press.

Mitchell, James E. 1974. "Pennsylvania vs. Lynn: The Rest of the Iceberg." *University of Detroit Journal of Urban Law* 52:421–58.

Mohl, Raymond A., and James F. Richardson, eds. 1973. *The Urban Experience: Themes in American History.* Belmont Calif.: Wadsworth Publishing Co.

Mollenkopf, John H. 1975. "The Post-War Politics of Urban Development." *Politics and Society* 5 (No. 3):247–95.

– – –. 1983. *The Contested City.* Princeton, NJ: Princeton University Press.

Morrall, J. F. III, and E. D. Olsen. 1980. The Cost-Effectiveness of Leased Public Housing. *Policy Analysis* 6 (Spring):151-70.

Moynihan, Daniel P. 1967. "The Professionalization of Reform," in Marvin E. Gettleman and David Mermelstein, eds. *The Great Society Reader.* New York: Random House, 461-476.

– – –. 1969. *Maximum Feasible Misunderstanding.* New York: Free Press.

Myers, Dowell. 1975. "Housing Allowances, Submarket Relationships and the Filtering Process." *Urban Affairs Quarterly* 11 (December):215-40.

Nakamura, Robert T. and Frank Smallwood. 1980. *The Politics of Policy Implementation.* New York: St. Martins Press.

Nathan, Richard P. 1983. *The Administrative Presidency.* New York: John Wiley and Sons.

Nathan, Richard P., and Charles F. Adams, Jr. 1977. *Revenue Sharing: The Second Round.* Washington, D. C.: The Brookings Institute.

Nathan, Richard P., and Paul R. Dommel. 1978. "Federal-Local Relations Under Block Grants." *Political Science Quarterly* 93 (Fall):421-42.

Nathan, Richard P., et al. 1977. "Monitoring the Block Grant Program for Community Development." *Political Science Quarterly* 92 (Summer):219-44.

National Commission on Urban Problems. 1969. *Building the American City: Report of the National Commission.* Praeger Special Studies in U. S. Economic, Social and Political Issues. New York: Praeger Publishers.

National Low Income Housing Coalition. 1983a. The 1984 Reagan Budget and Low Income Housing. Special Memorandum No. 18 from the Low Income Housing Information Service. February, 1983.

– – –. 1983b. Low Income Housing Appropriations for 1984. Statement of Cushing N. Dolbeare, President, before Subcommittee on HUD-Independent Agencies, Senate Committee on Appropriations, May 24, 1983. Mimeographed copy supplied to author.

Nelson, Kathryn P. 1980. "Recent Suburbanization of Blacks: How Much, Who and Where?" *American Planning Association Journal* 46 (July):287-300.

Nenno, Mary K. 1983. "The Reagan Housing, CD Record: A Negative Rating." *Journal of Housing* 40, Number 5: (September/October): 135-141.

Neustadt, Richard E 1980. *Presidential Power: The Politics of Leadership from FDR to Carter.* New York: John Wiley.

Nixon, Richard M. 1971. *Nixon: His Second Year in Office.* Washington, D. C.: Congressional Quarterly, Inc.

O'Loughlin, J., and Douglas C. Munski. 1979. "Housing Rehabilitation in the Inner City: a Comparison of Two Neighborhoods in New Orleans." *Economic Geography* 55 (January):52-70.

Olsen, Edgar O., and David W. Rasmussen. See: U. S. Dept. of HUD, 1979b.

Palen, J. John, and Bruce L. London. 1984. *Gentrification, Displacement and Neighborhood Revitalization.* Albany, NY: State University of New York Press.

Palmer, John L., and Isabel V. Sawhill, eds. 1982. *The Reagan Experiment.* Washington, D.C.: The Urban Institute Press.

Peabody, Malcom E., Jr. 1974. "Housing Allowances: A New Way to Abuse the Poor." *New Republic* 170 (March 9):20–23.

Pechman, Joseph, ed. 1979. *Setting National Priorities: The 1980 Budget.* Washington, D. C.: The Brookings Institute.

— — —. 1981. *Setting National Priorities: The 1982 Budget.* Washington, D.C.: The Brookings Institute.

— — —. 1982. *Setting National Priorities: The 1983 Budget.* Washington, D.C.: The Brookings Institute.

Perry, David C., and Alfred J. Watkins, eds. 1977. *The Rise of the Sunbelt Cities.* Urban Affairs Annual Reviews, vol. 14. Beverly Hills, CA.: Sage Publications.

Peterson, Paul E. and J. David Greenstone. 1977. "Racial Change and Citizen Participation: The Mobilization of Low Income Communities Through Community Action," in Robert H. Haveman, ed., *A Decade of Federal Anti Poverty Programs.* NY: Academic Press, 241–278.

Pettigrew, T. F. 1979. "Racial Change and Social Policy." *Annals of the American Academy of Political and Social Science* 441 (January):114–31.

Phares, Donald, ed. 1977. *A Decent Home and Environment: Housing Urban America.* Cambridge, Mass.: Ballinger.

Phillips, James G. 1973a. "Housing Report/HUD Proposes Cash Allowance as Link to Broad Plan for Welfare Reform." *National Journal* 5 (August 25):1225–61.

— — —. 1973b. "Housing Report/Standoff Likely Between Nixon and Hill: Democrats Hit Delay on Low Income Programs." *National Journal 5.* September 29):1448–1451.

Piven, Frances Fox, and Richard A. Cloward. 1966. "Desegrated Housing? Who Pays for the Reformers' Ideal?" *New Republic* 155 (December 27): 17–21.

— — —. 1971. *Regulating the Poor: The Functions of Public Welfare.* New York: Pantheon Books.

— — —. 1982. *The New Class War.* New York: Pantheon Books.

Pomper, Gerald M. 1981. *The Election of 1980: Reports and Interpretations.* Chatham, NJ: Chatham House Publishers.

Priest, D. E. 1977. The Uncharted Trend: Toward Increased Public-Private Co-operation in Housing Development. *American Real Estate and Urban Economics Association Journal* 5 (Summer):242–53.

Pynoos, Jon, Robert Schafer, and Chester W. Hartman, eds. 1980. *Housing Urban America.* New York: Aldine.

Raskin, Marcus G., and Tim Yarborouogh. 1978. *The Federal Budget and Social Reconstruction: The People and the State.* Washington, D. C.: Institute for Policy Studies.

Reagan, Michael D. 1963. *The Managed Economy.* New York: Oxford University Press.

— — —. 1972. *The New Federalism.* New York: Oxford University Press.

Reeb, Donald J., and James T. Kirk, Jr. 1973. *Housing the Poor*. New York: Praeger Publishers.

Reed, Richard Ernie. 1979. *Return to the City: How to Restore Old Buildings and Ourselves in America's Historic Urban Neighborhoods*. Garden City, NJ: Doubleday.

Resources for the Future, Inc. 1975. *Financing the New Federalism: Revenue Sharing, Conditional Grants, and Taxation*. Baltimore: Johns Hopkins University Press.

Reynolds, Malvina. 1964. "Little Boxes," in *Little Boxes and Other Hand Made Songs*. New York: Oak Publishing Co.

Ripley, Randall B. and Grace A. Franklin. 1980. *Congress, The Bureaucracy, and Public Policy*. Homewood, IL: The Dorsey Press.

Rokeach, Milton. 1979. *Understanding Human Values: Individual and Societal*. New York: Free Press.

Roos, L. John. 1975. "Experimentally Testing Alternative Housing Policies." *Policy Studies Journal* 3 (September):298–301.

Rose-Ackerman, S. 1977. "The Political Economy of a Racist Housing Market." *Journal of Urban Economics* 4 (April): 150–69.

Rosenfeld, Raymond A. 1980. "Who Benefits and Who Decides? The Uses of Community Development Block Grants," in Donald B. Rosenthal, ed., *Urban Revitalization* Urban Affairs Annual Reviews, vol 18. Beverly Hills, CA: Sage Publications.

Rothenberg, Jerome. 1967. *Economic Evaluation of Urban Renewal: Conceptual Foundation of Benefit Cost Analysis*. Studies of Government Finance. Washington, D. C.: The Brookings Institute.

Ryan, William. 1976. *Blaming the Victim*. Rev., updated ed. New York: Vintage Books.

Safire, William. 1975. *Before the Fall: An Inside View of the Pre-Watergate White House*. Garden City, New York: Doubleday.

Saltzstein, Alan L. 1977. "Federal Categorical Aid to Cities: Who Needs it versus Who Gets it." *Western Political Quarterly* 30 (September):377–83.

Sanders, Heywood T. 1980. "Urban Renewal and the Revitalized City: A Reconsideration of Recent History." in Donald B. Rosenthal *Urban Revitalization* Volume 18, Urban Affairs Annual Reviews: Beverly Hills, CA: Sage Publications.

Savitch, H. V. 1979. *Urban Policy and the Exterior City: Federal, State and Corporate Impacts Upon Major Cities*. New York: Pergamon Press.

Schafer, Robert, and Charles G. Field. 1969. "Section 235 of the National Housing Act: Home Ownership for Low-Income Families." *Journal of Urban Law* 46 (No. 3):667–85.

Schattschneider, E.E. 1960. *The Semi-Sovereign People*. New York: Holt, Rinehart, and Winston.

Scudder, Samuel. 1972. "(Cities and Suburbs) HUD Seeks to Reduce its Ownership of Inner City Abandoned Properties." *National Journal* 4 (February 26):371.

Seidel, Stephen R. 1978. *Housing Costs of Government Regulations: Confronting The Regulated Maze.* New Brunswick, NJ: Center for Urban Policy Research.

Seiders, D. F. 1981. "Changing Patterns of Housing Finance." *Federal Reserve Bulletin* 67 (June):461-72.

Semer, Milton. See: U. S. Dept. of HUD, 1976.

Silver, Christopher, 1982. "Neighborhood Planning in Historical Perspective: New Uses for an Old Idea." Paper presented to the 1982 meeting of the Urban Affairs Association, Philadelphia, PA.

Solomon, Arthur P. 1974. *Housing the Urban Poor: A Critical Evaluation of Federal Housing Policy.* A Publication of the Joint Center For Urban Studies of the Massachusetts Institute of Technology and Harvard University. Cambridge, Mass.: The MIT Press.

Solomon, Arthur P., ed. 1980. *The Prospective City: Economic, Population, Energy, and Environmental Developments.* Cambridge, Mass.: The MIT Press.

Stanfield, Rochelle L. 1977a. "Civil War Over Cities Aid: The Battle No One Expected." *National Journal* 9 (August 6):1226-27.

— — —. 1977b. "Government Seeks the Right Formula for Community Development Funds." *National Journal* 9 (February 12):237-43.

— — —. 1977c. "The Latest Community Development Flap: Targeting on the the Poor." *National Journal* 9 (December 3):1877-79.

— — —. 1977d. "Three Rays of Hope for the Ailing Large Cities." *National Journal* 9 (April 16):589-91.

— — —. 1981. "Cashing Out Housing: A Free Market Approach That Might also Cost Less." *National Journal* 13 (September 18):1660-64.

— — —. 1982a. "Low-Cost Housing Aid Battle May Be a Zero-Sum Game Without Any Winners." *National Journal* 14 (December 18):2164-67.

— — —. 1982b. "Losing Friends." *National Journal* 14 (May 22):918.

— — —. 1983a. "If Vouchers Work for Food, Why not for Housing, Schools, Health, and Jobs?" *National Journal* 15 (April 23):840-44.

— — —. 1983b. "Housing Focus-Ramshackle Planning." *National Journal* 15 (October 15):2122.

— — —. 1983c. "Pierce, HUD's 'Nice Guy' Secretary—'Its Almost as if He Isn't There'." *National Journal* 15 (August 6):1642-46.

Steiner, Gilbert Y. 1971. *The State of Welfare.* Washington, D.C.: The Brookings Institution.

Stegman, Michael A., ed. 1970. *Housing and Economics: The American Dream.* Cambridge, Mass.: MIT Press.

— — —. 1979. *Housing Investment in the Inner City: The Dynamics of Decline.* Cambridge, Mass.: MIT Press.

Sternlieb, George, R.W. Burchell, and J.W. Hughes, 1975. "The Future of Housing and Urban Development." *Journal of Economics and Business* 27 (Winter):99—111.

Sternlieb, George, et al. 1980. *American's Housing: Prospects and Problems.* New Brunswick, NJ: Rutgers U. Center for Urban Policy Research.

Steven, A. 1975. "Home Ownership for the Poor: A Case Study." *Journal of Economics and Business* 27 (Winter):99–111.

Stone, Clarence N., Robert K. Whelan, and William J. Murin. 1979. *Urban Policy and Politics in a Bureaucratic Age.* Englewood Cliffs, NJ: Prentice Hall.

Straszheim, Mahlon R. 1979. "The Section 8 Rental Assistance Program: Costs and Policy Options." *Policy Studies Journal* 8 (No. 2):307–23.

Struyk, Raymond J. 1977. "The Need for Local Flexibility in U. S. Housing Policy." *Policy Analysis* 3 (Fall):471–83.

———. 1979. *Saving the Housing Assistance Plan.* An Urban Institute Paper on Housing. Washington, D. C.: The Urban Institute.

———. 1980. *A New System for Public Housing: Salvaging a National Resource.* Washington, D. C.: The Urban Institute.

Struyk, Raymond J., and Marc Bendick, Jr. 1981. *Housing Vouchers for the Poor: Lessons From a National Experiment.* Washington, D. C. The Urban Institute.

Struyk, Raymond J., Sue A. Marshall, and Larry J. Ozanne. 1978. *Housing Policies for the Urban Poor: A Case for Local Diversity in Federal Programs.* Washington, D. C.: The Urban Instiute.

Sumka, Howard J. 1979. "Neighborhood Revitalization and Displacement: A Review of the Evidence." *American Planning Association Journal* 45 (October):480–87.

Suttles, Gerald D. 1968. *The Social Order of the Slum: Ethnicity and Territory in the Inner City.* Chicago: The University of Chicago Press.

Szabo, Joan C. 1975. "Urban Report/Community Development Program Shows Signs of Progress." *National Journal* 7 (November 29):1634–40.

Szulc, Tad. 1978. *The Energy Crisis.* Lexington, Mass.: D.C. Heath.

Thurow, Lester C. 1981. *The Zero-Sum Society: Distribution and the Possibilities for Economic Change.* New York: Penguin Books.

Tobin, Gary A. 1979. *The Changing Structure of the City: What Happened to the Urban Crisis.* Urban Affairs Annual Reviews, Vol. 16. Beverly Hills, CA.: Sage Publications.

U. S. Advisory Commision on Intergovernmental Relations (ACIR). 1977. *Community Development: The Workings of a Federal-Local Block Grant.* Washington, D. C., GPO.

———. 1978. *Categorical Grants: Their Role and Design.*

U. S. Bureau of the Census. 1971a. *Characteristics of Low-Income Population, 1970.* Current Pouplation Reports, Series P–60, no. 81. Washington, D. C.: GPO.

———. 1971b. *Income in 1970 of Families and Persons in the U. S.* Current Population Reports, Series P–60, no. 80. Washington, D. C.: GPO.

———. 1981a. *Characteristics of the Population Below the Poverty Level: 1979.* Current Population Reports, Series P–60. no. 130. Washington, D. C.: GPO.

———. 1981b. *Geographical Mobility: March 1975 to March 1980.* Current Population Reports, Series P–20, no. 368. Washington, D. C.: GPO.

————. 1981c. *Money Income of Persons and Families in the United States: 1979.* Current Population Reports, Series P-60, no. 129. Washington, D. C.: GPO.

————. 1981d. *Statistical Abstract.* Washington, D. C.: GPO.

————. 1984. Characteristics of the Population Below the Poverty Level: 1982. Current Population Reports, Series P-60, No. 144. Washington, D. C.: GPO.

U.S. Bureau of the Census, and Department of Housing and Urban Development (HUD), Office of Policy Development and Research. 1975. *Annual Housing Survey 1973: U. S. and Regions.* Part B: Indicators of Housing and Neighborhood Quality; and Part C: Financial Characteristics of the Housing Inventory. Current Housing Reports, Series H-150 73B. Washington, D. C.: GPO.

————. 1979. *Annual Housing Survey 1977: U. S. and Regions.* Part B: Indicators of housing and neighborhood quality. Current Housing Reports, Series H-150 77. Washington, D. C.: GPO.

————. 1981a. *Annual Housing Survey 1978: U. S. and Regions.* Part B: Indicators of Housing and Neighborhood Quality by Financial Characteristics. Current Housing Reports, Series H-150 78. Washington, D. C.: GPO.

————. 1981b. *Annual Housing Survey 1980: U. S. and Regions.* Part C: Financial Characteristics of the Housing Inventory. Current Housing Reports, Series H-150-80. Washington, D. C.: GPO.

————. 1984. *Annual Housing Survey 1983:* U. S. and Regions. Part C: Financial Characteristics of the Housing Inventory. Current Housing Reports, Series H-150-83. Washington, D. C.: GPO.

U. S. Bureau of Labor Statistics. CPI Detailed Reports (monthly publication) 1970 through 1984. Washington, D. C.: GPO.

U. S. Commission on Civil Rights. 1971. *Home Ownership for Lower Income Families: A Report on the Racial and Ethnic Impact of the Section 235 Program.* Washington, D. C.: GPO.

————. 1975. *Equal Opportunity in Suburbia.* Washington, D. C.: GPO.

U. S. Congress. Budget Office. 1977. *Real Estate Tax Shelter Subsidies and Direct Subsidy Alternatives.* Washington, D. C.: GPO.

————. 1982. *Federal Housing Assistance: Alternative Approaches.* Washington, D. C.: GPO.

————. 1983. *Federal Subsidies for Public Housing: Issues and Options.* Washington, D. C.: GPO.

U. S. Congress. Joint Economic Committee. 1972. *The Economics of Federal Subsidy Programs. Part 5 — Housing Subsidies.* Joint Committee Print. 92nd Cong., 2nd sess. Washington, D. C.: GPO.

————. 1981. *Housing and the Economy: Hearings.* 96th Cong., 1st sess. Washington, D. C.: GPO.

————. Subcommittee on Priorities and Economy in Government. 1973. *Housing Policy: Report.* Joint Committee Print. 93rd Cong., 1st sess. Washington, D. C.: GPO.

U. S. Congress House Committee on Appropriations. 1972. Subcommittee on HUD-Space-Science-Veterans. Surveys and Investigations Staff Report. Bound in *HUD-Space-Science-Veterans Appropriations, 1973: Hearings.* Part 3, at 1294. 92nd Cong., 2nd Sess., Washington, D. C.: GPO.

— — —. Committee on Appropriations. Subcommittee on HUD-Independent Agencies. 1977. *Department of HUD-Independent Agencies Appropriations for 1978: Hearings.* Part 8: Subsidized Housing. 95th Cong., 1st sess. Washington, D. C.: GPO.

U. S. Congress. House. Committee on Banking and Currency. 1970. *Investigation and Hearing of Abuses in Federal Low and Moderate Income Housing Programs.* Staff Report and Recommendations. Washington, D. C.: GPO.

— — —. 1971a. *Emergency Home Finance Act of 1970 and Housing and Urban Development Act of 1970.* Committee Print. 91st Cong., 2nd sess. Washington, D. C.: GPO.

— — —. 1971b. *Interim Report on HUD Investigation of Low and Moderate Income Housing Programs: Hearing.* 92nd Cong., 1st sess. Washington, D. C.: GPO.

— — —. Subcommittee on Housing. 1972. *Real-Estate Settlement Costs, FHA Mortgage Foreclosures, Housing Abandonment, and Site Selection Politics: Hearings on H.R. 13337.* Parts 1 and 2. 92nd Cong., 2nd sess. Washington, D. C.: GPO.

— — —. 1974a. *The Administration's Housing and Community Development Proposals.* Committee Print. 93rd Cong., 2nd sess. Washington, D. C.: GPO.

U. S. Congress. House. Committee on Government Operations. 1971. *Overview Hearing on Operations of the Dept. of Housing and Urban Development.* 92nd Cong., 1st sess. Washington, D. C.: GPO.

— — —. 1972a. *Defaults on FHA-Insured Mortgages: Hearings.* Parts 2 and 3. 92n d Cong., 2nd sess. Washington, D. C.: GPO.

— — —. 1972b. *Defaults on FHA-Insured Mortgages (Detroit): Hearings.* 2nd Cong., 2nd sess. Washington, D. C.: GPO.

— — —. 1974. *Management of HUD-Held Multi-Family Mortgages: Hearings.* 93rd Cong. 2nd sess. Washington, D. C.: GPO.

— — —. 1978. *Section 8 Leased Housing Assistance Program. Hearings.* 95th Cong., 1st and 2nd sess. Washington, D. C.: GPO.

U. S. Congress. Senate. Committee on Appropriations. 1971. *Senate Hearings: Dept. of HUD, Space, Science, Veterans, and Certain Other Independent Agencies Appropriations.* Appendix I, Mortgage Bankers' Ass. of America Report at 777. 92nd Cong., 1st sess. Washington, D. C.: GPO.

— — —. Committee on Banking, Housing and Urban Affairs. Subcommittee on Housing and Urban Affairs. 1971. *1971 Housing and Urban Development Legislation: Hearings.* Parts 1 and 2. 92nd Cong., 1st sess. Washington, D. C.: GPO.

— — —. 1973. *Oversight on Housing and Urban Development Programs: Hearings.* Part 1. 93rd Cong., 1st sess. Washington, D. C.: GPO.

— — —. 1974. *Critique of "Housing in the Seventies"*. Prepared by the Congressional Research Service, Library of Congress. Committee Print. 93rd Cong., 2nd sess. Washington, D. C.: GPO.

— — —. 1976. *Community Development Block Grant Program: Hearings on Oversight on the Administration of the Housing and Community Development Act of 1974*. 94th Cong., 2nd sess. Washington, D. C.: GPO.

— — —. 1978. *Distressed HUD-Subsidized Multi-Family Housing Projects: Hearings*. 95th Cong., 1st sess. Washington, D. C.: GPO.

U. S. Congress. Senate. Committee on the Judiciary. Subcommittee on the Separation of Powers. 1971. *Executive Impoundment of Appropriated Funds: Hearings*. 92nd Cong., 1st sess. Washington, D. C.: GPO.

U. S. Department of Housing and Urban Development (HUD). 1970. *The Model Cities Program: A Comparative Analysis of the Planning Process in Eleven Cities*. (Office of Community Planning and Development). Washington, D. C.: GPO.

— — —. 1972. *Report on Audit of Section 236 Multifamily Housing Program* (Office of Audit). Washington, D. C.: GPO.

— — —. 1973a. *The Model Cities Program: Ten Model Cities: A Comparative Analysis of Second Round Planning Years*. (Office of Community Planning and Development). Washington, D. C.: GPO.

— — —. 1973b. *The Model Cities Program: A Comparative Analysis of Participating Cities—Process, Product, Performance and Prediction*. (Office of Community Planning and Development). Washington, D. C.: GPO.

— — —. 1974a. *Housing in the Seventies: A Report on the National Policy Review*. Washington, D. C.: GPO.

— — — —. 1974b. *Summary of the Housing and Community Development Act of 1974*. Washington, D. C.: GPO.

— — —. 1976. *Housing in the Seventies Working Papers: National Housing Policy Review*. 2 vols. Washington, D. C.: GPO.

— — —. 1977. *Block Grants for Community Development*. First Report on the Brookings Institution Monitoring Study of the CDGB Program. Washington, D. C.: GPO.

— — —. 1978a. *Decentralizing Community Development*. Second Report on the Brookings Institution Monitoring Study of the CDGB Program. Washington, D. C.: GPO.

— — —. 1978b. *Final Report of the Task Force on Housing Costs*. Washington, D. C.: HUD.

— — —. 1978c. *Lower Income Housing Assistance Program (Section 8)*: Interim Findings of Evaluation Research. (Office of Policy Development and Research). Washington, D. C.: GPO.

— — —. 1978d. *Lower Income Housing Assistance Program (Section 8): Nationwide Evaluation of the Existing Housing Program*. By Margaret Drury, Olsen Lee, Michael Springer, and Lorene Yap. (Office of Policy Development and Research). Washington, D. C.: GPO.

– – –. 1979a. *City Need and Community Development Funding.* (Office of Policy Development and Research). Washington, D. C. GPO.

– – –. 1979b. *Designing Rehab Programs: A Local Government Guidebook.* (Office of Policy Development and Research). Washington, D. C.: GPO.

– – –. 1979c. *Occasional Papers in Housing and Community Affairs.* Vol. 6. (Office of Policy Development And Research). Washington, D. C.: GPO.

– – –. 1979d. *Problems Affecting Low-Rent Public Housing Projects: A Field Study.* (Office of Policy Development and Research). Washington, D. C.: GPO.

– – –. 1979e. *Statistical Yearbook.* Washington, D. C.: GPO.

– – –. 1979f. *The Tenth Annual Report on the National Housing Goal.* (Office of Policy Development and Research). Washington, D. C.: GPO.

– – –. 1980a. *The Conversion of Rental Housing to Condominiums and Cooperatives: A National Study of Scope, Causes, and Impacts.* (Office of Policy Development and Research). Washington, D. C.: GPO.

– – –. 1980b. *Fifth Annual Community Development Block Grant Report.* (Office of Community Planning and Development). Washington, D. C.: GPO.

– – –. 1980c. *1980 National Housing Production Report.* (Office of Policy Development and Research). Washington, D. C.: GPO.

– – –. 1980d. *The President's National Urban Policy Report 1980.* Washington, D. C.: HUD.

– – –. 1980e. *Targeting Community Development.* Third Report on the Brookings Institution Monitoring Study of the Community Development Block Grant Program. Washington, D. C.: GPO.

– – –. 1981a. *Implementing Community Development.* A Study of the Community Development Block Grant Program prepared by The Brookings Institution. Washington, D. C.: GPO.

– – –. 1981b. *Participation and Benefits in the Urban Section 8 Program: New Construction and Existing Housing.* (Office of Policy Development and Research). Washington, D. C.: GPO.

– – –. 1982a. *Community Development Block Grant Report.* Washington, D.C., GPO.

– – –. 1982b. *The Costs of HUD Multifamily Housing Programs: A Comparison of the Development, Financing and Life Cycle Costs of Section 8, Public Housing, and Other HUD Programs.* 2 vols. (Office of Policy Development and Research). Washington, D. C.: GPO.

U. S. Federal Home Loan Bank Board Journal. January, 1974, January, 1976, December, 1976, January, 1980, January, 1981, October, 1983. Monthly Data on Mortgage Activity in the U. S.

U. S. General Accounting Office. 1973. *Opportunities to Improve Effectiveness and Reduce Costs of Rental Assistance Housing Program.* Washington, D. C.: GPO.

– – –. 1978. *Section 236 Rental Housing: An Evaluation With Lessons for the Future.* Report to Congress by the Comptroller General. Washington, D. C.: GPO.

– – –. 1980. *Evaluation of Alternatives for Financing Low and Moderate Income Rental Housing.* Report to Congress by the Comptroller General. Washington, D. C.: GPO.

– – –. 1983. *Block Grants for Housing: A Study of Local Experiences and Attitudes.* Report to Congress by the Comptroller General. Washington, D. C.: GPO.

U.S. President's Commission on Housing. 1982. *The Report of the President's Commission on Housing.* Washington, D. C.: GPO.

Van Horn, Carl E. 1979. *Policy Implementation in the Federal System: National Goals and Local Implementors.* Lexington, Mass.: D. C. Heath, Lexington Books.

Warner, David C. 1977. *Toward New Human Rights: The Social Policies of the Kennedy and Johnson Administrations.* Austin, Texas: University of Texas, Lyndon B. Johnson School of Public Affairs.

Weicher, John C. 1972. *Urban Renewal: National Program for Local Problems.* Evaluative Studies 4. Washington, D. C.: American Enterprise Institute.

Weicher, John C., and J. C. Simonsom. 1975. "Recent Trends in Housing Costs." *Journal of Economics and Business* 27 (Winter):156–62.

Wellborn, Clay H. 1972. "(Cities and Suburbs) Project Rehab is Upgrading Rental Housing in Effort to Rehabilitate Neighborhoods." *National Journal* (January 8):78–79.

Welfeld, Irving. 1977. "American Housing Policy: Perverse Programs by Prudent People." *The Public Interest* 48 (Summer):128–44.

Welfeld, Irving, et al. 1974. *Perspectives on Housing and Urban Renewal.* American Enterprise Institute Perspectives 2. Praeger Special Studies in U. S. Economic, Social and Political Issues. New York: Praeger Publishers.

Weltner, C. L. 1977. "The Model Cities Program: A Sobering Scorecard." *Policy Reviews.* 2 (Fall):73–871.

White, M. J., and L. J. White. 1977. "The Tax Subsidy to Owner-Occupied Housing: Who Benefits?" *Journal of Public Economics* 7 (February): 111–26.

Wildavsky, Aaron. 1979. *The Politics of the Budgetary Process.* Boston, Little Brown.

Wilensky, Harold L. 1975. *The Welfare State and Equality: Structural and Ideological Roots of Public Expenditures.* Berkely and Los Angeles: University of California Press.

Williams, Walter, and Betty Jane Narver. 180. *Government by Agency: Lessons from the Social Program Grants-In-Aid Experience.* Quantitative Studies in Social Relations. New York: Academic Press.

Wilson, James Q., ed. 1966. *Urban Renewal: The Record and he Controversy.* Cambridge, Mass.: MIT Press.

Wolman, Harold. 1971. *Politics of Federal Housing.* New York: Dodd, Mead and Co.

Zukin, Sharon. 1982. *Loft Living: Culture and Capital in Urban Change.* Baltimore: The Johns Hopkins University Press.

Index